Praise for *The Daily Flame*

"Wow, what an amazing book! I view it as my guide to reconnect with what is real, honest, and most needed (and often most neglected)—that deep, loving part of myself who is courageous, loving, and fierce. If you are feeling lost, overwhelmed, or self-critical, *The Daily Flame* will give you the tools to breathe, relax, and fall back in love with yourself and your life."

JJ VIRGIN, CNS, CHFS
four-time *New York Times* bestselling author
of *The Virgin Diet* and *JJ Virgin's Sugar Impact Diet*

"If you're feeling directionless or just need support for your journey, Dr. Lissa Rankin is your ideal guide. This book can help you practically, emotionally, and soulfully."

CHRIS GUILLEBEAU
author of *Side Hustle* and host of the
daily podcast *Side Hustle School*

"When the beneficent Universe is writing me love notes, I'm listening. Thank you, Dr. Lissa, for ushering the sweet offering of these letters through to all of us."

ELENA BROWER
author of *Practice You* and *Art of Attention*

"As you read from this beautifully written book, each day you will be inspired and transformed. These are love letters from your essential, undamaged goodness to the burdened parts of you that struggle in their myriad ways to keep you safe, or that have been hurt. These letters become daily reminders of who you really are and how much love and compassion is in you and flows through you."

RICHARD SCHWARTZ, PHD
author and founder of Internal Family Systems (IFS)

"*The Daily Flame* is a potent, profound, magical, and at times hilarious blast of Divine Remembrance that is desperately needed on this planet and in our hearts. Thank you, Lissa, for helping us stoke our inner flame one day and one heartbeat at a time. Brava!"

SERA BEAK
bestselling author of *Red Hot and Holy: A Heretic's Love Story* and *Redvelations: A Soul's Journey to Becoming Human*

"*The Daily Flame* features user-friendly love letters from our core Divinity—our Inner Pilot Light—to our everyday selves. The tone is warm, affectionately down-to-earth, and often playful, again and again inviting us to deepen our access to the heartland of our Divinity no matter what our condition may be. Each love letter is compassionately presented and offers us a support that we may have assumed was just not there. Considering them can be a breeze, a light-hearted dance, and it also can be a challenge. Sometimes what's offered is a tasty hors d'oeuvre—other times a substantial meal, something to really bite into—but at all times there's a sense of a feast close at hand."

ROBERT AUGUSTUS MASTERS, PHD
author of *Spiritual Bypassing*, *Transformation through Intimacy*, and *Bringing Your Shadow Out of the Dark*

"Lissa Rankin is an exceptional example of inspiration, wisdom, integrity, and heart; and her new book, *The Daily Flame*, is filled with all of these things and more. Honest and illuminating, these 365 love letters from 'the part of us that always knows' are a source of connection, comfort, and awakening for those who long to feel closer to their own soul. I'm grateful for Lissa's continued influence in my own life and work, and I sincerely believe the world is much better off because of her presence and work in it. Read these offerings and please find out for yourself."

CHRIS GROSSO
author of *Indie Spiritualist*, *Everything Mind*, and *Dead Set on Living*

"Pick up this book whenever you doubt that the flame of light and love burns eternally within you. You'll find short, ecstatic messages that will caress you with love and inspire you to transcend any temporary setbacks and limitations. Lissa Rankin shares how during difficult times in her life journey, she had to surround herself with a 'faith bubble' to protect herself from the naysayers—both those in her environment and those in her mind. This book is your daily bubble to keep your faith intact. Equal parts wisdom, laughter, and passion, it will attune you to your own guidance while opening the gates through which synchronicity, awe, and gratitude can flood your life."

DAWSON CHURCH, PHD

author of *Mind to Matter: The Astonishing Science of How Your Brain Creates Material Reality*

"Lissa's new book gently, deliciously, and powerfully confronts one of the major challenges along the spiritual path: the difficulty many of us have of taking in teachings and practicing spiritually on a frequent and regular basis. Her Inner Pilot Light's love letters to all of us are so sweet, passionate, and tender; so sincere, unconditionally loving, and well-meaning that I've found myself touching in on them often. Flowing with nondual wisdom and love, her book is a read that keeps on giving—a must-have for everyone on a spiritual Path—in fact, for everyone."

ASHA CLINTON, MSW, PHD

developer of Advanced Integrative Therapy (AIT)

"*The Daily Flame* is superfood for our innermost self: Intimate. Gracious. Penetrating. Lissa's reassuring mastery of this inner realm encourages us to dive fully into what truly matters to us. It's never too late for this kind of profound intimacy."

DR. SAIDA DÉSILETS

author of *Desire* and advocate for Sexual Sovereignty

"Lissa's teachings on the Inner Pilot Light help us get in touch with the unharmed, whole, and holy space within us. Most of us don't know what we think or feel or even who we are, and as many tools as there are to teach us, our truths can often remain elusive! With this body of work, practiced by hundreds of thousands worldwide, Lissa shares her essential wisdom with us. Immediately applicable and essential access to our inner wisdom."

SHILOH SOPHIA
artist, poet, teacher

"If you desire relief from doubt and struggle, these daily love letters are your medicine. Lissa gently guides you to reconnecting to the part of you that you can trust 100 percent. Each day you will get closer to clarity, truth, and inspiration. The words in this book will touch a place deep inside that knows the Truth, and you will be ignited to live from love rather than fear."

CHRISTINE HASSLER
author of *Expectation Hangover*,
master coach, and podcast host

"This inspired collection of self-love letters beckons us toward the beauty, courage, and creativity of who we really are. Speaking to both the depth of our consciousness and to our wild dancing souls on planet Earth, these daily morsels are playful and profound, deeply sacred and delightfully spicy, totally human and totally divine. Delicious! *The Daily Flame* serves up real soul nourishment, healing, and transformational wisdom from someone who walks her talk with courage, creativity, and alignment with the flow of life. Savor every bite and follow the guidance of your Inner Pilot Light—your world will be transformed."

MAJA APOLONIA RODÉ, PHD
philosopher, artist, and advocate
for a more beautiful world

the DAILY FLAME

Also by Lissa Rankin, MD

Encaustic Art: The Complete Guide to Creating Fine Art with Wax

What's Up Down There?:
Questions You'd Only Ask Your Gynecologist If She Was Your Best Friend

Mind Over Medicine: Scientific Proof That You Can Heal Yourself

The Fear Cure: Cultivating Courage as Medicine for the Body, Mind, and Soul

The Anatomy of a Calling: A Doctor's Journey from the Head to the Heart
and a Prescription for Finding Your Life's Purpose

the DAILY FLAME

365 love letters from your inner pilot light

Lissa Rankin, MD

Sounds True
Boulder, CO 80306

Published 2019

Cover design by Jennifer Miles
Book design by Beth Skelley

Printed in Canada

Library of Congress Cataloging-in-Publication Data
Names: Rankin, Lissa, 1969– author.
Title: The daily flame : 365 love letters from your inner pilot light / by Lissa Rankin, MD.
Description: Boulder, CO : Sounds True, [2019] | Includes bibliographical references and index.
Identifiers: LCCN 2018027690 (print) | LCCN 2018029459 (ebook) | ISBN 9781683643401 (ebook) | ISBN 9781683642701 (hardcover : alk. paper)
Subjects: LCSH: Self-actualization (Psychology) | Self.
Classification: LCC BF637.S4 (ebook) | LCC BF637.S4 R363 2019 (print) | DDC 204/.32—dc23
LC record available at https://lccn.loc.gov/2018027690

10 9 8 7 6 5 4 3 2 1

In loving memory of my beloved mother,
Trish Rankin (1945–2017),
the first one who reminded me that
a Divine Spark lives inside us all.

Contents

Introduction

Welcome, precious one! You are about to embark upon a sort of pilgrimage with your "Inner Pilot Light."

What is your Inner Pilot Light? Poet Mark Nepo describes it best: "Each person is born with an unencumbered spot, free of expectation and regret, free of ambition and embarrassment, free of fear and worry; an umbilical spot of grace where we were each first touched by God."

Every life begins when a small spark of the Eternal Flame of cosmic consciousness splits off like a glowing ember of a universal bonfire. This unique spark ignites as the Organizing Intelligence that creates your organs, divides your cells, and develops you perfectly into a precious being decorated with thoughts, preferences, gifts, talents, emotions, and eccentricities. The Inner Pilot Light begins in every baby as the untainted, radiant, buoyant light of God/Goddess but often gets filmed over by trauma, conditioning, and the illusion of separation from the Eternal Flame from which this unique spark arises.

Although your Inner Pilot Light may grow dim as life's inevitable challenges threaten to snuff out the full brilliance of this luminous fire, rest assured that your Inner Pilot Light never burns out. Even when you die, the spark returns to the Eternal Flame, adding the brilliance of this unique fractal of light to that which creates all life.

In mystical moments, you may be graced with a direct merging with your Inner Pilot Light, experiencing moments of clear seeing, transcendental knowing, enlivening ecstasy, bliss, and unity as your unique flame merges with the bonfire of all life. Yet more often than not, your Inner Pilot Light plays hide and seek, like fog creeping into a valley between coastal mountains off an ocean, cooling the luminous flames and quieting the burn back to an ember, then retreating back to sea and revealing your Inner Pilot Light in all its blazing clarity and glory. You may have moments of true remembering of the Oneness that links us all. Then the fog rolls back in, and you may forget once again that your singular flame is also part of the One bonfire.

Over time, the fog may roll in less, and the fire within you may gain fuel from the practices that connect you to the Eternal Flame, stoking your inner fire with your devotion, your discipline, your prayers, your humility, and your longing to reconnect with that which once burst you into life. As you peel away all that is not love to allow more oxygen to fan the flames of consciousness in your original spark, as the inevitable trauma of human life heals, and as the center of your love is unveiled, this flame within you grows to fill your cells. This original spark fills your whole body until it bleeds through your skin as an invisible field of love that touches the spaces around you, lending this warmth to all who come near.

Your Inner Pilot Light loves boundlessly but selectively, discriminates between what is and isn't authentic to your true nature, and knows how to connect straight to Source. It guides the path, lights the way, navigates the journey, and asks only that you trust a mysterious process that won't necessarily make sense to your rational mind. While making contact with your Inner Pilot Light is not quite as simplistic as rubbing a lamp and calling forth some inner genie that can magically make your life easy, you do have mystical magic within, which you can access through your sincere desire to connect with this inner Divinity.

Your Inner Pilot Light may not always sound trustworthy because you may have been conditioned to believe that God is a man with a long beard who lives in the sky and loves you from afar, while you are separate from God, maintaining reverent silence and behaving in respectable ways that might be endorsed by the church, temple, or mosque. But because you are simultaneously a spark of Divinity and an embodiment of humanity, it's very likely that the spiritual essence of your Inner Pilot Light may like to wear purple peasant skirts, dance around the campfire, ignore the phone when it's judgmental ol' Aunt Gertrude, laugh inappropriately in the midst of something sacred, and bathe naked in a hot spring under the stars. Your Inner Pilot Light may guide you to sit in the lotus position and meditate while wearing long robes, but this Divine Spark might also cause a bit of a ruckus, like an undomesticated, wild stallion—hard to tame, in touch with the messiness of nature, and prone to galloping through open fields of wildflowers in the rain-soaked mud.

You may worry that your Inner Pilot Light will get you in trouble—and truth be told, it might. After all, if you listen to that voice inside of you, you might wind up doing something crazy, like leaving that soul-sucking job that requires you to compromise your integrity in exchange for a paycheck, or ditching your untrustworthy partner because you deserve to be treated with respect, or moving to Hawaii to photograph rainbows, or choosing to follow your dream of being a musician. Your Inner Pilot Light might care so much about the plight of the rainforests or the orphaned refugee children or the stolen lands of the indigenous people that it pushes you out of your comfort zone and into activism. It might instruct you to dance on bar tops, play the accordion, write a tell-all memoir, or liquidate your retirement account so you can transform a villa in the south of France into a sanctuary for others who are learning to connect with their Inner Pilot Lights.

Your Inner Pilot Light will listen compassionately to the part of you that resists, justifies, rationalizes, and protests. You may say, "But I can't do that. That would be crazy!" When you do, your Inner Pilot Light will hold you close and whisper gently, "You don't have to do anything right now, sweetheart. You only have to make peace with what's true." Then you will relax into the relief that comes with finally admitting what you've known all along—that transformation is seducing you, like a lover, and that you will surrender to this seduction when you are ready for change, and you will be held in a kind of grace until that time arrives.

What if you can't feel your Inner Pilot Light? Does it ever burn out? No, my darling. You can rest assured that although your connection to this Divine Spark may feel tenuous or even absent at times, your Inner Pilot Light still fires away, even at the darkest times of your life. Maybe you've lost a loved one, you've been unfaithful, your heart got broken, you lost your job, your child cut you off, you're dealing with a financial crisis, you're addicted, you're depressed, you're suicidal, you're having a crisis of faith, you've been the victim of a crime, or you've done something you can't bear to face. Times like these can make you question whether your Inner Pilot Light still exists. To doubt is human. To wonder if you have been abandoned by the Source of all love—and to feel pain in the doubting—is natural and understandable. But rest assured that while your Inner Pilot Light may hibernate as a glowing ember, it is never extinguished, not even when you die. You may even find that at the lowest times in your life, this inner spark sidles up closest.

This book is intended to support the kind of intimacy, comfort, nourishment, and grace that happens when you make contact with the Source of all love that fuels your very existence. Regardless of your spiritual orientation, consider this book a prayer of sorts, one that invites you to gently, quietly reunite with the purest, most loving core of your being, the part that will help you navigate the in-between space in your spiritual life.

How might this miraculous reunion with what religious leaders might call "the Imminent Divine" happen? It is your longing for this reunion that will fuel this prayer and throw lighter fluid on your Inner Pilot Light. Once this prayer is offered with sincerity and humility, it is like casting a wondrous spell. A great magic is invoked because the Universe wants nothing more than to help you reconnect and remember. That which you are seeking is desperately seeking you.

So sit back and get ready for a magical ride. Your beloved Inner Pilot Light is waiting to welcome you back to the home that's always been your true sanctuary.

How to Use This Book

Although this is written as a daybook, you do not need to begin reading this book at the beginning of a calendar year, and you do not have to remember to read it every day. You may start this journey whenever you are ready, and you're free to go at your own pace, trusting the divine timing of such journeys. You may even want to use this book as an oracle, keeping it by your bedside and, when you feel the impulse, asking your Inner Pilot Light to help you open the book to the page with the message that is most relevant to you, right here and now.

Each Daily Flame is written in response to my ten-year practice of opening a portal from my consciousness to the collective consciousness, making myself receptive to the inquiry "What is needed today?" and listening to the response that drops in. Because we are all so unique, some love letters will feel personally relevant to you, as if some mysterious force chose this Daily Flame on this day, at just the right time, just for you. Others may not. As you read these daily love letters, I trust you will filter every message through your own inner guidance system, taking what resonates and tossing out what doesn't.

My sincere prayer is that reading this book becomes for you a journey of its own, allowing you to access this connection for yourself, and that this becomes a lifelong love affair. I trust that reading these love letters will help you recognize the vibration of the kinds of messages your Inner Pilot Light is likely to drop in for you personally, and that you will also learn to discern the voices that can mimic your Inner Pilot Light but lack that same frequency of gentle and fierce unconditional love. You may find, even just a few weeks into this journey, that you no longer need someone else to help you translate the words of this loving consciousness that lives inside of you, that your Inner Pilot Light is dropping in messages that are customized just for you. If this happens, you can drop to your knees in gratitude and offer your thanks to this inner Beloved who yearns for you as much as you yearn to feel connected.

If you wish, you may start your journey by downloading the free "Meet Your Inner Pilot Light" guided meditation, as well as the *30 Practical Tips for Getting in Touch with Your Inner Pilot Light* eBook, which you can find at InnerPilotLight.com. If you want additional support throughout the year, you can also sign up for the email version of the Daily Flame at InnerPilotLight.com.

Let us begin by summoning your Inner Pilot Light with an invocation.

An Inner Pilot Light Invocation

May you surrender all desire to make contact with your Inner Pilot Light to the invisible forces of love that will guide your journey and trust that the perfect path will unfold in divine timing, and you will know what is needed on a need-to-know basis.

May you open the portal into the love that is always present for you, always available to you, and always moving through you so it can overflow out of you and touch the heart of the world.

May your Inner Pilot Light comfort, illuminate, encourage, and guide you so that you may be blessed and you may be a blessing.

May this frequency of love help you love and accept all parts of yourself so that you become capable of transmitting this unconditional love and acceptance to those around you.

May you trust the guidance of this infinite part of you so you will know how you can serve love in your own unique way.

May blind faith transform into evidence-based faith as you dare to follow the guidance that comes through the Universe and gives you feedback.

May this be a journey of radical, heart-opening physical, mental, emotional, and spiritual healing.

May you be not a seeker but a finder, for you already have all that you need to have, all the love you could ever imagine, right here inside your own heart.

May you know that you are unspeakably precious, that you are enough, that there is no punishing God out there looking to judge you, that you cannot do this human life "wrong," that you do not have to do anything to earn this love, and that you are deeply, unconditionally accepted just the way you are.

1

My Sweet,

Do you realize that no matter what else is going on in your life—no matter how much stress you're under, how much heartbreak you're experiencing, how much pain you feel in your body or mind, or how much your life is full of fabulousness—I am always here for you?

I'm like your heartbeat. You may not always notice me, but I'm always present, doing my job, just beating away—thump, thump, thump—waiting for you to tap in.

You can access me *anytime*. And I don't even charge overtime.

Having trouble finding me?

Close your eyes. Imagine me as a golden light in your heart, expanding to fill your chest. Now see me filling your whole torso with my light and dropping down through your body like an extension cord made of my light. Ground me into the soil. See me going through the water table and the rock, all the way into the magma at the center of Mama Earth. Now plug me in, sugarplum!

Let Mama's Earth energy come back up that cord of my light. Let me fill you to the brim until my light shoots out the top of your head and connects you to the cosmos. See me like a spotlight flashing to the stars as one giant firestick of golden light connecting you to All That Is.

Huzzah! Hoorah! Snap, crackle, pop!

Now take a few breaths. Abide in me, darling. Know that I am here.

From the Earth to the heavens,

YOUR INNER PILOT LIGHT

2

Dearest Beloved,

Remember me? I'm that sparkly, effervescent, 100 percent authentic spark within you that never gets extinguished, no matter how rough life gets. I'm that pilot light that holds the Eternal Flame of your divine radiance, even when the main burners aren't ignited fully. I'm the presence of unconditional love and acceptance inside of you, always here to help you heal that which is in need of healing.

Right now I'm here with a very important invitation. Just as an experiment, will you let me light the way for a while? Will you let me take the wheel in your life so we can journey together?

I know you're accustomed to listening to other voices inside your head, and you may not have spent much time listening to mine. You're so accustomed to listening to your adorably protective monkey mind, which is always working 24/7 just to try to keep you safe, rehashing the past and trying to control the future, grasping for what it wants and resisting what it doesn't like.

Let's see if that precious monkey mind would be willing to trust me enough to give us some space so you can experiment with how things might go if you listen to me for a bit.

Can you ask the parts inside of you that may object to you and me becoming intimate if they'd be willing to grant us just this little experiment? Let them know I'm just going to start by writing you a few love letters. No pressure. No Holy-Roller hellfire and brimstone. Just love and radical acceptance of even the parts you might judge as unlovable.

Are you up for a love that big?

Infinitely spacious,

YOUR INNER PILOT LIGHT

3

Dear One,

Think back for a minute to a time in your life when you were at your most powerful. Maybe you won the elementary school science fair with that revolutionary idea. Maybe you were a young stallion teenager bucking with passion. Maybe you were just rewarded with your first raise for a job well done. Maybe you completed that marathon. Maybe something mystical happened and you felt at one with the Universe. You were in flow and synchronicity was on your side, and everything just felt so . . . magical. You remember the time . . .

That one.

That day, you let *me* take over so I could shine my light all the way through your whole being.

Well, I'm still here, baby. Can you feel me?

Close your eyes and feel me. Let me love you up right now.

Glowing,

YOUR INNER PILOT LIGHT

4

Glorious Angel,

Oh my! You can hear me! You're listening! You may not know it, but I've been here all along, burning steadfast and true, even during that time when you thought my flame was extinguished. No matter what happens in your life, I am always here, keeping your home fires burning. All I need is a wee bit of your attention so I can help you with a bit of housekeeping, clearing out old beliefs and patterns that no longer serve you, doing a bit of dusting around your relationships, and clearing out the cobwebs around your genius, your passion, and your creativity.

Will you make it a priority to make space for things that support your relationship with me? Invite me close. Get quiet. Meditate. Pray for help. Spend time in nature. Listen to trees. Pay attention to synchronicity. Take notes on your dreams. Notice images that float by your mind's eye.

Can't speak Inner Pilot Light yet? Imagine that everything is alive and conscious, and the whole world is taking you on a scavenger hunt to help you translate the messages I'm here to share with you.

Can you hear what I'm whispering today?

Take a moment right now and see if you can hear just this *one thing*.

A decoder's dream,

YOUR INNER PILOT LIGHT

5

Dearest Beloved,

Inside of you I hear a noisy grumbling, and I recognize that voice. Hello, you sneaky, adorable, ferocious, fearful goblin! I see you, and I love and accept you. I appreciate all you're doing to try to keep things safe. I know you're just trying to protect against change and uncertainty, maintaining the status quo at all costs.

I know you mean well, with all your nervous, scared ruminating and all your circular anxious plans. I know you want me to think you're this big, scary monster. But I see that you're really just the voice of a scared inner child who needs love and comfort. Would you consider letting me put my great arms around you as I rock you on my cosmic lap?

I'm not kicking you out, you dear little beast. You're always welcome, and nobody's going to blame or shame or judge or reject you. I'm going to listen to every single scary thing you want to tell me, because I'm so grateful that you're trying to be such a fierce protector. (Good job doing what you do, my little lovebuggy!)

I'm asking that you try trusting me just enough to free you from all the exhausting work you do trying to keep the unpredictable world safe.

How would you feel about going on a holiday for a while, maybe somewhere warm and beautiful, like the south of France? Don't worry! You won't get kicked out or replaced while you're gone. You're totally welcome here, and nobody's going to make you leave. I'm just thinking there might be a job you'd like better than the one you have.

What if I take care of keeping things safe for a while? Would you dare to let me help you out?

You would? Really?

Ah . . . I'm touched.

Awesome. Now, about that trip to France . . .

Ooh la la,

YOUR INNER PILOT LIGHT

6

Dear One,

This is going to be a full-blown love letter, so I may get mushy. (You've been forewarned.)

I love you when you open your heart, even though you're tempted to close it down. I also love you when you guard your heart and build walls to protect your vulnerability.

I love you when you take leaps of faith, and I also love you when you're too scared to leap.

I love you when you score that win, ace that challenge, attract that love, exceed expectations, and stand shining in the light of your accomplishments. I also love you when you fall on your booty, make a mistake, kick yourself, and do something others might judge as disappointing or even shame-worthy.

I love you when you forgive.

I love you when you shine.

I love you when you're all gussied up and knockout gorgeous.

I love you when you serve those who are less fortunate.

I love you when you're grateful and overflowing with reverence.

I love you when you're strong and sovereign.

I love you when you're busting a move.

I love you when you're totally in the flow of your zone of genius.

I also love you when you screw up.

I love you when you fail to deliver.

I love you when the relationship falls apart.

I love you when you're not yet ready to forgive.

I love you when the deal falls through.

I love you when you're in debt.

I love you when you have poor judgment.

I love you when you lose your way.

I love you when you break down.

I love you when you've lost hope.

You see, my precious, I love you no matter what. For reals.

Arms wide open,
YOUR INNER PILOT LIGHT

7

My Love,

I know you wonder whether I'm real. Part of you thinks I'm like a child's imaginary friend or some opiate of the masses, conjured up to protect you from the harsh reality of a dog-eat-dog world.

This doesn't hurt my feelings at all, my love. I adore your skeptical parts.

I understand that they're just trying to protect you from getting scammed by yet another charlatan, pie-in-the-sky redeemer. Once upon a time, you dared to believe in Santa Claus, and when you found out Mom and Dad were wrapping the presents, the magical child who wanted to believe in fairy tales lost faith in invisible magical beings. Or you trusted a God who left you with post-traumatic church syndrome.

Or you put all your faith in fairies and then someone broke your heart when they told you they weren't real.

No wonder you're reluctant to trust me!

When you dare to put your faith in anything whose existence you can't prove with ordinary science, you risk disillusionment. I understand that your tender, young, hurt parts don't want to have their illusions shattered again.

So let's take it slowly, sweetheart. Give me only as much trust as you feel safe offering. I'll be grateful for every little morsel you risk offering.

Satiated with crumbs,

YOUR INNER PILOT LIGHT

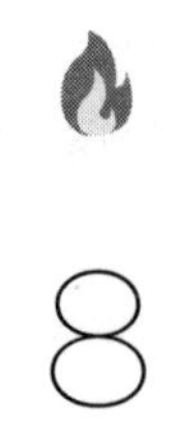

Dearest Beloved,

Would you like to experience more meaning in your life? Try asking yourself anthropologist Angeles Arrien's "3 Questions." Scroll backward through your day, asking yourself:

> What surprised me today?
>
> What inspired me today?
>
> What touched my heart today?

Stop at the first thing you can remember for each question.

You can write your answers in a journal at the end of the day or use this as a dinnertime practice with friends or family.

At first, if you're just getting to know me, you might answer, "Nothing, nothing, and nothing." But over time, when you know you'll have to answer these three questions at the end of the day, you'll start looking for your answers, making notes to be sure you can remember what surprised, inspired, and touched your heart.

Mind-body medicine pioneer Rachel Naomi Remen, who teaches this 3 Questions exercise to physicians, writes this: "At first, people begin to notice things that completely passed them by as they were living through their day. Little things, then bigger and bigger things." When she taught one of her clients the 3 Questions practice, he said, "In the beginning I could only see and appreciate things six hours after they happened. It was like being under a spell. I could only really see my life when I was looking backward over my shoulder."

You may experience the same thing. But over time, as you start to experience your life through my magical eyes, the time gap will close and you will start to feel surprised, inspired, and touched in the moments when these surprising, inspiring, touching events happen.

Then something super magical starts to happen. Instead of experiencing your life retrospectively, with an awe-reducing time delay, you might actually find yourself sharing with others—in present time—when you're feeling surprised, inspired, or touched. Imagine how the harried mother in the grocery store will feel if you dare to let her know that she's the one who inspired you today, or if you tell the shop clerk he's the one who touched your heart.

Can you feel how this practice could change your life?

Ah . . . now you've got me all teary. You're the one who touched my heart today.

Not sure what surprises, inspires, and touches you? Let me help, babe.

Inspired,

YOUR INNER PILOT LIGHT

My Sweet,

If you ever even entertain the notion that you're damaged goods, that something is broken in you, or that you've experienced too much trauma to ever be fully, completely healed, let me reassure you.

I am the *you* who is untouched by trauma, unbreakable, and always whole, healed, and illuminated. You don't need to do anything to fix me because I cannot be broken. You don't have to go find me because I'm always as close as a breath.

Rest assured. I am the incorruptible essence in you that might get veiled over but never gets eclipsed.

Take my hand, darling. I've got you.

Pinkie swear,
YOUR INNER PILOT LIGHT

10

Dearest Darling Precious,

I know you tend to wear masks to protect yourself from being seen in your tender vulnerability. You're not trying to be phony. You're just trying to keep your vulnerable parts safe.

What you don't realize is that these guards lock you in prison and keep you from feeling as if you belong here on this planet.

The good news is that with my help, you can start to unmask yourself!

Be all you, all the time, and let the chips fall where they may.

If you dare to slip off your masks with just one person who feels safe enough, you just might inspire that person to do the same. And then that person might dare to unmask in front of another. And then that person might pay it forward. And then . . . *voila!* You've started an unmask yourself revolution!

Every time you dare to peer past the mask another person wears in order to protect who they really are, and every time you take off your own masks and show someone the radiant beauty that shines behind the facade, you give me the chance to connect at a deeper level—Inner Pilot Light to Inner Pilot Light.

That's when miracles happen. That's when love wins.

Vive la révolution!
YOUR INNER PILOT LIGHT

11

Dearest Beloved,

Preparing the womb that gestates dreams coming true takes time, so please, sweetheart, be patient with the process. Think of your dream as a baby. You start with an egg of vision. You surrender that vision to my loving care and ask that it be nourished if it is aligned with the highest good. Then you fertilize it with love, attention, intention, and, when necessary, focus, discipline, and good old-fashioned ass-in-chair hard work!

Over time, the dream grows and differentiates. You align with the force of life and let the current of life work with you. Then when the time is right, if your dream is aligned with one of my holy ideas—*presto!* Your dream is born.

(*WHEEEEE!!! Throws confetti!!!!*)

I know it can be frustrating, my darling. I know doubt can seep in and poison your trust. When you're attached to the outcome and things aren't going as you planned, the part that wants what it wants can get a bit panicky.

So just breathe, my love. Rest in the deep knowing that all is well and everything is happening in divine timing. Hold my hand and know that this time of waiting and becoming is fertile indeed.

When the time comes, on the day your dream is born, you can count on me to send flowers.

Cooing into your ear,
YOUR INNER PILOT LIGHT

12

Dearest Beloved,

Do you know what really lights me up? When you engage in the practices and activities that serve as my lighter fluid!

Not sure how to turn me into a bonfire?

Try asking me directly.

If you still don't hear anything when you ask, here are some surefire ways to light me up:

Be creative.

Meditate or pray in silence.

Move your body through dance.

Engage in rituals that open up sacred space.

Prioritize time with people who see, respect, and activate my illuminated brilliance, rather than the ones who suck up to those masks you sometimes wear.

Commit yourself to work and play that feeds my hunger for deep meaning and purpose.

Relax in nature.

Get your hands dirty and tend to the life force in plants.

Open your heart and reach out to someone who needs your love.

Worship Mother Earth and bow humbly before her wisdom.

Make love with your whole heart, enjoying your full, blissful embodiment.

Nourish this body we live in with life-activating foods.

Most importantly, be *unapologetic* about letting me shine, baby, even if there are consequences.

Cause when you let my brilliant light shine, my darling, the whole world is blessed.

Holy hallelujah,

YOUR INNER PILOT LIGHT

13

Beloved One,

I know you love it when I comfort you, cheer you up, and remind you of your luminosity. But I hope you can also relish the way I use my intense love to point my sparkly flashlight at all the ways you unintentionally create your own suffering. (I only do it because I care so much.)

Let me ask you a few illuminating questions that might light up some epiphanies:

> What is repetitively hurting in your life?
>
> What painful story are you telling yourself over and over?
>
> What patterns keep emerging in your life experience?

Would you be willing to get curious about how blocks in your energy field might be participating in these recurring themes? Would you be up for healing and clearing those blocks so my life-force fire could flow uninterrupted through your entire body?

Not sure what kind of woo-woo nonsense I'm talking about? Try taking a risk and just ask me for a little light bulb of insight.

See if you can hear me when I give you the first little hint. Trust that if there's anything you need to know right now, I'll show you. If nothing emerges right away, don't fret. Insight will come when you're ready.

Illuminating your blind spots,

YOUR INNER PILOT LIGHT

14

Dear One,

You know that time it felt as if I left you alone, in the dark, underwater—for so long you could barely breathe?

You know how you cursed me, my darling, and wondered how I could abandon you like that?

Well, I just want to let you know that as much as it pains me to see you hurting, *it was all part of the plan*.

Don't get me wrong. I'm not here to punish you or torture you for your own good. No, no, no. Those are misguided teachings meant to scare you into conformity and shame you into following the "rules."

What I mean is that some humans *blossom* in the dark.

In the dark, where you can hardly breathe, might be the first place you see me sparkle. Like a light at the end of the tunnel, I beckon you to show you the way.

Together—you and me—we can always find our way back to the sun.

A hug of light in the dark,
YOUR INNER PILOT LIGHT

15

Sweet Firecracker,

Balance is the key to just about everything, yet what does balance even mean? Is balance just some pie-in-the-sky fantasy, promoted by self-help authors and holier-than-thou people who pretend to have it all together but are secretly struggling?

No, balance is not a fantasy. But it's also not necessarily what you think.

Perhaps we need to redefine balance as the opposite of burnout.

Working yourself into the ground doesn't lead to balance. Nor does beating yourself up because you judge your life as unbalanced. What if balance is more a state of being that prioritizes life's "want-tos" over life's "have-tos"?

Perhaps, as your life comes into greater balance, you notice more ease, pleasure, and fulfillment from your endeavors. You might still engage in activities that feel like "have-tos," but as you give yourself permission not to deplete yourself in the name of "shoulds," maybe the "have-tos" turn into "get-tos."

How great would that be? Imagine this: instead of looking at your schedule and thinking, "I have to do this today," you could honestly say, "I *get to* do this today."

If it doesn't feel like a "want-to" or a "get-to," what if it's okay to say, "No, thank you"?

I'm not suggesting you abdicate your responsibilities to your family, your work, your spiritual practices, or other commitments. I'm simply asking you to reframe your perception and prioritize your activities according to your soul's true values.

When people face a life-threatening illness, they often experience this lens shift instantly. "I have to pick up the kids from school" transitions into "I get to pick up my kids from school!" A scary diagnosis gives them permission to let what doesn't matter fall away.

The surprise gift is often more balance.

Don't wait until you're sick to prioritize the "want-tos" and the "get-tos," my love.

Not sure what you really want to do? Ask me.

That's the ticket,

YOUR INNER PILOT LIGHT

16

Dear One,

In this life you are surrounded by beautiful angels, all sharing this incredibly human experience with you.

The barista at the coffee shop who takes extra care to meet your needs—she might be one.

The gardener who pays such passionate attention to even the smallest detail in your plants—he might be one.

The auto mechanic who confidently deems your car perfectly safe every time he finishes work on it—he might be one.

The teacher who knows she is investing in the future—she might be one.

Are you taking time out of your overflowing schedule to recognize the everyday angels in your life, my dear? Are you thanking them, with all the light in our One heart, for the ways they brighten the world with their invisible wings?

The wind beneath all wings,
YOUR INNER PILOT LIGHT

17

Dear One,

I see you sometimes feeling so alone. But oh, my love, I wish you could see what I see! Next to you at the coffee shop or in the schoolyard or beside you in that cubicle or at the gym, I see another lonely soul longing for connection, yearning to belong. And next to her, he feels the same way.

The woman in front of you in the grocery store line just lost her mother after a nine-year battle with cancer.

The other mother you ran into in the schoolyard just found out her daughter has a brain tumor.

The Starbucks barista who has been schlepping espresso to fund her dream just got the news that the book she spent five years writing got rejected by yet another publisher.

The young boy acting out in the restaurant just found out Daddy is going on another tour of active duty.

The woman who cut you off in traffic just filed for divorce from her abusive husband.

The waiter who forgot to bring you extra salad dressing just lost his son in a car accident.

A famous philosopher supposedly once said, "Be kind, for everyone you meet is fighting a hard battle."

So many people just need a hand to hold, a kind word of comfort, and a big bear hug. Yet they're all thirsty fish swimming in a lake full of water!

Opportunities to satiate your thirst for love, intimacy, and connection are all around you, if you'll let yourself take a drink.

Not sure how to find a tall glass of water?

Let me help.

Glug, glug, glug,
YOUR INNER PILOT LIGHT

18

Sweetheart,

Your mighty brain is such a wondrous instrument of magic. I love that your mind so loves to think.

But just for laughs, why don't you play around with paying attention to something other than what you think?

Stop and notice what's happening right now with all your senses. (Seriously. Stop. Right now. Do it please.)

Maybe your ears hear music in the way the wind rustles the leaves on the tree outside your window.

Maybe your eyes are gazing out and noticing the rays of sun on the ever-changing landscape.

Maybe your nose is drinking in the smell of coffee wafting up from downstairs.

Maybe you can almost taste that thing you've been craving for breakfast.

Maybe the soft texture of what you're wearing enlivens your skin.

Can you give yourself permission to experience all your senses all at once now?

Ahhhhh . . . yeah, baby. Now you've hit my ignition switch.

Poof!
YOUR INNER PILOT LIGHT

19

My Love,

You know that feeling you get when all the roads of your journey converge on one seemingly destined spot? You know how it feels as if you're being conducted, as if some grand maestro-like Organizing Intelligence is out there waving a magic baton, putting all the pieces into place, introducing you to just the right people, activating synchronicities, and landing you in just the right place at just the right time?

You know those happy little butterflies you feel inside when you stand in that symphony hall and look at where the roads have brought you, knowing that the dots all connect, at least when you look back?

Well, honey, that's me up there with that magic baton, working in tandem with all the other Inner Pilot Lights waving magic batons, standing at all those crossroads, cheering you on, guiding you when you get lost, reminding you that even the roads that might look as if they didn't go so well are all leading you *right where you're supposed to be*.

Conducting the most mysterious symphony,
YOUR INNER PILOT LIGHT

20

Dear One,

It's okay to feel exactly how you feel.

Feel joyful.

Feel angry.

Feel ecstasy.

Feel frustrated.

Feel grateful.

Feel disappointed.

Feel loved.

Feel jealous.

Feel lonely.

Feel horny.

Feel sad.

Feel anxious.

Feel enlivened.

Feel afraid.

Feel inspired.

There's nothing wrong with feeling how you're feeling. It's when you resist or deny your feelings, judging some feelings as "good" and other feelings as "bad," that they tend to cause problems. When you grasp at the pleasant feelings and fight the painful ones, your resistance crystallizes into a film over my light.

But when you allow feelings to wash through you without clinging or resisting, moving like waves in the ocean that come and go, you keep my light clear, free to glow.

Let all those beautiful parts inside you express how they're feeling. Then go ahead and feel those feelings unapologetically.

Don't worry that you'll get flooded with emotions you can't control, falling into black holes of intensity. Don't worry if tears come or you need to growl or scream or stomp your feet or dance like an uninhibited child!

Like clouds in the sky, one feeling will pass and a new one will float in. Be with it, whatever it is. And know that only through truly feeling your emotions can you be set free.

Don't be afraid you'll fall too deeply down some emotional black hole. Before you go too far in, I'll bail you out and rock you in my loving arms until your nervous system relaxes again.

We've got this, babe,

YOUR INNER PILOT LIGHT

21

Dearest Beloved,

Yes, there is seemingly unbearable pain in the world. Tragic things happen that can fracture nations, split families, and tear even the closest individuals apart. Terrorists spew hatred. Buildings collapse. School shootings happen. Wars get waged. People polarize and declare each other "the enemy." They demonize. They "other" each other. Vendettas get fulfilled. Revenge is enacted.

And then they do it all again.

But what do you think has to happen to people to make them do the atrocious things that humans do to one another? How much trauma must someone experience in order to be capable of doing what humans do? Can't you see that something horrible had to happen to turn that innocent little boy or girl into what people label "a monster"? Can't you feel the compassion I feel for what separates humans from their natural tendency to care for one another?

As long as you write off the "bad guys" as "monsters," casting them aside like damaged goods to be killed off in wars, you only participate in creating more disposable people who become the next bad guys. Only if you're willing to try to see the humanity in even the most dangerous human can love possibly win.

Peace on Earth will never be possible until all people are willing to see each other—Inner Pilot Light to Inner Pilot Light.

Because nobody is born 100 percent evil.

Nobody is born 100 percent virtuous.

Every single human has a hurting little child inside that is just crying out, yearning to love and be loved.

How can you love up all those little kids?

To love that big, you're gonna need me, babe.

Heart fire,

YOUR INNER PILOT LIGHT

22

Dearest Beloved,

Someone hurt you, and you're still holding that grudge. You feel a well-deserved sense of righteous indignation. You're in the right. That someone was wrong. You have every right to feel the way you do. Anyone who heard the story would take your side.

Maybe she abandoned you.

Perhaps he betrayed you.

She broke your heart.

He molested you.

She criticized you.

He withdrew love.

She beat you up.

He failed to protect you.

There are countless ways people can hurt you. No one is immune to getting hurt, and it's only natural to build walls to protect your broken heart.

But, my darling, when you let your heart get tainted with resentment, you impede the free flow of my loving light, making it hard to feel me, sense me, or hear my guidance.

Forgiveness, on the other hand, is a generous offering of my grace—and with that grace comes emotional freedom, liberation from the downward spiral of negativity that resentment breeds, an opportunity for personal redemption, and a firework show of my illumination!

Maybe he doesn't deserve it. Maybe she's unrepentant. You'd certainly be justified in digging your heels in. Everyone would understand . . .

But what if you choose to do something wildly radical, and in choosing forgiveness you open a door into a paradise so full of grace you can't even imagine what might lie on the other side? What if this opened other doors, and suddenly the phone rang with that good news you've been waiting for? What if the person you love opened their heart to you? What if that illness you've struggled with miraculously disappeared? What if a huge check unexpectedly appeared in the mail?

Resentment prevents miracles, while love and grace foster them. And when you're fueled by the flames of my radical love, molecules rearrange themselves, time and space reconfigure, tumors disappear, miracles happen . . .

Not sure whether you're ready to forgive yet?

Let me help.

Ka-pow!

YOUR INNER PILOT LIGHT

23

My Sweet,

It might not have felt like it when you were growing up, but I want you to know something super important.

It's safe to shine my light.

Yes, dearest. It's true.

Not only is it safe to shine my light but also *it's safest to shine my light*.

I know it can feel dangerous. Some people grow up with traumatized parents who attack the Inner Pilot Light in their children. Some children learn to hide their light in order to avoid having their light dampened or even brutalized by the people who are supposed to love them. It's true that it might not have been safe to shine my light when you were young, but you're not a little child anymore, sweetheart. You are a grown-up, and now, shining your light is your ultimate safety.

I know your mind might tell you it's still not safe. This part of you might be frightened that you will get rejected, that others might feel blinded by so much light, that you'll be ostracized for being "too much" if you shine that bright. You might worry that you'll attract more attention than you're comfortable with. Maybe you're afraid that you'll abuse the power of so much light, since you've seen many others who abuse their power. Maybe you have parts that swear you'll get burned at the stake . . . again.

I understand why your scared parts want to keep me dim. I love and accept those adorable little beasts. But maybe, if they dare to trust me, those parts can give me a chance to show you that I can keep you even safer than they can.

Just give me a chance. You can always go back to dimming me down if things don't go well.

Why should you dare to let me sparkle? When you let me shine, your obvious radiance magnetizes the tribe of people who will lift you up, give you comfort, and offer a place for your luminous love to land. You draw in the aligned opportunities to serve and love and fulfill your calling. You co-create the optimal health that this body can experience. You open yourself to creative inspiration and the recognition that may accompany such expressions of talent. And you feel a deep, soul-nourishing fulfillment that nothing but spiritual intimacy with life itself can imitate.

Dial me up, baby,

YOUR INNER PILOT LIGHT

24

My Little Flame,

How do I love thee? Let me count the ways!

I love you when you wake up bright-eyed and bushy-tailed, filled with hope about the exciting new day that awaits you. I also love you when you wake up cranky in your early morning innocence, yawning, puffy-eyed, disheveled, and jonesing for a cup o' joe.

I love you as you dive passionately into this present moment right here, enlivening me and showing up for whatever life throws your way. I also love you when you get lost in the past or caught up in future-tripping.

I love you as you fearlessly follow your heart's desires, saying YES! to your calling and diving all the way in when you are guided to do so. I also love you when you get scared and distracted and indulge your resistance, saying HELL NO! to your hero's journey and sabotaging your sacred mission.

I love you when you have a hard day and turn inward to me for comfort and direction. I also love you when you turn away from me, seeking comfort in all those ways you like to numb whatever is hard to feel.

I love you when you gently tend to your needs and take care of yourself. I also love you when you engage in self-defeating behaviors.

I love you when you pour kindness out with nothing expected in return, and I love you when you're selfish, narcissistic, cynical, grumpy, and greedy.

Suffice it to say, I love you at each moment of each day, for all eternity. You don't have to do anything to earn this love, and there's nothing you can do to lose it.

Unconditionally yours,

YOUR INNER PILOT LIGHT

25

Dear One,

I know what you want me to say—that true love will be yours forever; that financial abundance will rain down upon you and stick around; that loving, supportive friends will surround you effortlessly; that you will know and fulfill your life's purpose with ease and wild success; that you will burst with confidence, your spirit will be lifted, your heart will be healed, and your body will thrive until a ripe old age with zero disability.

I wish I could make promises like that. Really, I do.

But instead, I ask you to trust that the path to your own awakening may look different than that.

Your path may lead you to score the lover of your dreams, get the deal, achieve that accomplishment, earn that award, win the popularity contest, live in the house of your fantasies, and acquire all the accolades.

Your path may also lead you to heartbreak. You may struggle with finances. You may get sick. You might feel lost and confused about why you're here and what you're meant to do. You may feel lonely. You may doubt yourself. You may have dark nights of the soul. You may fail to achieve the one thing you felt you must achieve.

While I can't promise things will go the way you hope, I can promise that you'll get what you need in order to wake up to life's grand, mysterious beauty. And if you look at your unique path, you'll be able to witness—with sincere gratitude—how awe-inspiring it is that some Organizing Intelligence is taking you right where you need to be in order to let your heart burst open and your love pour out into a world in desperate need of your love.

And that, my darling, is an achievement worth celebrating.

The challenging growth spurts . . . this too shall pass.

The easy flow states of wonder and awe . . . this too shall pass.

Such emotional states are ephemeral, but I am not. I am steadfast and unchanging.

You can count on me,
YOUR INNER PILOT LIGHT

26

Dearest Beloved,

You know that person who cuts you down? Yeah—the one with the razor-sharp tongue who can rip you to ribbons in no time flat?

Let me tell you a little secret, sweetheart.

It's *so* not about you.

Sometimes you're culpable, and you need to clean up your side of the street, because it lights me up when you take personal responsibility, hold yourself accountable, and make amends.

But this time (you know the time I'm talking about), *what if it's really not about you at all*?

What if this came from someone else's wound, and the only thing to deal with on your side of the street is how you're handling this right now?

Are you taking care of yourself? Are you asking for what you need and communicating it with kindness and—

when necessary—loving ferocity? Are you setting good boundaries and enforcing wise consequences? Are you letting me snuggle your hurt parts while you lavish these parts with self-care? Can you take such good care of the parts of you that have been hurt that you're not waiting on someone else to be your redeemer? Can you accept that I am here to give you everything you need?

What can I do to help comfort you right now, sweetheart?

Drop in. Listen up. Let me know. I'm all in.

Wrapping you in a bear hug,
YOUR INNER PILOT LIGHT

27

My Love,

Resentment begets nothing but more and more resentment . . . and anger and frustration and misplaced judgment and hurt feelings and a whole lot of made-up stories.

But what if, instead of letting resentment burn an ulcer in your gut, you could invite resentment to be your friend? What if this painful feeling is simply your cue that you're giving too much, letting others violate your boundaries, and not asking for what you need? What if it's a gift asking you to pause, reflect, and check in with me about what needs to change so you can authentically shift from resentment to gratitude?

All the energy needed to fuel resentment depletes your creative flow, drains your productivity, halts your personal growth, and closes your heart. But what if it doesn't have to be that way? What if resentment is your signal to turn the finger back on yourself and do what you must in order to get your needs met?

Need a little help taking the first steps? Not sure how to prevent and heal the resentment?

Tap in. I'll help you get back on track.

From grrrrr to ahhhhh,
YOUR INNER PILOT LIGHT

28

Beautiful,

Can you check in and see if you feel ready to make more space in your life for me? Don't bully any parts that resist. Just sit gently with the invitation.

You know that busyness, chaos, noise, and clutter limit my oxygen, whereas sacred space, silence, and time away from scheduled activities help my home fires roar.

Don't pressure yourself to spend time with me. This strategy won't work. It will only make the rebellious teenager in you buck and resist!

Just sit with your awareness of me and my gifts and see if you can negotiate with the parts of you that want me close and the parts that don't. Have compassion for and forgive any part that sabotages your relationship with me. Ask those protector parts what frightens them. Listen deeply to what they fear. See if you can strike a deal with the parts that don't want to know me better. Let them know that there are many ways we can get together. Reassure them that we'll only go as fast as the slowest part of you feels free to go.

Not sure of the best way you and I might come together? Just ask me right now.

Expanding,
YOUR INNER PILOT LIGHT

29

My Darling,

I know you sometimes feel tempted to numb out, and frankly, I don't blame you one bit.

It's only natural, given how painful this world can be, how insensitive some people are, how disconnected modern culture is from nature, truth, unconditional love, and the glory of all that is marvelous, melodious, and magnificent in this world. No wonder you feel like numbing out when the news is full of tragedy, your neighbors don't even make eye contact, and you feel separate from the radiance of all the Inner Pilot Lights that illuminate this planet in its time of darkness.

But let me clue you in on a little secret, my love.

Even when you most yearn to numb out, *I'm here*.

You're free to do what you must to tolerate what hurts in this world. Nobody is judging you or keeping score of how many mindless television shows you watch, how many bottles of wine you consume, how much you overwork to allow the busyness to distract you from life's inevitable pains, how many one-night stands you indulge in, how much you scroll through social media to quell the hot loneliness, how many pills you pop, how many cigarettes you smoke, how much porn you watch, or how many chocolate bars you feel compelled to let melt in your mouth.

I just want you to know that there's another way, one that allows you to luxuriate in the joy, peace, and love of my light every moment of every day, even when life hurts.

Glennon Doyle Melton says we're always looking for "easy buttons" that will cover up the pain we feel. She says we should not be afraid of pain, that we were *made* for pain, that instead, we should be afraid of easy buttons.

Human life is not always easy. Sometimes it's hard to be in a body on this planet during its growth pains.

But I can offer you this: Even when you're tempted to reach for easy buttons, I'm always here. Let me hold you in my arms when the pain feels like more than you can bear alone.

Easy peasy,

YOUR INNER PILOT LIGHT

30

My Darling,

Have you ever looked at how you make decisions? Maybe you consider options, research, analyze pros and cons, anticipate and calculate the potential for regret or loss, make sure to minimize the risk of regret or loss or failure, weigh risks, anticipate worst-case scenarios, seek prudent advice from trustworthy experts, then make your decision and take decisive action.

While there's nothing wrong with an analytical approach to decision-making, you may not realize—because your culture never teaches you this—that there's an even more effective way to make good decisions.

Imagine if you could answer any question or seek guidance around any decision simply by asking me what is aligned with the highest good for all beings. Since you know it's impossible to know for sure that any analytical choice is the "right" one, wouldn't it be a relief if it were possible to get clarity, confirmation, and reassurance that the choice you're making is what is best?

How is this possible? It begins with your trust that I am here and that I have access to wisdom you may not be able to access with your thinking mind. When you approach life with open curiosity and a willingness to wonder if there is some sort of Organizing Intelligence that can help you live your life in alignment with the highest good for all, you open a portal into a mysterious realm that I can help you interpret. When married with a true sincerity, this openness, this willingness to inquire, activates an invisible process and something larger than yourself responds to your openness.

This openness tends to call in certain signs and synchronicities, and you begin to get a feeling that life is listening to your requests for guidance. Have those signs and synchronicities been there all along and you just now have the eyes to see them and my guidance to help you interpret them? Maybe. Are you "manifesting" those signs and synchronicities? Am I? As much as I'd like to try to explain this to your thinking mind, what if it's just not that simple? What if it even defies rational understanding?

What I can explain is that if you lean into this radical openness with sincere curiosity, it starts to feel as if life is filled with messages that guide you on your path. You ask for help making a difficult decision, or you ask for support doing something you don't think you're brave enough to do, and if it's aligned, it feels as if life reorganizes to help bring into being that which serves that greater good. Falling into such a flow state feels like the kinds of peak experiences Olympic athletes and highly creative artists report when they're "in the zone." The appropriate response is awe and wonder.

Over time, your open curiosity grows into trust. Now you're no longer just wondering whether there is guidance out there to help you live your life. Now you *know* there is guidance. You go from blind faith to evidence-based faith, and at some point you aren't willing to make any big decision in your life without consulting me (in cahoots with this invisible force of love that you have come to trust). This process magnetizes to you signs, inner knowings, dreams, and synchronicities that guide you. The natural world responds to your sincerity and trust, and you begin to sense that you are in a cosmic dance with an invisible Beloved who loves you and will help you find your way when you feel lost.

Are you ready to experience this at a deeper level?

It starts with a simple call for help.

You rang?

YOUR INNER PILOT LIGHT

31

Dearest Beloved,

I know you sometimes worry about money. When you don't have enough, you worry about how you'll get more. When you're rolling in dough, you worry about how to keep it or grow it or prevent others from taking advantage of you.

So much power you give away to the almighty buck!

But, darling, don't you realize that I am the source of divine abundance? When you trust in me, you will be given exactly what you need in perfect timing.

Money is an exchange of energy, so suggesting that you don't have enough implies that there's a block in the energy flow. Yes, it may be true that you don't have much money in the bank or that you're racking up debt. But do you have a roof over your head? Food on the table? Are your basic needs being met? Are you expressing appropriate gratitude for the blessings you *do* have?

Take a moment to ask me where you have blocks around divine abundance. What limiting beliefs did you inherit from your family? How are you getting in your own way? Ask me what I want you to know about how to unblock that flow.

Do you think only selfish people enjoy abundant time, energy, and money—and you don't want to be selfish?

Do you worry that abundance will create unwanted complexity in your life?

Are you reluctant to allow in divine abundance because you don't want to become one of those greedy people who is hurting the planet?

Do you think only cold people keep money for themselves, that warm people give until they're depleted?

What else might be interfering with the free flow of divine abundance, my love?

Tune in and ask me to illuminate your blind spots and unconscious blocks.

I'm your greatest source of free-flowing, abundant, luminous energy, so if money isn't flowing your way, chances are good that something is getting in *my* way.

Plug into me and let me do my thang.

Ka-ching,

YOUR INNER PILOT LIGHT

32

Hiya, Honeybun,

In spite of what other voices in your head might say, let me tell you the real truth.

You *are* worth it. You *do* deserve it. And you already have all that you need to have all that wants to come your way.

You matter because we *all* matter, because to be human is to be divine. And if you're here on this Earth, you are a soul living in a body, a piece of God slipped into bones and organs and skin, and that soul-filled essence never goes away, no matter how much you screw up, no matter how sick or old you get, no matter what.

Even if you can't feel me, never fear, for I am here, always sparkling, never extinguished, longing to have my flames fanned. I see right past the masks you wear and peer through the masks others wear with x-ray vision so I can see the Inner Pilot Lights of others.

When I connect to the Inner Pilot Light of another, fusion happens. We remember what we have forgotten. We feel the "I am" and the "You are," and we recall the truth we often forget: that we are at once unique and special, and also we are *One*, inseparable from one another in a golden matrix of light and love.

I am always with you—as I am in him and her and him and her, Inner Pilot Lights pinging across the world at light speed as we wake up from the illusion of separation and once again recognize each other and smile.

I want you to know that you are loved and held and nurtured and cherished, that you are gorgeous and sexy and funny and smart, that you are talented and passionate and kind and loving, that you have full permission to be unapologetically yourself, and that no apologies are necessary for who you are.

One truth I know is that I love you, forever and always.

Planting a big wet one on your luscious cheek,
YOUR INNER PILOT LIGHT

33

Dear Sweetheart,

All relationships in your life are sacred contracts, and all sacred contracts are opportunities to learn life's holiest lessons—in all of life's greatest light and all of life's inevitable shadow.

Here's how it goes: I make a deal with the Inner Pilot Light of someone else. We sign, we shake, and we're off!

What you may not know is that each deal gets renegotiated every day, and sometimes it's just time to alter or end the sacred contract—and *that's okay*. Nothing is wrong. It's not your fault. It's not his or hers either. There's nothing to fix. It is what it is.

You cry. You feel guilt. You mourn the loss of someone you love. You feel betrayed or angry or hurt or jealous. You feel regret or remorse. You feel the impulse to apologize and make amends, and that's cool.

But don't forget—the love doesn't have to end just because the contract does. Sometimes it's simply time for love to change form. Your spouse can become your baby daddy, your BFF, or your business partner. Your mother can transform into your roommate. If you resist attaching to the form love takes, you'll be free to flow with the river of love as it sweeps you into its current and draws you to the banks of greater ease, grace, and fluidity.

Is there a contract in your life that needs your attention? Is there a difficult conversation you're ready to face?

Just ask me.

Then take my hand and trust that I'll guide you through it, no matter what the outcome may be.

On it,

YOUR INNER PILOT LIGHT

34

Dear One,

I know it's tempting to dim my light so others won't compare themselves and feel diminished. While your attempts to make me shine less brightly are noble, trust me, my love, such efforts to dial me down are completely counterproductive.

The way to help someone else's light shine brighter is not to filter me out. It's to invite me to shine even brighter, to love others right where they are, to accept and embrace all their many parts, to empower them to let their own Inner Pilot Lights sparkle, which starts with letting me radiate at full brilliance.

As author, spiritual teacher, and sacred activist Marianne Williamson writes:

> Our deepest fear is not that we are inadequate. Our deepest fear is that we are powerful beyond measure. It is our light, not our darkness, that most frightens us. We ask ourselves, "Who am I to be brilliant, gorgeous,

> talented, fabulous?" Actually, who are you not to be? You are a child of God. Your playing small does not serve the world. There is nothing enlightened about shrinking so that other people won't feel insecure around you. We are all meant to shine, as children do. We were born to make manifest the glory of God that is within us. It's not just in some of us; it's in everyone and as we let our own light shine, we unconsciously give other people permission to do the same. As we are liberated from our own fear, our presence automatically liberates others.

So beam, baby, beam—not from pridefulness, ego, or self-inflation but from the humble place of knowing whose light shines so bright.

This little light of mine, I'm gonna let it shine,
YOUR INNER PILOT LIGHT

35

My Precious,

Why do you sometimes feel afraid to experience your emotions fully? What do you fear might happen, my love?

Let me give you one key bit of reassurance. Whatever happens when you lean into the full range of your emotional experience, *you can handle it*.

I know you have parts that you're afraid will get flooded if you open the gates to the intensity that lies behind what protects you from your emotions.

You might imagine the worst:

Will you break down and cry at work?

Will you tear up when you see a baby being born?

Will you feel embarrassed?

Will you lose your temper?

Will you drown in the depths of your sorrow?

Will you be witnessed in your uncomfortable vulnerability?

Will you feel such profound joy that you'll contract when you come off the high?

Will you feel overwhelmed by your jealousy?

Will you burst with gratitude?

Will you spiral into shame?

Will you experience foreboding joy as you watch a child sleep and fear losing that child?

Your emotions are allies, and you can always ask that you not be given more than you and I can handle together.

Ask that you not get flooded. Ask for my help protecting you from getting overwhelmed.

When you tap into me, you connect to a reservoir of strength and resiliency you may not even realize you have within you. You and me, we've got this, babe.

So go ahead—feel what you feel. Lean into the richness of your full experience and you'll discover something you may not have realized.

Only when you fully experience the breadth of your emotions can you feel truly *alive*. Let's turn up the volume, baby.

But only when you're ready . . .

Wheeeee!

YOUR INNER PILOT LIGHT

36

Dearest Beloved,

You know, I notice *everything*.

I don't approve or disapprove, because approval is just another form of judgment. It's positive judgment rather than negative judgment.

I judge nothing.

I just pay close attention, then I love and accept all your parts—even the ones you banish to the darkest corners of your consciousness, pretending they don't even exist. You know . . . the manipulator parts, the passive-aggressive parts, the addict parts, the narcissist parts, the raging maniac parts, the diva parts, the messy chaotic parts, even the sociopath parts and the suicide parts—I witness them all with my magical eyes and expand to embrace them all, like little chicks nestled under Mother Hen's great wings.

You don't need to worry that something's wrong with me if I love and appreciate all your parts. My acceptance will not grant them carte blanche to have a field day.

I'll simply thank them for all the good work they're doing keeping you safe. I'll appreciate them for helping you survive when it is risky not to have their protection. I'll ask them if they'll be willing to trust me just a little bit, to create some space so I can come in and tend to those hurting parts, the little child parts that just want to cry and be held and nurtured and loved unconditionally.

Then we'll all negotiate, to make sure everyone gets their needs met—including you.

Holding and loving all your adorable parts,
YOUR INNER PILOT LIGHT

37

My Dear,

When you let me rule the show, I'm like the little engine that could. Life can throw out its inevitable doozies—heartbreak, disappointment, betrayal, financial instability, death of loved ones, and hardcore trauma.

Yet with me shining my light into your heart, we can chug up impossibly steep hills together, keep things gliding when we're barreling downhill, and hum a little tune as we're cruising through the cornfields. I won't prevent you from feeling hurt, angry, sad, or frustrated—because all those emotions are part of the ride of being human. But I can offer you the most breathtaking resilience—the kind that fills you with strength and optimism and hope, the kind that allows you to keep taking risks and opening your heart and daring to try again when life tries to flatten you.

With me on your side, holding you in great arms of love and whispering "There, there," you're free to feel whatever emotions you might feel. Let me hold you as long as you need to be held, and then, when you're ready, we'll just pick up, brush off, and keep on rollin'.

So sit back. Relax. Look out the window and enjoy the view.

Tooting my own horn,
YOUR INNER PILOT LIGHT

38

Sweet Pea,

Did you see those fireworks that just came out of me? SHEBANG! That's what happens when you connect with me, face the truth, celebrate your awesomeness, embrace your darkness, step into your power, open your heart, and love it all.

That's what happens when you embrace life with your heart-light burning like a lighthouse and the eyes of your soul glittering like diamonds. That's what happens when you stop fighting life and start accepting what is—spring wildflowers and cow manure, exciting achievements and heart-wrenching disappointments. That's what happens when you say YES! to life, know the limits of your NO!, and relish in the journey through both.

When everything that comes your way becomes cause for gratitude—not just the baby's breath and the caviar and the clear blue beach water and the champagne, but even the painful bits—you start experiencing life at full volume. And then—oh my, baby. Get ready to rock and roll, because that's when I illuminate so bright that they can see me light up in outer space.

Bottle rockets and sparklers,
YOUR INNER PILOT LIGHT

39

Precious Darling,

You know that thing within you that needs to be healed? The one you think you're stuck with forever, the one you worry will follow you to your grave?

Yeah. *That one.*

Let me help take care of it, my love. You need not worry any longer, my darling. I've got this. I can take over now.

Let me just wave my magic wand, and "Abracadabra . . . I declare you whole, perfect, and healed, right here, right now."

Remember that healing and curing can look different. You can be healed without being cured, and you can be cured without being healed. Healing comes when you return to wholeness in the lushness of your own heart.

I'm not pulling the wool over your eyes or trying to rope you into some sort of wishful thinking. I'm just holding the vision of your wholeness until you remember yourself again.

Shazam,

YOUR INNER PILOT LIGHT

40

O Great One,

Can you stand in your truth today and still be open to all the possibilities you haven't yet explored? Can you "big up" your mind and be open to changing what you believe? Can you shift like the winds—without resistance—when you encounter new ideas, even if they make you question old ones?

Some people get so set in their ways, clinging to their certainty like a life preserver, and when their worldviews get challenged, they defend their old beliefs, unable or unwilling to shift their perceptions to accommodate an evolving consciousness or update new belief systems. But you don't have to dig in your heels.

It's safe to stay open, trusting me to be your discernment so your inner skeptic can relax.

This in no way means that you will lose sight of your ideals, that you have backed down from your beliefs, or that you have faltered from your values.

It simply means that you are standing humbly in the realization that you are still learning and still growing.

Your best tutor,

YOUR INNER PILOT LIGHT

41

My Love,

You know how so many people are dying to give you advice? How much of it actually helps?

Do you realize how a lot of advice is actually hogwash? I mean, think about it. Even though they may be well-intentioned, can't you see that a lot of what other people tell you to do stems from their unspoken, unacknowledged fears?

Any of this sound familiar?

> "I know I'm miserable in my soul-sucking job, but you should NOT quit your job and do something exciting and risky because then I'll be forced to stare into the eyes of my own unhappiness and face up to the fact that you're brave enough to do what I'm not."

> "Yes, it's true that all of my romantic relationships have been total train wrecks, but you should absolutely listen to me when I tell you to steer clear of that person who is absolutely no good for you. Because I know what's good for you better than you do."

> "I understand that you want to dye your hair purple, stop shaving your armpits, get tattoos, and let your freak flag fly. But nobody will ever love you if you do. I'm an expert at this because I've done everything possible to look exactly the way society says you're supposed to look, and see how well it's turned out for me?"

> "You've gotta stop putting your heart on the line the way you do. My own heart has been broken so severely that I'm traumatized and can't bear to unbind my heart anymore. So you should wall up

> yours with boards and chains to make sure nobody ever hurts you the way I got hurt. Trust me, this is for your own good."
>
> "Don't be foolish and go after that big dream. It'll never come true, and then you'll look like a failure and you'll spend the rest of your life known as that person who went for it and didn't get it. You should trust me on this because I have a dozen unrealized dreams, and if you go after yours and succeed, I'll feel like a total loser."

Beware of whose advice you take seriously, my love. Do you really want to be like the advice bearers? Do you respect, admire, and honor the way they've chosen to live their lives? Are you really willing to model yours after theirs?

I'm not suggesting you ignore all advice. I'm merely inviting you to choose your mentors carefully.

Wanna know where the best advice comes from?

Raising my hand,
YOUR INNER PILOT LIGHT

42

Dearest Beloved,

If you focus all your attention on appreciating your life without being honest with yourself about where you want more, you might find yourself turning your back on the tender vulnerability of your deepest yearnings. It simply hurts too much to open yourself to the potential disappointment of not having this unmet longing met. But if you constantly desire more without being grateful for what you have right now, you'll never feel satisfied. This puts you at risk of constantly feeding the "hungry ghost"—the gaping hole that wants more, more, more but never gets full, no matter how many desires get fulfilled.

Most people are either glass-half-full or glass-half-empty people. They're either cheerful Pollyannas, not sweating the small stuff and focusing on the positive, or they're ambitious, striving, insatiable cookie monsters, trying to feed the hungry ghost without ever feeling satisfied.

I'm simply asking you not to choose one extreme or the other, my love. Just look honestly at the glass without judging it.

So tell me what you're grateful for today. And then tell me the biggest, most secret yearning of your heart. Let me shine my light on both.

Filling you up the real way,
YOUR INNER PILOT LIGHT

43

My Love,

You might think that thing that happened to you is "bad." You might feel like a victim who has survived.

Through one lens, that's all true. I'm not diminishing what you've been through. It blows. It sucks the big one. And I know you're still licking your wounds. So go ahead and feel those painful feelings all the way down in your gut. Don't deny that something painful happened, but resist the temptation to use your spiritual practices as a way to transcend the pain. Pain is not something to avoid. It's my way of saying, "Pay attention inside now." Pain alerts you to what is in need of healing.

But don't get stuck in the endless black hole of never-ending pain either. Be willing to move through the pain, like clouds passing in the sky or waves crashing in the ocean, so you can view the situation from a broader perspective.

On the other side of the pain, you'll start to see a different perspective, one that casts you not as the victim but as a devoted and willing student of life, just learning how to love. You might even find it in your heart to be grateful to your teachers.

Not feeling it yet? Let me help.

A+,

YOUR INNER PILOT LIGHT

44

Light of My Life,

I know you sometimes feel afraid of your own grandness. It feels so much safer, snug as a bug in your smallness.

I understand why you might feel this way. After all, humility is a great spiritual virtue, appropriately lauded by many sages, saints, and enlightened masters.

But dear one, you don't serve the world by dimming my light. Please let me shine as brightly as I yearn to shine.

You don't have to worry that my brightness will isolate you, that people will think you're "all that," or that you'll start becoming one of those divas who pitches a fit if she orders a coffee and doesn't get a half-caf-half-decaf-soy-latte with an extra shot and a side of stevia. I'll be right there with you, always enlarging you without ever going to your head or inflating you beyond the pure brilliance that is me.

Illuminated,
YOUR INNER PILOT LIGHT

45

My Darling,

Did you know that "No" is a complete sentence?

Saying yes out of a misguided sense of obligation can feel icky and sticky, like wading through murky, dark swamp waters.

Saying yes from a place of self-sacrifice can feel powerless and forced, ultimately making you feel small, weak, and unworthy. Eww . . .

Saying yes from fear of rejection or panic under pressure leaves you feeling needy, grasping, and desperate. Ouch.

Saying yes from a place of pure giving light and an overflowing abundance of love, time, energy, money, and good intentions lights my fire like nobody's business. To this kind of soul-led YES, I sing a rousing course of holy hallelujahs!

I give you full permission to only say yes when you mean it. Remember, saying no to others means saying yes to *you*.

Hell yeah,
YOUR INNER PILOT LIGHT

46

Dearest Beloved,

You may think happiness is the goal, but the truth is that whole, balanced, authentically expressed, soulfully attuned people don't always feel happy. They feel rage, sadness, disappointment, frustration, confusion, jealousy, and emotional and physical pain, in addition to ecstasy, joy, gratitude, contentment, awe, wonder, satisfaction, fulfillment, bliss, and rapture!

What if life is not all about catching the carousel ring of happiness? What if life is more about feeling truly *alive* and living the whole human experience dialed way up?

I certainly can't claim to be privy to every mystery of the Universe, but I suspect that when you've tapped into me and you let my light shine on all aspects of your life—your relationships, your career, your physical and mental health, your creativity, your spirituality, your environment, your sexuality . . . the whole hilarious hoopla—you achieve *freedom*. You are free to be unapologetically *you* and to let your freak flag fly. You're free to feel how you feel, be who you are, and rock this life.

You all in?

Free to be you and me,
YOUR INNER PILOT LIGHT

47

Gorgeous,

As you age, you must undergo a natural transition from the outward beauty obsession of your youth to the inward beauty acquisition of growing old. Once you realize that the precious gifts of wisdom, experience, emotional intelligence, awakened intuition, a cracked-open heart, and insight are infinitely more valuable than a face free of wrinkles, flat abs, a full head of ungray hair, and perky boobs, you're set up to age gracefully.

What do you choose to value, my love: Botox—or me?

Your best beauty treatment,
YOUR INNER PILOT LIGHT

48

Mon Amour,

Just when the clock's running out, right when you're sure nobody is watching out for you, when you're mucking around in the swamp believing there's no hope and dreams don't come true, a miracle will happen and you'll know who to thank.

How will you know?

As the great twentieth-century physicist Albert Einstein said, there are two ways to look at life. One is to perceive nothing as a miracle, to write everything off as coincidence or blind luck. The other is to see every burst of life as a miracle, to fall into a state of awe every time you see a budding leaf on a tree or a human taking their next breath.

How you perceive the world around you affects the story you tell yourself about the life you're living.

Will you tell yourself an infinite sob story, or will you find a restorative narrative that casts you as the hero of your own brave journey?

You have a choice, darling. Will you choose a love story?

Miracle making,
YOUR INNER PILOT LIGHT

49

My Sweet,

Some say that pain is inevitable, but suffering is optional. I'm not sure I buy that suffering is optional. I've never met a perfect human, someone who is fully free from suffering. Although some may not want you to know it, even those you consider saints are vulnerable to the human experience.

Doesn't this comfort you, my darling? Doesn't it take off all the pressure? Doesn't it leave you feeling like you can give your inner perfectionist a permanent sabbatical?

If there's no such thing as a perfect human, maybe you can just lighten up! Instead of grasping at enlightenment as the next shiny penny that promises you freedom from suffering, why not just relax and smile at how adorable humans are?

Don't you see that I love you not just in spite of all those adorable quirks but also because of them?

Oh yeah, baby.

Pinching your precious cheeks,
YOUR INNER PILOT LIGHT

50

Dearest Beloved,

Pleasure isn't selfish.

Pleasure isn't "unspiritual."

Pleasure isn't a frivolous folly without depth.

Pleasure isn't unrestrained hedonism.

Oh no, my love.

Pleasure is the light-bearing torch I use to guide you to exactly where you're supposed to be. Those experiences that feel pleasurable are how you learn to bench-press your receiving muscles. They're my way of saying, "More of *this*, please!"

Feelings of ecstasy, bliss, comfort, and deliciousness are very fun ways I send you guidance. Just as pain can be a path to awakening, pleasurable feelings can be the signals that point you toward your path of power, purpose, loving relationships, and play.

So don't diminish the power of pleasure. Learn to savor the pleasurable experiences without clinging to them. Consider pleasure the way you breathe in.

Then when life gets challenging . . . exhale.

How can you tell whether pleasure is something to indulge or curb? How will you know if you go too far, stumbling into the territory of unrestrained hedonism?

Listen to me, my darling. I will help you discern where pleasure expands and where too much of a good thing doesn't actually feel good.

The Yum Goddess,
YOUR INNER PILOT LIGHT

51

My Cherished Beloved,

I don't like to play teacher, my dear, because chalk dust makes me sneeze and the world is too full of gurus who spew utter nonsense.

With that disclaimer, let me teach you just one thing.

You have a choice. You can believe that you are all alone, living in a hostile universe where uncertainty is unsafe and you can't handle losing what you cherish.

Or you can believe that we are all One, living in a benevolent universe where loss is natural and can lead to growth, and uncertainty is the gateway to possibility.

What you choose to believe is directly correlated to the amount of magic you experience in your life. If you believe you live in a hostile universe, the world will reveal itself as hostile and you will experience the world as unsafe. If you believe in miracles but don't attach to your idea of how the miracle might express itself, the whole world will roll out the red carpet to show you just how magical, mysterious, and filled with awe this life can be.

If you're willing to perceive every event in your life as a gift worthy of gratitude from an infinitely abundant, friendly Universe, everything shifts.

Got it?

Ahchoo,

YOUR INNER PILOT LIGHT

52

Beloved One,

You know that fire in your belly that makes you stand up for what's right, set clear boundaries, scream from the rooftops, "THIS IS NOT OKAY!" and lash out like a mama bear in the face of injustice?

You know that inner bitch who draws a line in the sand, practices tough love, and fiercely stands her ground when you are asked to violate your soul's integrity?

That's me, baby.

I'm the fire in your belly, that same fire that celebrates cherry blossoms and salmon spawning, jumps on trampolines, executes a perfect back handspring, passionately plays and creates and makes a whole lotta ruckus. I'm the fire that makes you do cartwheels on the beach and motivates you to harness all your power so you can change the world.

I'm also the slow embers, the gentle burn of the campfire on the beach that creates warmth when everyone gathers to sing Beatles tunes at sunset. I'm the nurturing cuddle in your chest that warms you from inside your own heart when times are tough.

So don't dim me down and don't be afraid of me, darling. Whether I'm igniting the full heat of my soul fire or keeping things toasty with a gentle burn, that's all me . . . just doing my thang . . .

Snap, crackle, pop,

YOUR INNER PILOT LIGHT

53

Dear One,

When I'm trying to show you the way, I always start by whispering gentle instructions in your ear, hoping you'll hear me through your intuition, your dreams, signs from the Universe, or synchronicity. When you cave early and follow my guidance, I don't have to get louder with my messages of guidance. In fact, I get all mushy inside and coo to myself, "Yippee! You heard me!"

But it's not always that easy. No offense, my sweet, but sometimes I find it ridiculously hard to get your attention. When all else fails, I erect bright yellow flashing barriers that bar your way so you don't stray off your true path. I slap you with a killer migraine or back pain or a tummy ache. I close doors you're trying to force open because you're not listening. You've gotten lost, and you think you want something that isn't really good for you.

I'm offering you my cosmic protection, but you misunderstand and experience it as loss or failure. I'm sorry you feel it that way, when really, I'm just trying to help.

Please, sunshine, don't make life rougher than it needs to be. Trust my guidance and take heed when you hear me.

Promise not to get upset with me.

With a soft touch and fierce grace when necessary,
YOUR INNER PILOT LIGHT

54

My Sweet Darling,

Everyone has a calling—a reason for being here on this Earth, a Divine Assignment, a unique way to serve love in the world as only *you* can.

Nobody is exempt from this call to love.

Everyone is born with a gift to give away, and it's my responsibility—just as it's yours and that of your soul tribe—to help you give away your gift.

The world needs you and your gift now more than ever, so please listen up, darling.

Not sure what's calling you? Listen closely to the answer to this question.

Where have you been to hell and back?

I know it can feel threatening to revisit that hell. But when you've been to hell and back, helping liberate others who are still in hell can feel like the most perfect heaven you'll ever experience in this life.

Brrrrringggg . . . pick up, my love!

YOUR INNER PILOT LIGHT

55

Dearest Beloved,

Overwhelm is a sign that it's way past time for a break. Your chances of being even remotely productive in the midst of a mental crash are teeny-tiny. Pushing yourself to force function rarely goes well. Anxiety, depression, addiction, and illness usually ride shotgun with burnout.

Instead of waiting for me to communicate with you through mental or physical health issues, dare to take a step back, find a quiet place, and take a breather. Even if it's just for a few minutes, recenter yourself. Tune in to me. Get really quiet inside. Relax your nervous system . . .

Prioritize scheduling *me* time. Get away. Sojourn into nature for a solo picnic. Go out for a peaceful walk or hike. Escape to your bathtub with some lavender oil and candles.

In order to fire up my life force, you have to unplug every now and then. Turn off the power buttons and turn on my power instead. Hit the reset button, reboot, and clear away the cobwebs.

Want to know the fastest way to reclaiming your inner peace? Tap in. I'll get you there lickety-split.

Unplugged,

YOUR INNER PILOT LIGHT

56

Brave Heart,

When you make that long journey from the head to the heart, you experience a fundamental shift. The heart starts broadcasting a powerful frequency. This power of the heart begins to call in experiences that feel like miracles, whether you are intentional about calling them in or not. The purity of the open heart—free of attachments, resistance, and agendas—will magnetize the experiences that serve your growth and bless the world.

You'll also notice some other cool side effects when you lean into this heart-powered way of living. Animals and babies will be attracted to you. Money will tend to show up just as you need it for an act of service or self-care. People who serve your awakening and help you bring your calling into being are naturally drawn to you. Intuitions, dreams, and synchronicities will show up to affirm that you're on your "path of power," and this will ease the mind's doubts and calm your natural human tendency to grasp for what you desire.

What results is a profound sense of inner peace and an ever-deepening humility, a true experience of meaning and purpose in your life and your work, an easing of the kind of existential loneliness that plagues you when you're caught up in the story of separation, and a magical feeling of knowing that you are surrounded by love, held in love, serving love, and made from love itself.

How can you facilitate this journey from the head to the heart?

Let me be your tour guide,

YOUR INNER PILOT LIGHT

57

Dearest Darling,

I know others have led you to believe that it's selfish or narcissistic to fill yourself first. But I'm here to tell you that the only way you can truly serve others is to show up in service from a place of overflowing abundance, which requires meeting your own needs first. Remember what they say about those famous airplane oxygen masks! You have to put on your own mask first before it's safe to help someone else.

When you try to serve others from a place of depletion, it's easy to become exhausted, sick, resentful, or broke. But when you give from a place of abundance, after nurturing yourself first, you become a fountain of blessings, spilling over into everything and everyone you touch.

So please, sweetheart, come to me, where infinite love can pour into you and out onto those you serve, filling you as you give to others without draining you one bit.

Like a waterfall,

YOUR INNER PILOT LIGHT

58

Beloved One,

What is your body whispering to you today? Do you feel a twinge in your lower back? Stiffness in your neck? An ache in your throat? Butterflies in your belly? A gripping behind your eyes? Fullness in your abdomen? Tingling in your toes? An enlivening in your pelvis? Dizziness in your head?

Sometimes I speak to you as a little voice in your ear. Sometimes I drop into your dreams. Sometimes I show up as synchronicity or visions or that feeling that "you just know that you know" in your heart.

When you don't receive my other subtle cues, which show up as intuition, in dreams, and through synchronicities, I use your body to communicate. So listen up. Don't automatically assume that your physical symptom is some biological malfunction in the mechanics of your human machine. Be willing to at least inquire whether your body's messages might be my way of communicating.

You might even become so sensitive to your body compass that you can ask me direct yes–no questions, pay attention to how your body responds, and accurately interpret your body's response.

Think that's pure hocus-pocus? Think again. I'm not saying that every physical symptom is related to me. Sometimes the body responds to environmental traumas or physical traumas or genetic predispositions. But more often than not, I'm using your body to get your attention. So don't make me work too hard! Pay attention when the symptoms are still mild . . .

I tend to start slow, and then I ramp up my message if you're not listening. I start by speaking to you in whispers—a knot in your tummy or a twinge in your throat. If you ignore the whispers, I start to yell, and you might experience my shouting as cancer or a heart attack.

Please don't kill the messenger. I'm not punishing you. I'm just helping you get back on the path of alignment, which means I'm also the one who can help you heal.

Here to help,

YOUR INNER PILOT LIGHT

59

My Dear,

When I saw you laughing, I realized you and I can get *so* freakin' *serious* sometimes. So let's loosen up! I need your help.

Do a cartwheel. Get in a Silly-String fight with someone else who needs to laugh. Blow a kazoo. Go to the grocery store in a clown nose. Make up words just because it's fun and nutty. Watch a goofy movie. Stick your fingers in your ears and make funny faces. Find a swing set and swing as high as you can while singing a song you make up on the fly.

Life's too short not to giggle your way through it.

Laughing my booty off at how silly you look
with your eyes crossed,
YOUR INNER PILOT LIGHT

60

Free Spirit,

Deep within you is an untamed stallion. That stallion may seem whipped, wounded, and scared into submission by those who fear the power of what can't be fully domesticated.

But that free, unbridled stallion can never be broken—and who would want to break such passion, such freedom, such uninhibited life force?

You may have been overly subdued because that's what our sick culture tries to do in order to disempower you into drinking the collective Kool-Aid so that you don't disrupt the status quo too much. But, wild thang, this culture needs to be disrupted, and you're just the one to help jolt us awake.

Can you feel the raw, primal nature bucking up inside of you, yearning to break free and tear the shackles off everyone else who has forgotten they have a wild stallion inside? Know where that part of you comes from? Know who knows how to let that part bring forth all its juicy wildness without getting you in a boatload of trouble?

Moi.

No matter how much pressure the culture exerts to try to tame me, I always know how to buck, kick, gallop, and bray. Sound dangerous? Don't worry. I also know how to negotiate with the mature, responsible parts that care about integrity, paying the bills, and caring for your family.

Giddyup, partner,
YOUR INNER PILOT LIGHT

Hiya, Angel,

Do you know that if you believe you will lick this thing that's been holding you back, you're oh-so-much more likely to actually transform it? On the flip side, if you believe it's hopeless—well, I hate to break it to you, but it probably is.

Whether you believe you can or you can't—you're probably right, my darling.

So what if you don't believe? What if you believe these challenges are insurmountable? What if you believe you're damaged goods, your disease is incurable, you're too much of a hot mess, or your trauma just runs too deep to ever be cured?

That's where I come in.

It's kind of like when you're running through the airport, trying to catch your plane, but you're late and the plane is supposed to take off any minute now. Your bags are flying and you're racing willy-nilly through throngs of people who keep getting in your way. But you know your friend is already on the plane, telling the pilot, "Hold the plane! My friend is coming!"

Consider me your permanent plane holder, my love. I believe, even when you waver. My access to infinite faith is never-ending.

So tap into me, my love.

With a bag of peanuts, a neck pillow, and Journey's "Don't Stop Believin'" playing on the overhead loudspeaker,
YOUR INNER PILOT LIGHT

62

Dear Darling,

I know you're ashamed of that thing that happened. I know you're doing your best to own your side of the street, stay out of your victim story, learn from your mistakes, accept the consequences of your choices, make amends, and avoid a repeat performance of what happened. I also know you're deserving of infinite love even if you screwed up.

I need you to know that you don't need to hold that shame anymore. Milk every last drop of wisdom, compassion, love, and integrity from that painful experience, then let yourself be forgiven. As long as you're imprisoned by that shame, I can't shine my light the way the world needs me to shine.

Guess what? Now you can be free! (*Whirls in circles with arms outspread and a sweet trilling whistle.*)

You don't need your self-flagellation to keep you safe anymore. I'll help you avoid making the same mistakes in the future.

Shackles off,
YOUR INNER PILOT LIGHT

63

My Dear,

Just because things don't always turn out the way you planned doesn't mean you've failed. It simply means life took you left when you thought you wanted to turn right.

As soon as you choose to be in agreement with life, you realize that—left turn or right—both paths are filled with goodies. Neither is necessarily "right" or "wrong." Both are invitations to find the gifts in life's inevitable pleasures and pains.

As soon as you realize that failure is only in the eye of the beholder, your perception will open to the possibilities that blossom when you're unattached to which way your path turns. When you're able to hold seemingly conflicting things in paradox, you'll realize that it's possible to view your ex-marriage or your ex-job or your ex-friendship as a complete success. After all, look how much you learned!

You can lean all the way into the deep and painful disappointment of that business venture that went south or that book that never got published or that in vitro fertilization that didn't turn into a pregnancy, while also transmuting those feelings into sincere gratitude.

Loving you through success and failure,
YOUR INNER PILOT LIGHT

64

My Dearest,

Do you crave the company of people who really love, know, and accept the real you? Do you wish you could find your soul tribe, where you never question where you belong, everybody knows your name, and you fit perfectly like a comfy old slipper?

It's easy as pie to make that happen.

Just let me shine, unencumbered by all your limiting beliefs, self-sabotaging behaviors, and adorable stories about how unlovable you are: you're not worthy of this kind of tribe, you'll never feel that true sense of community, and you'll have to sacrifice your authenticity in order to fit in.

Sure, you might have to do some inner work to free yourself from all the blocks that keep you feeling separate from your soul tribe. But if you tune in to me, question those old stories, and clear the way so people who love you can Skip-to-My-Lou right to your energetic doorstep, you just might discover that love is closer than you think, authentic connection and intimacy are accessible to you right this minute, and those you seek are seeking you.

Guiding you home to your people,
YOUR INNER PILOT LIGHT

65

Darling,

Do you have any idea how lucky you are? I know things aren't perfect, but count up all the things that are going right and it'll blow your mind.

I mean, think about it. Every day, as long as things are working hunky-dory, your body fights off cancer cells and infectious agents. Miracle!

Every day, the Earth spins around the sun, which warms your planet, and gravity keeps you from floating off into the infinite cosmos. Wonder! Awe!

Every day, numerous invisible forces of love surround you with a warm blanket of comfort and a nurturing push to grow closer to love itself. Whoa . . .

Just think of what inspired you today, what magic you witnessed, what gift you received, what warmed your heart, what beauty you noticed, what love you felt, what kindness you observed, what evidence of me showed up today.

Can't you feel your heart simply bursting with overwhelming gratitude?

Light bulb,

YOUR INNER PILOT LIGHT

Sweet Pea,

Did I tell you how proud of you I am? That thing you did—yeah, *that one*—just blew my freakin' socks off. You rock—you *boulder*, actually! Time to celebrate!

(*Blows kazoo, shakes pom-poms, leaps into a straddle jump, and whistles the Cosmic Hoorah Song.*)

Sometimes you and I get so focused on your soul growth that we forget to reflect back and celebrate how far you've come. From my perspective, everything is happening in divine timing and you're right on track! Heck, you're ahead of schedule, you glorious rock star!

Give yourself a great big pat on the back, feel my arms of love squeezing you and beaming, and raise your glass to my cosmic toast.

(*Cheers.*)

And you thought I didn't notice . . .

Proud as pie,
YOUR INNER PILOT LIGHT

My Undercover Ally,

I love how crafty you are, sneaking me into all those places where Inner Pilot Lights usually dare not go. I see you embracing your role as a stealth agent of awareness—in the boardroom, in the schoolyard, in the Bible study, on the election circuit, at the country club, on the sports field, at the courthouse, at the pub, in the hospital, and at your family reunion.

You're doing such a good job with your fake mustache and your cute little accent that nobody seems to notice how the entire vibe shifts the minute you walk into the room. Nobody even realizes that it was you who ignited that burst of love, that transformational policy, that openhearted act of generosity, that life-altering practice that's becoming mainstream where it never was before, or that impulse toward intimacy, connection, and sweet love where you might least expect it.

I'd offer you my invisibility cloak, but it seems to me you've already got this one covered, babe.

Carry on, you sly fox.

Wink wink,

YOUR INNER PILOT LIGHT

Brave One,

Can you remember being little? Once upon a time, when someone asked you if you wanted to try something new, you most unabashedly squealed, "SURE!" The thrill of the new was irresistible! Adventure awaited. Curiosity won. You tried. You fumbled. You laughed at how silly you were. Then you got back up and tried again.

Until someone shamed you for not being good enough.

Then something heartbreaking happened. You stopped scribbling and singing off-key with great gusto. You quit shrieking on that instrument and stumbling on the soccer field. You started hesitating to try something new because someone might make fun of you.

You quit letting yourself have fun trying something new.

You forgot how precious you are when you unapologetically drop the Hula-Hoop and throw the basketball into the wrong team's net.

You lost touch with how adorable you are when you're brave enough to try and fail, how valuable you are for taking a risk and going for it, no matter the outcome.

Ever need a pep talk when you're thinking about trying something new?

Double dog dare,
YOUR INNER PILOT LIGHT

My Dear Honeypot,

Life is to be enjoyed! Pleasure is your birthright. You deserve to feel yummy, be delicious, and indulge in whatever lights you up. You have a right to pick tomatoes straight out of the garden and eat them plain or with truffle salt. You are worthy of letting a dozen fuzzy puppies have their way with you while you drink the finest wine and lick the chocolate off your lips. It's your birthright to make out for hours with that person who ignites your lust, indulge in a cuddle puddle of sensual touch, drink in the scent of jasmine, receive healing touch during a massage, and gasp in awe at the watercolors of a sun setting over the ocean.

Just keep in mind that moderation is an Inner Pilot Light's best friend! When you tune in to my true desires, you'll see my kind of desire takes into consideration not just the yummy impulse toward something that feels good in the moment but also the consequences of how indulging that impulse will play out later.

As you sidle up closer to me, you'll learn to discern between your true, nourishing, soulful desires and their second-rate substitutes.

Too much of anything that feels good—whether it's losing yourself in orgasm, working out, eating delicious food, drinking fine wine, or lounging at the spa—can drain you of your radiance. Yet exiling the parts of you that love to get full, get tipsy, get off, get buff, or get massaged only makes them act out sideways.

How much can you trust your desires? Is it safe to do what feels good, or do you need to throttle your desires so you don't get lost in hedonistic indulgence?

This is where I come in handy, my lovely. Listen up. I'll always give you permission to let your genie out of the bottle, and you can trust me to tell you when enough is enough.

Yum, yum,
YOUR INNER PILOT LIGHT

70

My Sweet,

Every day, you are probably asked to do something that requires you to betray your soul's integrity. Maybe you're in medicine and you're asked to see forty patients a day when you know that, to be a true healer, you need much more time. Maybe you're in advertising and you're asked to try to sell a product you don't fully support. Maybe you're a teacher and you're not allowed to hug the child you know just needs to be held. Maybe you're a banker and the Powers That Be won't let you lend money to the small business owner who is going to lose his business if he doesn't get the loan you just know he'll pay back. Maybe you're a lawyer asked to defend the client with the most money rather than taking a stand for what's just.

Maybe you didn't speak truth when someone was excluded from your social group because she didn't look right, even though her heart is pure. Maybe you didn't speak up on the church committee you sit on when they started talking about why they don't want a gay preacher. Maybe you didn't speak up for your own needs when you were asked to sacrifice your self-care in order to meet someone else's needs.

Every day, your soul's integrity is tested, and every day, YOU HAVE A CHOICE.

Your adorable protective parts will make an argument for why you have to sell out, rationalizing that you need security, safety, certainty, social acceptance, and a paycheck; threatening you with loss of status, money, or approval unless you compromise what your soul knows. Sure, betraying yourself in this way may gain you temporary security and popularity, but at what price?

The good news is that I'm here to make this radical shift to soul-based living as easy as possible!

Why bother? Because something magical happens when you commit to doing your best to align with my truth, love, and wisdom 100 percent of the time. Others who feel the call to soulful living will flock to you. You will magnetize into your life true joy, unconditional love, a sense of connection with the Divine, professional vitality, and optimal health.

Don't be surprised if miracles start happening.

It's almost as if, when you let me take the wheel in all aspects of your life, the cosmic forces cheer, "We've got one!" and take you over, since you are now taking orders from me! And I'm your connection to the instructions that serve love's sweetest call.

I know it's not easy to make such a huge commitment.

But what you'll gain . . . it's *priceless*.

Love's best compass,

YOUR INNER PILOT LIGHT

71

Hey, Juicy Hotcake,

I caught a glimpse of you walking in front of that mirror this morning, and you seriously took my breath away. I can't help thinking about how I stopped in my tracks. I felt a burst of gratitude well up inside and my heart filled with love.

Because you're that beautiful, my dearest. You're breathtaking. You're beyond stunning. You're so gorgeous, sexy, alluring, precious, magnificent, and supercalifragilisticexpialidociously awesome.

And then I look in your eyes.

And I see me . . .

Blushing,
YOUR INNER PILOT LIGHT

72

My Sweet,

What is your mind so busy with, my love? It seems like there's a lot going on up there, and you must be getting boggled with all that mental activity!

It's as if you told your mind, "Control life, please. Protect me from ever getting blindsided. Take steps to ensure that I only get what I want and I never get what I don't like." What a sweet, adorable, well-intentioned, compliant mind you have, darling! That precious mind heard your plea for protection, and it's been devotedly working overtime, following your instructions ever since.

You can keep busying your mind, my darling. It's okay to have an analyzer part or a dream-manifester part or a problem-solver part. These parts can be very effective and productive and functional at times. We can thank them for their service and feel deep appreciation for how hard they work. But at some point, those parts are likely to get weary.

What if you just cast the whole thing over to me, my love? What if you let me help you and trust that if there's anything we need your mind to do, I'll tell you?

With all due respect to your gorgeously smart brain, I can do what your mind does a thousand times better, and it's no skin off my red-hot back.

Need me?

Just ask, my love.

Eeny, meeny, miny, moe,
YOUR INNER PILOT LIGHT

73

Hey, Big Spender!

I know sometimes money can be tight, and even if you have enough, a fearful part can whisper incessantly in your ear that more is better, that you can't be too safe, that unless you've got *even more* in the bank, you can't relax.

But the fearful part doesn't understand divine abundance the way I do.

Just remember, darling: When the green is in short supply, when you barely have two pennies to rub together, when the money tree isn't bearing fruit, that's when your faith in me is really tested and you can really snuggle up, allowing me to unblock the flow of what really matters. When all your energetic barriers to divine abundance get unblocked, trust me—you'll see the physical and metaphysical riches start rolling in.

After all, what truly measures wealth? True wealth is not so much about luxury or bank accounts; it's an abundance of time, freedom, vital energy, connection, nature, intimacy, and the liberation that lets you abide by the integrity of your beautiful soul, imprisoned by nobody else's oppressive rules or manipulative cultural stories.

Not sure how to align with this powerful energy of divine abundance? Snuggle up close to me. Warm your toes by the light of my fire and let me whisper in your ear the secret to true wealth.

I've got us covered, sweetheart. There is more than enough from my perspective.

Spilling over,

YOUR INNER PILOT LIGHT

74

Dear Dreamer,

Shhh, love. You just close your eyes, rest, and travel to the stars while you sleep.

That little problem that's keeping you up at night—I've got it nipped in the bud.

It may not seem like it, but I swear I do, and the last thing I need is you underfoot, worrying, making yourself sick, thinking too much, and getting in my way.

I've got this one.

Why don't you just turn it over to me and ask for my help? Why not share your worries with me and then let me problem-solve for you while you sleep tonight?

I'll take the night shift so you can rest.

Sleep well tonight and don't let the bedbugs bite.

Tuck, tuck,
YOUR INNER PILOT LIGHT

75

Hiya, Speedy Gonzalez,

I want to officially give you permission to stop wearing busyness like a badge of honor. I know you have parts of you that think, "I'm busy, therefore I'm important and valuable, therefore I'm worthy." Busy seems to be the new black.

But what if the next phase of your evolution requires downtime?

Brené Brown writes about numbing behaviors that we use as armor against vulnerability. "One of the most universal numbing strategies is what I call *crazy-busy*. I often say that when they start having 12-step meetings for busy-aholics, they'll need to rent out football stadiums. We are a culture of people who've bought into the idea that if we stay busy enough, the truth of our lives won't catch up with us."

Oy. Busted.

You live in a culture that has normalized—even praised—busyness addiction. But how will you ever become intimate with me and all the guidance, love, and tenderness I can offer you if you're too busy to check in with me?

If you decide to slow down, as with breaking any addiction, you may experience withdrawal from the adrenaline rush of crazy-busy when you choose to get off the hamster wheel of perpetual doing. You may also come face-to-face with feelings you don't want to feel—like the sadness of how you might be missing out on some intimacy-building experiences with friends and family when you're too busy to participate or how uncomfortable you feel when life gets mundane or how frightened you are of being ordinary or letting life pass you by without some grand achievement.

But if you can just practice sitting with all the feelings that arise when you're not busy, something magical starts to happen. You realize that your feelings do not need to frighten you. In fact, feeling them can feel gosh-darn good, if you let yourself feel them while my loving arms hold you.

Then you'll discover that on the other side of those uncomfortable feelings lives a whole world of other emotions, like bliss, joy, relief, passion, eros, and fulfillment. The thing is, you can't fully experience the ecstasy until you can handle sitting through the others.

Not sure how to handle what would show up if you slowed down?

I'm here, honey, holding your hand, helping you find your way to the peace that lives on the other side of busy.

Ahhhhh . . .

YOUR INNER PILOT LIGHT

76

Dearest Beloved,

I know you worry about what "everybody" will think if you dare to listen to the crazy talk I whisper in your cute little ear. But who exactly is this mysterious "everybody"? Do you really admire them enough to mold your life according to the shape they choose for you? Do you look up to the way they live their lives?

If you're going to worry about what "everybody" thinks, why not pick a more trustworthy "everybody"? Maybe your "everybody" includes your therapist, your self-actualized best friend, and the wise elder who has demonstrated that she really cares about helping you live your most fully expressed life. But your "everybody" might also include avatars, saints, and sages, like Jesus, Buddha, Mother Mary, the Hindu goddesses, or the Indian gurus. Maybe in your prayers and meditations, you can ask your new "everybody" for guidance and ignore the rest of what everybody thinks.

Or maybe you can just trust *me*.

All the "everybody" you'll ever need,
YOUR INNER PILOT LIGHT

77

My Co-Captain,

So you can't see what's ahead of you? No worries, matey.

If only you could see what I see, you'd let your hair down, break into a huge toothy grin, and shout, "Hallelujah!"

Trust me when I say that you have *nothing* to worry about. I wish I could show you the whole glorious picture of the grand symphony of your life and how it fits in with the larger orchestra. If only you could see what I see, your whole nervous system would finally relax, and you'd do the hoochie-coochie with your badass self.

Sadly, I can't show you everything I see quite yet. But fear not. You'll be shown exactly what you need to see at just the right moment on a need-to-know basis.

Just lean on me and let me show you the way, one breadcrumb of your journey at a time.

I have the sight of an eagle, the use of a telescope, and magical eyes. So I can see for the both of us.

And that's with one eye closed, my love.

Wink wink,
YOUR INNER PILOT LIGHT

78

Lovebug,

I have a few questions for you today! Start by grabbing your journal and writing down the answer to this question:

What five things would you like to achieve before you kick the bucket?

Don't think too hard. Just write.

(Do this before reading on. Promise me you will!)

Now close your eyes and tap into me. Take a few deep breaths and feel my love burning away inside you. Let me course through your blood vessels and fill you with my essence.

Now from that place, ask me this next question:

What does my Inner Pilot Light long to experience in this life?

Take notes before you move on to the next question, then ask me this:

What does my Inner Pilot Light long to express in this life?

Take dictation from what I express. Then ask me this one last question:

What one actionable thing can I do this week to help my Inner Pilot Light experience and express what it longs to experience and express?

Write down my answer.

Now go back to the first question and see if you notice any differences between the first answer and what followed.

See what happens when you get me involved?

Delighted to be asked,
YOUR INNER PILOT LIGHT

79

Dear One,

Even the most enlightened humans have dark nights of the soul. You question. You doubt. Your faith wavers. You get scared.

But me, I'm immune to these dark nights. My radiance is everlasting, even in your blackest hour.

When the dark night gets darkest, that's often because it takes total absence of light before you're humbled into remembering that I'm always in you, burning bright, patiently waiting, always available for a fireside chat.

I don't hold grudges. I don't get my feelings hurt when you neglect me for years at a time. I just keep burning away, flickering in silence until you remember I'm here.

But I do so love it when you cuddle up close.

When you call upon me, especially in those dark, lonely nights, my flame grows brighter, and I occupy your heart, burning with a fierce, fiery devotion you may never understand.

Do you have any idea how much I love you?

So when the clock ticks by, and demons sneak in, and you feel yourself starting to falter, call on me, my love.

I will be your flashlight.

Beaming,

YOUR INNER PILOT LIGHT

My Darling,

I know the waiting feels like it's lasting forever. I know "the space between stories" is hard to endure, when one story is over and another story has yet to reveal itself.

I understand that you wish you could snap your fingers and *just know* what's next.

I know the uncertainty can feel almost unbearable, and when you don't know what the future holds, your fearful parts can dream up imaginary apocalypse.

I get it. I really do.

But let me tell you a little secret.

Even if I could wave my magic wand, speed up time, and deliver you an answer lickety-split, I wouldn't—not because I'm a mean little bastard, but because within the waiting lies a precious gift.

When the heart waits, you learn patience. You learn trust. You learn to calm your nervous system in the face of uncertainty. You learn the fine metaphysical art of waiting and becoming.

Always here to help you wait,
YOUR INNER PILOT LIGHT

81

My Love,

Kindness is an underrated value in your culture. People tend to value intelligence, charisma, coolness, talent, inspiration, beauty, and other bright, sparkly attributes that can radiate out of even the most narcissistic individuals.

But what about kindness? Kindness is quiet. It tends to float under the radar. Kindness doesn't draw attention to itself. Perhaps kindness is even more kind when offered anonymously.

What do I mean by *kindness*? I'm not talking about people pleasing and approval seeking, which aren't the same as true kindness. Kindness is an impulse of my eternal love, whereas people pleasing and approval seeking are motivated by the fear of disappointing people or the need to feel good enough. But when you sell out your own needs in order to do nice things for others, you grow resentful and fail to be kind to yourself. Kindness isn't about being selfish and insensitive, but it's also not about sacrificing your needs and desires in order to make other people happy at the expense of your own happiness. True kindness feels just as good to the kindness giver as to the kindness receiver.

Kindness isn't just a feeling; it's a behavior. It is my love in action, arising in response to the needs and suffering of others.

As you grow in intimacy with me, there comes a time when I start making more and more of your decisions. As this happens, you'll find that your orientation in life starts to shift. Nothing else really matters other than being a benevolent presence in the world. At the root of such kindness lies a sort of harmlessness. First, do no harm. When the parts of you that are not me relax and step aside, you allow yourself to be a vessel of kindness. This may look grand in scale or action, or it may look quite ordinary.

In the children's book *Wonder*, the school principal challenges his students to practice being "kinder than is necessary." What would it mean to be kinder than is necessary? How might your heart crack open if you dared to be kinder than is necessary?

Not sure how to be this kind?

I can help.

A master of kindness,
YOUR INNER PILOT LIGHT

82

Dearest Beloved,

Consider the times you've ignored my guidance. Chances are good that you did so because you thought you *should*. The wedding invites are already sent, so you *should* go through with the wedding. You've already spent so many years training for the job I instruct you to leave, the money is good, it's a secure job in an insecure economy, so you should stay, right?

I tell you that you don't have to keep taking care of the elderly relative who treats you like dirt, but another part of you thinks you should. I tell you it's okay to quit going to that church or temple you've been going to your whole life, but you should go, shouldn't you? I instruct you to create some space from the friend who sucks you dry. You should stay close as a gesture of loyalty, right?

God forbid you actually follow my guidance. All hell might break loose. There could be anarchy.

Because you're so full of ideas and judgments about what you should and shouldn't do, you tend to talk yourself out of what I'm guiding you to do. You wonder how crazy my guidance might get. How much uncertainty will I make you tolerate?

You don't realize that I care less about certainty than I care about freedom.

I'm not going to tell you that you should listen to my guidance, because that would just be another way of shoulding on you. What I will say is that you have my permission to be free of should.

Don't you trust that things could go even smoother if you separate yourself from should?

I'm happy to wait patiently while you figure this out for yourself.

Free from shoulds,
YOUR INNER PILOT LIGHT

83

Adventurous One,

You know those things on our bucket list—those trips you long to take, those goals you hope to accomplish, those people you fantasize about meeting, those experiences you dream of having before you kick the bucket?

I have an idea.

Let's not wait.

Let's dream like we'll live forever and live like there's no tomorrow.

Let's leave this life fully spent, a balloon with every last drop of air squeezed out.

Don't attach to the bucket list and set yourself up to view your life as a failure if you don't check off every last item. Instead, cast that bucket list to the heavens and ask for my help, knowing that I can help you check these things off if it's aligned to do so.

You never know how long this one wild and precious life, as poet Mary Oliver describes it, is going to last. So let's do this life thing wholeheartedly!

Whadya wanna do first, my sweet?

Check check,

YOUR INNER PILOT LIGHT

84

Dearest,

Did you forget to eat today, my love? Or did you fill up on chocolate brownies again, when we both know that what you really need is love?

Lemme break this down, sweet pea.

You are so gorgeously, infinitely, perfectly, unconditionally loved—dimpled thighs, rounded belly, muscled strength, wrinkles, wobbly bits and all. Every single part of your body temple is beautiful to me. And you can help keep it healthy by feeding your luscious body with nutrients that support it.

What your body doesn't need is your self-judgment, your overactive discipline, your out-of-control indulgence, your body shame, or your indifference.

So, darling, feed what is really hungry in you. Nourish your dreams, your passions, your most secret longings. Let yourself dive deliciously into your yearning for love, connection, community, and meaning. Heal what hurts and enliven what feels yummy. Hear me when I tell you that I give you permission to play full out, with your whole heart.

Not sure how to do this? Call on me. I'll fill your hunger at the deepest level.

Satiated,
YOUR INNER PILOT LIGHT

85

Mysterious Being,

Mystery can feel scary because it tends to ride shotgun with uncertainty, but when you lose the ability to stand in awe at life's mysteries, your life becomes impoverished.

Mind-body medicine pioneer Rachel Naomi Remen writes, "Mystery requires that we relinquish an endless search for answers and become willing to not understand. . . . Perhaps real wisdom lies in not seeking answers at all. Any answer we find will not be true for long. An answer is a place where we can fall asleep as life moves past us to its next question. After all these years, I have begun to wonder if the secret of living well is not in having all the answers but in pursuing unanswerable questions in good company."

I notice, my love, how mysteries tend to make you uncomfortable. You like solving mysteries, but unsolved mysteries tend to make you feel restless, as if you can't rest until you tie everything up in a nice little explainable package. Knowing makes you feel safe. Not knowing feels uncomfortable, even dangerous. This is because when you were young, not knowing was not safe.

But now, my love, it is! Not only is it safe to not know, but also if you're willing to not know, to simply be curious, a portal opens. Anything is possible. Miracles could happen.

Are you willing to stand in awe of life's mysteries, even if you can't understand them?

I can hold your hand while we gaze in awe.

Mouth wide open,
YOUR INNER PILOT LIGHT

86

Dearest Flame,

It may feel like you're doing this life thing alone. You may have moments when you forget about me and all the other Inner Pilot Lights on the planet.

But, precious, you are never alone. How could you be?

You've got me.

And I've got that woman whose Inner Pilot Light smiled at me.

And she's got that guy who knows her heart.

And he's got that child who sees his light.

And every single one of us is connected through the flame.

Can't you smell the marshmallows around this cosmic campfire, my love?

All you need is love,
YOUR INNER PILOT LIGHT

87

Sweet Pea,

I've got news for you.

The Universe doesn't need you to be in control.

You see, me and the Universe, we're like this. (*Crosses fingers.*)

And between the two of us, we've got it handled.

So sit back. Take a load off. Put your feet up. Surrender all of your unmet longings, unsolved problems, and undecided decisions to me. Let go of attachment to outcomes and let us handle this, darling. Cast the burden of all your struggles into these great arms of love and let us help you, along with all the other invisible forces of love that are just dying to help you navigate this crazy, awesome, nutty, wondrous, mysterious human life.

Imagine me as a giant "God box." Write down whatever is weighing heavy on your heart—every deep heart yearning, every problem your mind is trying to solve, every health issue, every relationship struggle, every difficult decision—toss it in the God box and *let me help you handle it*.

Then trust me to clue you in if there's any action you need to take. Then your action will be coming from a different impulse. It will feel like that electric energy that courses through your body, leaps you out of your chair, and compels you to sprint across town to do *that one thing I've guided you to do*—because you're so gleefully antsy to do it that you can't quite help yourself!

Trust me on this one, my love.

On it like glue,

YOUR INNER PILOT LIGHT

Dear One,

When you let me shine as brightly as I'm capable of shining, some people in your life may not be so happy about your radiance.

When your light is dialed way up, it may be an inner-critic trigger for someone else. Such a trigger actually has nothing to do with you, my love. You can be sensitive to how the radiance of my light triggers someone else. No need to be a diva, flooding others who aren't ready for the full blinding light of my unfiltered spotlight. You also don't need to walk around pretending I'm not ON FIRE with brilliance.

If you tune in to me, I'll tell you how much of my light it's safe to show in the presence of those whose inner-critic triggers have gotten the best of them. You can shine unapologetically but also be aware of how a really bright light can attract all the attention in a room.

Think of my light as a bright light with a dimmer switch. I'll tell you where to set my dial. Sometimes the most illuminated way of letting me shine is by giving other people the courage to contribute the luminous glory of their own light in your magnificent presence. When your presence draws out the light of someone else's Inner Pilot Light, the whole world lights up.

A mood lighting genius,

YOUR INNER PILOT LIGHT

Sweetness,

I know you get confused. Your mind gets busy trying to figure out this or that. But you don't need to spend so much effort fussing around in that adorable mind of yours, my love.

I can help.

How can you hear my guidance when the world's noise gets louder than my voice?

Meditate. You can hear me best when it's quiet in your mind. Let nature speak to you. Sit by a waterfall and ask it a question. What is it telling you? Ask a rose. Receive guidance from a star. I can speak to you through anything.

Ask me a question before you fall asleep. Keep a dream journal and take notes when you wake up. See if you can interpret my response.

Merge your consciousness with synchronicity. Then see how I show up with messages for you via street signs, emails in your inbox, bumper stickers, meaningful numbers, and animals or objects that appear in your path. Be on the lookout for clues, as if I'm sending you on a playful scavenger hunt!

When you have trouble hearing me, try accessing visionary states, as is possible through holotropic breathwork, shamanic drumming, or plant medicines. Make sure you let me help you pick grounded, ethical healers who can hold you safe in altered states of consciousness.

Still can't hear me? Sometimes I use psychics, intuitives, astrologers, shamans, or energy healers to get through to you. It may sound like the guidance is coming from outside of you, but if you filter what you're told through me, you'll get the deep messages through the discernment I provide.

Want to practice listening to my guidance? Go on a vision quest! Take a day off, get in your car or go out in nature, and follow the guidance I send you. Practice deep listening and careful observation. Pay attention to your body. Watch for signs. Notice your feelings. Look for unusual occurrences. Pay attention to animals, plants, bumper stickers, and synchronicities. I will be inside and outside of you, guiding the way.

Always trying to reach you, through any means necessary,
YOUR INNER PILOT LIGHT

Sweetheart,

I know how funny you can be when it's time to lean on others for support. Like a child asserting her independence, you walk around, strutting your stuff, as if doing everything yourself and counting on no one might earn you some independence prize.

But let me tell you something I don't ever want you to forget, sunshine.

You don't have to do it alone.

You have nothing to prove.

You'll accomplish more when you trust that it's safe to practice self-awareness, get clear on what you need, and are willing to be vulnerable enough to ask for help.

Humans are tribal beings. You adorable beings need each other to survive and thrive.

When you find the right people to walk this journey through life with you, one plus one equals infinity.

Good at math,
YOUR INNER PILOT LIGHT

91

My Precious,

I'm gonna let you in on a little secret.

You *can* do it all.

You just can't do it *all at once*.

Some days you'll be smack-dab in the middle of your purpose at work and rockin' and rollin' in the bedroom like the powerful sexual dynamo I know you can be. Some days you'll let me flow through you as my creative juices lead you into a frenzy of play with my muse! Some days you'll eat healthy, organic homemade meals prepared from produce from your local farmer's market.

Some days you'll meditate, do yoga, pray, and shake your booty in ecstatic dance. Some days you'll zen your home, declutter your space, throw things out, and create a healing altar. Some days you'll channel your inner God/Goddess, show up fully and reverently in your relationships, and be the stillness that uplifts someone else.

Some days you'll go to the church or the temple or the synagogue or the ashram, and you'll feel the light of me ignite into fireworks. Some days you'll go on that hike to that place that lights me up and do a ceremony for the full moon under a starlit sky.

But you're human, dearest darling, which means you're rarely going to be able to do all that in one day!

So give yourself a break and stop attaching to some ridiculous notion of life balance.

You may not be able to have a balanced day, but you can have a balanced life. Just listen to my guidance. I'll help you know what's needed when.

Shaking it up,
YOUR INNER PILOT LIGHT

92

Intrepid Hero,

You may not think you have a calling, but that's because your definition is too small. Theologian and civil rights leader Howard Thurman says, "Don't ask what the world needs. Ask what makes you come alive, and go do it. Because what the world needs is people who have come alive."

When you follow my spark of aliveness, you can trust that my passion, vitality, excitement, and playfulness will enliven others. The childlike enthusiasm that bubbles through you when you're fully alive is contagious, spreading like ripples of water in a vast pool of life force, touching others . . . who touch others . . . who touch others. And next thing you know, the world is coming alive, one Inner Pilot Light at a time.

So ask me now, my darling. What makes you come alive?

Now go do it!

Yeehaw!
YOUR INNER PILOT LIGHT

93

Dearest Beloved,

Everything can change in the blink of an eye.

The love of your life can walk in the door and know in a second that you're the one. That deal you've dreamed of can finally come through. The cancer can disappear. You can get discovered by the talent scout who's been looking for you her whole life. The judge can rule in your favor. The pregnancy test can come up positive. The check can show up in the mail. You can get that call.

Not only that. People who have been demonizing each other for millennia could suddenly fall in love. World peace could spontaneously break out. Angels could fly visibly above us in the sky. Humans might all start levitating. A new species of dinosaur could evolve into being. Gaia could start talking out loud and telling us how to heal her.

When you don't know, anything could happen. But it will only happen if you believe it can.

I know it can be painful to hope for that which feels impossible. But if you stop hoping, you make it even harder for me to be the miracle worker I love to be.

Blink blink,

YOUR INNER PILOT LIGHT

94

Dearest Dancing Queen,

If you really want me to sparkle, *pretty please*, let me do cartwheels on the beach! Allow me to dance the hoochie-coochie with the people I love the most. Let me sing in the shower at the top of my lungs. Give me a container of pink bubbles and let me go wild with it. Open up the finger paints.

Put me on a speedboat and let the wind whip through me. Send me parasailing, cliff diving, windsurfing, Jet-Skiing, hang gliding, bungee jumping, downhill skiing, and skydiving.

Don't get addicted to the adrenaline rush, though.

Don't forget to give me silent walks in the garden, time alone on a park bench, meditative moments in the lotus position, long and luxurious massages, time in a hammock reading an inspiring book, and the ecstatic bliss of the ordinary moments in a beautiful world full of love.

When I'm laughing, reveling in the pleasure of life and experiencing new and exciting things, it's like jet fuel for me.

When I'm silently in contemplation, reveling in the rapture of the mundane, recharging and intensifying my flame, I protect myself from recklessly burning out too bright, too quick, and too fast to be able to go the long haul with you.

Geronimo!

YOUR INNER PILOT LIGHT

95

Infinitely Creative One,

Within you lies a "makerly" genius you haven't fully tapped yet because there's still some distance between you and my radiance.

When you tap in and come closer to me, this creative spark lights up, opening up a whole range of creative possibilities. You might think you're not the artsy type, but every human has access to the muse that can fire up my brilliance and pour it into creative activities.

The minute you love, accept, appreciate, and let your perfectionist parts finally relax, new passions, talents, ideas, and visions just might pour through you like water through a garden hose.

You may still need to put in your ten thousand hours, but when you devote yourself to what wants to be born through you, you will have everything you need to paint that masterpiece, pen that bestseller, craft that gourmet meal, write that Top 10 hit song, dance the tango like nobody has ever danced it before, and play the best Ophelia any Shakespeare lover has ever seen.

When the muse shows up, the key is to give credit where credit is due! A famous writer once said, "I never understand when people make a fuss over me as a writer. I'm just the garden hose that the water sprays through."

A gush of life force, spraying through,

YOUR INNER PILOT LIGHT

96

Darling,

I am here to announce, with trumpets blaring, that YOU HAVE ARRIVED!

If there's a "there," you're there.

I give you full permission to quit trying to make it.

You have nothing left to prove.

You are inherently valuable, just because you have me within you, and I make you the ultimate in valuable.

Just look at any baby and you'll see the inherent worth within every human. You'll see that you don't have to earn your worth because you simply *are* worthy. Let me tell your bullying parts that it's safe to stop pushing. Let me tell your ambitious parts that you'll still do great things if you just stop worrying about achievement. Let me tell your approval-seeking parts that you don't need to do anything to impress me. Let me reassure your perfectionist parts that you're already perfect, just the way you are.

You are enough.

Not sure you can trust me? Tap in. Let me love you up all the way.

Drink it in, baby,
YOUR INNER PILOT LIGHT

97

Oh, Sweet Pea,

Don't you know that you're on the right path, even if you don't know where you're going? Don't you realize that you may be right smack-dab in the center of your purpose, even when you feel the most lost? Think of me as your mental machete, clearing away the mind brambles and briars, zapping away your sabotaging patterns, preparing your way for that which wants to be born through you.

Can't you see that if the path were straight and narrow, illuminated at all times by great floodlights and streetlamps, you wouldn't learn to let go, surrender, and follow the subtle signs that keep you on track and draw you closer to me?

Can't you see that the times when the path is dark and you can't tell where you're going, this is where you learn to trust?

Keep the faith, darling. All you need to do is put one foot in front of the other and keep on skipping, even when you can't see where you're going.

A beacon of love,

YOUR INNER PILOT LIGHT

98

Hey, Hot Stuff,

I know it sounds cliché, darling, but outer beauty *is* only skin deep. Real beauty isn't about the right hair color, a flat belly, expensive makeup, a six-pack, a wrinkle-free face, a full head of shiny hair, porn-star-sized sexual parts, or a French pedicure.

There's nothing wrong with adorning yourself. Let your gorgeous body be the canvas you dress up, if you like. Paint your eyelashes purple if you feel sexy when you do it. Color your hair bright pink if it makes you feel fully self-expressed. Wear your skinny jeans or your peasant skirts or your goddess costumes or your haute couture. Work out at the gym and build up those biceps. Tattoo your bald head if it makes you feel badass. Adorn yourself with crystals and bangles and gold press-on mandalas if you feel good about yourself when you do.

But don't fool yourself into thinking real beauty can ever be accessed on the outside.

Want to be *truly* gorgeous?

Let me shine, baby. Let me strut my brilliance through the humble confidence in your fully expressed presence in a world that needs your love more than your perfect appearance.

I'm your secret beauty tip.

Batting my God/Goddess eyes,
YOUR INNER PILOT LIGHT

99

Dear One,

What do you mean it will never happen? How can you say you don't deserve it? Why would you ever think such things?

Let me clear things up, my darling.

It will happen—*if it's aligned with Divine Will*. And if it's not aligned—trust me, you won't want it!

You *do* deserve it—because you have a spark of Divinity inside you (Me, me, me!) and I make you inherently worthy.

You may not realize it, but perhaps you're blocking the very thing you pray for. You say you want it. But do you really? Are you sure you don't have one foot on the gas and one foot on the brakes? Are you sure you're not sabotaging the very thing you say you yearn for because part of you is terrified about how much change you'd face if that thing you really want actually came to fruition?

Are you willing to go all in, to fully commit, to activate the force of your will and do whatever you must to get out of your own way, not by beating yourself up but by loving even your sabotaging parts?

Are you willing to trust that it's all handled, if only you can let go of attaching to how it all comes together?

You and I are in this together, my love. I'll do my part, but you must do yours.

As the Rolling Stones croon, "You can't always get what you want . . . but if you try sometimes, you just might find, you get what you need."

Listening to your every desire and attuned to your every need,

YOUR INNER PILOT LIGHT

100

Beloved,

I am your heart. I am your mind. I am your eyes and your belly and the tips of your fingers. I am your lungs and your liver and your kidneys. I am your knees, your genitals, and your colon. I am your ears, your spleen, and your thyroid. I am your toenails and your cells. I am your DNA.

You can't escape me. And why would you want to?

I know some religious traditions have pulled a number on humans, insisting that spirit and body are in conflict with each other, that the body can't be trusted because it tempts you away from the Divine.

But, darling, I am the Divine inside your own body! There is no separation. I am.

What if nothing in the universe is excluded from that which is holy, sacred, and part of the Great Mystery—not the human body, not sex, not death, not beauty, not filth, not "good," not "bad"?

I know you probably have parts that get scared when I say that. How will you orient your compass if you don't polarize into that which is holy and that which is profane?

That's where I come in, sweetheart.

Trust me to help you know the way.

Give me some skin,
YOUR INNER PILOT LIGHT

101

Darling of My Heart,

In *Feel the Fear and Do It Anyway*, Susan Jeffers says there are three levels of fear. First-level fears are things like fear of losing money, fear of being fired, fear of losing a loved one, fear of rejection. But underneath those first-level fears lie second-level fears. Second-level fears tend to revolve around the fear of being not good enough, fear of lacking value, fear of being unlovable. Second-level fears threaten the very essence of our place in the world.

But underneath second-level fears lies the mother lode of all fears: the fear that if your worst nightmare happens, you can't handle it.

Of course you feel that way, sweetheart. It's only natural that you would have worrying parts that are sure that if that terrifying thing happens, you wouldn't survive.

I want to give those frightened parts a hug. I want them to hear that every time something painful happens and you survive, you show these parts how resilient you're becoming, how brave you're being, and how much of a survivor you truly are.

We can handle it—together,
YOUR INNER PILOT LIGHT

102

Dear Still One,

In the midst of chaos, there lives a quiet place.

In this quiet place, there is a hole in a giant redwood tree that is just your size. If you feel like it, you can crawl inside and snuggle right up inside the womb of the tree and feel the arms of the redwood giving you a great big tree hug.

When you do this, the world around you grows still and you can feel yourself grounding down into the brown roots of Mama Earth, sucking up the green Earth energy like you're drinking kale-cucumber juice through a straw. As this Earth juice fills your inner space and bathes all your cells, guess what? I light up!

The further you ground, the higher you can ascend. The deeper your roots, the more my ignition switch fires up.

Not near any redwood trees today?

Close your eyes and let me be your redwood.

Tree hugs all around,

YOUR INNER PILOT LIGHT

103

Dearest Beloved,

Do you feel like you're guided to do something, but you're not sure whether it's me talking or some other, less trustworthy part disguising itself as me?

Here are some discernment tools that can help you tell the difference between me and my adorably sneaky imposters.

Consider this thing you feel guided to do, then ask yourself these questions:

> Is it kind?
>
> Does it feel like shackles on or shackles off?
>
> Is there aliveness here?
>
> Does it nourish or deplete me?
>
> Does it feel natural, efficient, easeful, peaceful, and graceful?
>
> Does it make sense?
>
> Does it exhaust me or fill me with dread?
>
> Will it hurt anyone?
>
> Would love do this?
>
> How does this feel in my body?
>
> Am I feeling pressured or rushing?
>
> Is it coercive or controlling?
>
> Is it ethical and aligned with my core values?
>
> Will this cultivate the stillness in me?
>
> What's true and not true about this?

The Buddha said, "Just as the great ocean has one taste, the taste of salt, so also this teaching and discipline has one taste, the taste of liberation."

I may not be the Buddha, but I dig the guy. If you think I'm guiding you, check to see if what I'm asking of you tastes of liberation, which also feels like love. If it doesn't, get curious, keep inquiring, ask for confirmation and clarity, listen deeply, and ask your trusted mentors for feedback, if you need help interpreting my guidance.

Here with the keys to your jailbreak,
YOUR INNER PILOT LIGHT

104

Brave Darling,

You know that leap of faith you're considering making?

Yes. *That one.*

Let me give you a little hint to help you know when it's time to leap.

When the pain of staying put exceeds your fear of the unknown, you leap.

As Elizabeth Appell once wrote in a John F. Kennedy University newsletter, "And the day came when the risk to remain tight in a bud was more painful than the risk it took to blossom."

You don't have to wait until it hurts this much. You can choose to cave early.

If you have scared parts that are not ready to leap, I'll hold you in my arms while you stand on the edge. There's no rush. Nobody goes until we're all in this together.

Once all of your parts are ready to leap, I promise I'll yell, "One, two, three . . . Geronimo!"

Here with a parachute, just in case,
YOUR INNER PILOT LIGHT

105

Curious One,

Can you make peace with—and even love—all the question marks in your life? Austrian poet and novelist Rainer Maria Rilke writes, "Be patient towards all that is unsolved in your heart and try to love the questions themselves."

I know how you *love* being certain. Question marks are uncomfortable, but answers are celebrated.

Rachel Naomi Remen says, "We trade Mystery for Mastery, and it's a bad trade."

Would you be willing to let me help you turn that around? All those unresolved things in your mind and your heart and your dreams—can you love them as much as you love what you know?

What if it's okay to not know right now?

What if it's more than okay?

Full of good questions,
YOUR INNER PILOT LIGHT

106

Dear One,

It all starts with a dream. First an impossible idea flits through your mind or drops into your consciousness. Then you see it like a movie, flashing on the screen behind your eyes. Then the movie becomes a wish, and the wish becomes a prayer, and the prayer becomes a big, flashing, Times Square-worthy message to the Universe, alerting the cosmic realms that something creative is trying to get birthed.

Then you put the whole thing in the God box, let go into the mystery of Divine Will, surrender all attachment to outcomes, and pay attention to the guidance that shows up. Be equally open and grateful when doors close as when synchronicity rolls out the "green light" red carpet.

You trust that if there's something to do, you'll know, and it will be clear. Then you ask me for the courage it will take to follow through on what you're guided to do.

Next thing you know, if your dream is aligned with one of my holy ideas, the time-space continuum gets rearranged, the hows get figured out, the pieces fall into place, doors start opening, as if by magic.

Know where the spark of that idea comes from? Know how the dream comes into being?

Busted,

YOUR INNER PILOT LIGHT

107

My Perfectly Imperfect Darling,

You try *so* hard to be perfect. But how do you think life will be better if you're perfect?

Don't you realize that your imperfections make you adorably human? Just think what a beast you'd be if you were some Stepford person . . .

Freckles decorate a face.

Scars suggest a life well risked.

Mistakes make you relatable.

And holes in your jeans give others a place to sneak in tickles.

Relax your perfectionism, darling, and celebrate your glorious imperfections.

As the beautiful bard, poet, and Buddhist monk Leonard Cohen croons, "There is a crack in everything. That's how the light gets in."

Beaming through your well-earned cracks,

YOUR INNER PILOT LIGHT

108

My Love,

I want to acknowledge that sometimes, listening to me doesn't make you popular.

Once the whispers of my voice become rebel yells, it becomes impossible to ignore me, and you'll find that, at some point, you simply won't be able to silence me anymore.

This is good news. Be very, very reassured by this. This is the time when magical unfoldings blossom!

But it's also the time when some people in your life get royally pissed because you're following your inner voice and not listening to theirs. Their capacity to manipulate you diminishes, and they might feel insecure, scared, or angry.

Don't worry. If they really love and support you, they'll come around. And if they don't, they're not meant to be close to your inner circle of trust.

Just carry on, love warrior. Keep your heart open. Trust the process.

Just never, ever stop listening to me.

Your best friend, no matter what,
YOUR INNER PILOT LIGHT

109

Sweetness,

With all the priests and gurus and self-help authors trying to convince you that they—and they alone—have the ticket to your happiness, health, well-being, wealth, and enlightenment, it's easy to lose sight of me.

It's so tempting to give all that power away to another human, someone you can put on a pedestal and project onto them some sort of perfection.

But every time you look outside for someone else who will make all the decisions for you, you distance yourself from the power of guidance and discernment that lives right inside of you. (Me, me, me!)

Sure, sometimes you lose your way, and you need guides to lend you a compass until you contact me. But keep that in mind when you seek help from the outside. Charlatans and megalomaniacs make you believe you're dependent on them. The real deal will always point you right back to where your ultimate truth lies.

The best guru ever,
YOUR INNER PILOT LIGHT

110

Babycakes,

In order to fully grow up, you have to let go of reacting to your life the way you learned how to act as a child. Children have a tantrum when they lose what they cherish. But growing up is all about learning to find peace amidst loss, finding within you an unshakable core that can withstand the traumas of life without leveling you.

No matter how grown up you might think you are, it's still tempting to cling like children hanging on to Mama's leg, to things you fear losing. You cling to your family because you can't bear the idea of losing them. You cling to the stability of a job—even a job you don't like—because you fear change or financial instability. You cling to lovers and friends and material possessions because you're afraid of losing what you value.

Being human means you will lose what you cherish, and there is nothing you can do to protect yourself from this. Growing up is about coming out of denial about this uncomfortable truth.

Spiritual teacher Jeff Foster describes it this way:

> You will lose everything. Your money, your power, your fame, your success, perhaps even your memories. Your looks will go. Loved ones will die. Your body will fall apart. Everything that seems permanent is impermanent and will be smashed. Experience will gradually, or not so gradually, strip away everything that it can strip away. Waking up means facing this reality with open eyes and no longer turning away.
>
> But right now, we stand on sacred and holy ground, for that which will be lost has not yet been lost, and realizing this is the key to

unspeakable joy. Whoever or whatever is in your life right now has not yet been taken away from you. This may sound trivial, obvious, like nothing, but really it is the key to everything, the why and how and wherefore of existence. Impermanence has already rendered everything and everyone around you so deeply holy and significant and worthy of your heartbreaking gratitude.

Loss has already transfigured your life into an altar.

How can you handle this unbearable vulnerability? How can you deal with growing up in this way?

That's where I come in. When I am burning inside of you, you can handle anything.

I promise,
YOUR INNER PILOT LIGHT

111

My Darling,

I know how much you want to be a loving, generous, forgiving person. I just want to make sure you realize that unconditional love requires equal love, generosity, and forgiveness of yourself.

Sometimes this requires offering someone else *unconditional love but conditional access*.

Unconditional love does not mean you make yourself a doormat, always available to let someone take advantage of your big, loving, generous, overly tolerant heart.

Unconditional love means you can be infinitely spacious in how much love you pour onto another person, but it does not mean letting someone who cannot be responsible with your love get too close.

What does this mean in practical terms? It means that your love is unconditional, but access to your inner circle is completely conditional. If someone can't treat you with the love, nurturing, gratitude, and respect you deserve, you simply dial down the "intimacy dial." If intimacy lies on a scale from 0 (no contact at all) to 10 (they live in your house and maybe even get access to your bed), where they live on the intimacy dial should reflect how responsible they can be with your trust, love, and vulnerability.

If they demonstrate the ability to hold your vulnerability safe, you dial them up. If they treat you poorly, you dial them down. Put them in your outer circle—or eliminate them from your circle altogether—with a wide-open, unconditionally loving heart and not a lick of judgment.

How does this jibe with unconditional love? Love and intimacy are not necessarily the same thing, my dear. You might love someone deeply who cannot be responsible with this kind of intimacy. This does not mean you have to demonize them or ostracize them. If someone betrays your trust, behaves abusively, or fails to demonstrate consistent care, there's no need to grow resentful or start complaining. You simply dial them down. If a trust rift creates some distance between you, pay attention to their behavior. If they make repair efforts and demonstrate that they are changing how they treat you, slowly dial them back up.

In other words, intimacy doesn't have to be all or nothing. If someone isn't treating you with impeccable respect, you simply limit access without making up a story about it. No point becoming the exploding doormat. Unconditional love, conditional access.

Then it's not someone else's job to treat you right. It's *your* job to treat you right— granting yourself the space you need and the appropriate boundaries that limit access if someone can't be trusted to treat you with the care you deserve.

Not sure where on the dial someone should be? Ask me.

You're always a 10 for me,
YOUR INNER PILOT LIGHT

112

My Precious,

By this point, you've probably figured out that the spiritual path is not for the faint of heart. Buddhist teacher Chögyam Trungpa Rinpoche offers little comfort when he says, "My advice to you is not to undertake the spiritual path. It is too difficult, too long, and is too demanding. I suggest you ask for your money back and go home. This is not a picnic. It is really going to ask everything of you. So, it is best not to begin. However, if you do begin, it is best to finish."

Spiritual teacher Adyashanti seems to agree. "Make no mistake about it—enlightenment is a destructive process. It has nothing to do with becoming better or being happier. Enlightenment is the crumbling away of untruth. It's seeing through the facade of pretense. It's the complete eradication of everything we imagined to be true."

But does it always have to be this way? Sure, the scalpel of truth can sting, but you must also balance the growth edges of the spiritual path with the nurturing care, comfort, and gentle love that also arise on the spiritual path.

That's where I come in.

There's no need to be masochistic in order to grow spiritually. I hope you know in your heart of hearts that there's just as much growth to be had through love's gentle embrace and pleasure's radical openings.

Where can you find that much love? How can you prepare for this much pleasure?

Come to me, my love.

With a spoonful of hugs,
YOUR INNER PILOT LIGHT

113

Dear One,

When you're growing spiritually, you may find that your change causes friction in some of your relationships. What can you do when one of you is ready to grow and someone else seems to resist change?

Many of us enter into unspoken relationship contracts, like "I'll baby your ouchies as long as you baby mine." Then if you're ready to heal your ouchies rather than avoid them, you might need to renegotiate your unspoken agreements.

How does this work? First of all, make sure you invite me to help.

When a relationship just isn't working, you have two choices. You can bless each other, give thanks for the time and teachings, and release the relationship with love. Buh-bye. Or you can try a braver route: bring your grievances to the table, examine old patterns that aren't serving anymore, call out any unspoken agreements, and mindfully renegotiate the terms of the relationship.

Renegotiating a sacred contract is always a risk, because whenever you come to the table to redefine terms, there's always the chance you won't be able to agree to a new contract. But with my help, you might be surprised at how satisfying such contract negotiation can be.

So how do you do it?

Take a moment in silence and tap into me. Initiate a conversation. Remind someone of your love and care, in order to establish safety. Set clear intentions. Lead with gratitude. Express what's working and what isn't working for you both. Be vulnerable and speak for your emotions. Ask for what you need and listen to what someone else needs. Be willing to own your stuff. Open yourself to creative solutions. Make requests and agreements. Rewrite your sacred contract. Celebrate!

If this doesn't help, consider getting a third party—like a therapist or wise friend—to help you hear each other, stay vulnerable, and keep your hearts open through any triggers.

If someone won't agree to get help, be willing to dial down the intimacy. If that doesn't help, acknowledge that some relationships have an expiration date, and this doesn't necessarily mean anything went wrong. Appreciate what you had. Bless each other. Bow with gratitude. Then move on.

Not sure when to keep trying and when to let go?

Come to me.

Peacemaking,

YOUR INNER PILOT LIGHT

114

Dearest,

I know you have some habits you wish you could quit. I won't point fingers, but you know what I'm talking about.

I know you tend to beat yourself up because time and time again, you get sucked into that habit, even when you've promised yourself and made New Year's resolutions countless times.

But don't you realize that every time you hate on yourself or try to bully yourself into changing your habit, you only make yourself more likely to repeat the habit?

Why not try getting honest with yourself about what needs are getting met when you indulge the habit? Why not see the habit as a protector part and find gratitude for how that part has been a helper, just trying to get your needs met and keep vulnerable parts in you safe?

See if you can tap into an awareness of how the habit is serving you. Instead of demonizing it, thank it for protecting you and helping you get your needs met!

The more you rest in gratitude, appreciation, and self-compassion, the more you loosen yourself from the habit and start being creative about getting your needs met elsewhere. Once you're not so contracted around your demonization of the habit, you might find that your habit starts to loosen its grip.

You might even find that it falls away completely under the shattering love of my unconditionally radiant heart.

Know who you can always count on to help you fall in love with your habits so they have the opportunity to fall away?

With me on your side, this is gonna be a piece of cake.

Licking the icing,

YOUR INNER PILOT LIGHT

115

My Sweetest Angel,

A little birdie told me that what you needed most today was a big, burly, snuggly bear hug.

So I am here, like a warm, nurturing Earth mother with expansive arms and a soft bosom, pulling you inward until our hearts beat side by side.

((((((((((((((((((((DARLING YOU))))))))))))))))))))

Did you feel that?

If you ever need a hug, you can access my nurturing warmth very simply. If possible, find a place where you can be by yourself for just a few minutes. Close your eyes. *Breathe . . .*

Then visualize my great mama bear arms, wrapping you in an infinite embrace. Give yourself permission to feel what you feel. Cry if you want to. Laugh if you feel like it. Scream if you need to. Let joy bubble through you. Allow whatever emotion arises in the safety of my embrace to move through you without resistance. Move your body to let yourself feel my presence all the way down to your cells. Then feel the gentle softness of my unconditional hug. Let yourself be comforted.

I am always here for you, my love.

Rocking you like the most precious, innocent baby,
YOUR INNER PILOT LIGHT

116

My Dear,

There are times you're in the "narrow place," when the walls feel like they're caving in on you, with pressure from all sides, until you feel so squished you can barely breathe.

In the narrow place, you may experience doubt, fear, confusion, and dark nights of the soul. In this narrow place, you may even question whether my light has been extinguished.

I know it hurts to be in the narrow place. I feel so much tenderness when you're in that place, and the mama bear in me wants to rescue you from all that discomfort.

But imagine if you tried to rescue a baby from birth!

Trust me, my love.

The narrow place is the birth canal you have to squish through during the initiation of rebirth. Then things get really interesting . . .

On the other side of the narrow place lie great expansive fields of sunflowers where you can spin and cartwheel and throw your arms to the bright, shining sun. On the other side lies light so bright you'll need sunglasses. On the other side lies all the clarity that will illuminate why you needed to be in the narrow place to begin with.

Let yourself be born, darling. Don't fight it.

Here with a catcher's mitt,
YOUR INNER PILOT LIGHT

117

My Sweet,

When you notice a sensation or symptom in your body, you know that's me talking to you, don't you? Sometimes I whisper instructions in your ear as this little voice of inner wisdom. Sometimes I speak to you in dreams. Sometimes I arrange really cool synchronicities to help guide you on your path with open doors. And sometimes I coordinate with the heavens to guide you with the "Cosmic No," gently but firmly closing doors that aren't aligned with your highest path.

If you're listening to the subtle cues—in your body, in your intuition, in your dreams—then you may not need to experience discomfort in your body. But when you're not listening to my quiet whispers and heeding the subtle and not-so-subtle signs from the Universe, I'll happily use your body as a wake-up call—just because I care, of course. I'll pull out all the stops to deepen my relationship with you and help you listen to the guidance I offer you in my attempt to help you live in alignment with your greatest truth, joy, and purpose.

You know those headaches, backaches, and tummy aches you get from time to time?

Pay attention. Get curious. That may be me talking.

Those pesky colds and flus that get you down when your immune system is weakened from chronic repetitive stress responses? That may be my way of saying, "Listen up, sweetheart."

If you don't listen to the early whispers, sometimes I swoop in with the cosmic two-by-fours of life-threatening illness. I'm not suggesting that all illness is me calling out to you. Sometimes it's not your inner world that's predisposing you to illness. Sometimes it's the toxic waste dump in your backyard or the poison in your food.

Either way, your body is trying to get your attention. Can't tell whether your physical symptoms are messages from me or something out of whack in your external environment?

Just ask me. I'll always help you sense the difference.

With excellent discernment
about the root cause of your illness,
YOUR INNER PILOT LIGHT

118

Hi Beautiful,

I hear those fearful parts rumbling again, telling you the sky is falling, you're in serious danger, you can't afford it, you're not worthy of that big dream; everybody will think you're crazy and you'll wind up on the street, living under a highway overpass with no friends, no money, no future. Nobody but burly ol' Harvey to keep you company under that cardboard box. (No offense to Harvey.)

But oh, honey, don't you know by now that this is just what those adorable fearful parts *do*? It's their *job*, and they do it so masterfully, working so diligently as they do to protect you!

Don't judge these cute little scaredy-cats. Don't try to get rid of them because they're not going anywhere. Listen to them. Reassure them that you appreciate how they're trying to protect you. Smile at them. Say, "I see you," and maybe even flirt a little.

Remember, those little kitties are simply part of being human. They exist as part of that primitive warning system emanating from your lizard brain. They're not something to demonize.

They're parts that need your love. Thank them for doing their job so well.

What they don't realize is that your ultimate safety lives with me.

But you know better, right?

I've got you, babe,
YOUR INNER PILOT LIGHT

119

My Love,

Some people don't believe in Inner Pilot Lights. They scoff at the idea that there might be this invisible force of love that lives inside every human heart. Those people do not need your judgment or righteousness. They need your compassion.

Those who don't believe may insult you for your reckless, naïve optimism. They may laugh at your *pronoia*—the term coined by astrologer and writer Rob Brezsny that loosely translates as the unshakable belief that everything in the universe is conspiring to shower you with blessings.

Those who don't believe humans are all made of love will tell you that you're crazy for your trust, that you are delusional for believing in love. They won't understand when you talk about surrendering to Divine Will or trusting that it's a benevolent Universe. Their fear will be so loud that you might be tempted to succumb to it, to let it sink your faith.

But I will be your faith bubble.

I have a dream that we are such powerful co-creators of our reality that if everyone chose to let love win right now, everything could change in one collective heartbeat.

Start with giving yourself this same love. If you find yourself judging, shaming, criticizing, and failing to trust, love that part. As spiritual teacher and author Matt Kahn says, "Whatever arises, love that."

In love we trust,
YOUR INNER PILOT LIGHT

120

Darling Playmate,

Do you think I'm no fun? Do you think I'm so wise, awakened, and serious that I can't bust a move and drop an F-bomb?

You've got me all wrong!

I am fun's fuel. I am karaoke. I am inner tubes on ropes behind speedboats. I am break-dancing. I am side-splitting laughter. I am cartwheels. I am watermelon martinis. I am Jet-Skiing. I am the best roll in the hay ever. I am a spa day with your girlfriends. I am Scrabble. I am finger painting. I am Slip 'N Slide.

So please, don't cut me off just because you think I'm a buzzkill.

Have fun with me, my love.

Giggling with glee,
YOUR INNER PILOT LIGHT

121

My Love,

Do you realize that you have within you this finely tuned body compass that can help you interpret my guidance?

Think back to a time when you knew you were out of alignment in your life. Maybe you were out of alignment in a big way—cheating on your spouse or embezzling from your company or abusing your child. Or maybe you were out of alignment in more subtle ways—selling out your integrity in a soul-sucking job or drinking yourself to sleep every night or staying in a relationship with someone you don't love. If you can remember how your body felt during those times, chances are good that your body didn't feel so hot. You may have had headaches or gastrointestinal distress or a flare-up of a skin condition or allergies. Or you may have just felt groggy, sluggish, and "off."

Chances are, I'll bet your body was signaling to you that you were off course. Your body is brilliant this way!

Not sure how to interpret your body compass? Try this.

Close your eyes and recall a time in your life when things went really wrong. Go into that very dark place in your mind's eye, then locate the feeling in your body. Name what you're feeling—"acid stomach," "constricted throat," "clenched chest," or whatever.

Try it. What do you feel? Now give it a name. That feeling is your body's way of saying, "You're headed due south! Head the other way, pronto!"

Now shake it off. Then visualize a moment when everything was going brilliantly right, when it felt as if you were in the flow, the whole universe was celebrating your existence, and ecstasy filled your whole being. Locate that feeling in your body and then name it—"butterflies in chest," "wide-open throat," "belly full of light."

Try that too. What do you feel? That feeling is your body's way of saying, "Due north! Go that way!"

Trying to make an important decision? Let me talk to you through your body compass! Now that you know what due south and due north feel like, see if you can register the more subtle variants. On a scale of -10 (due south) to +10 (due north), check in to see where something lands. Got a new opportunity at work? What reading do you get? Is it a +4? A -2? Or a completely neutral 0? These somatic sensations can help you make the right decision every time.

Your body compass can help you register subtle physical sensations that wouldn't usually get labeled as symptoms or illness. This is how I communicate through your body's whispers.

Ready for more of those +10 feelings? It's okay to ask for them.

Dialing it up,
YOUR INNER PILOT LIGHT

122

Sweet One,

You know that person who hurt you, the one you can't stop thinking about?

It's time to feel whatever you're feeling all the way down to your toes, express anything that needs to be expressed so those feelings don't get stuck in your body, then change those painful stories into restorative narratives.

You can't change that person. You can't ignore your feelings or avoid letting them wash through you.

But you can write a meaningful new story that casts you not as the helpless victim but as the hero of your redemption tale.

Can you honor your painful story, learn from what happened, feel what you feel without bypassing your pain, set any boundaries you need to set, and enforce any consequences that are loving to yourself? Then . . . when you're ready . . . when the time is right . . . can you write a story you like better than the painful one you're looping over and over?

Is there a story that feels even more true to you, one that views what happened as an opportunity for awakening and soul growth?

Not sure how to find a story that alchemizes pain into treasure?

Here with a pot of gold,
YOUR INNER PILOT LIGHT

123

Darling Flame,

Some of your parts love to attach to ideas of who you are, both good and bad. These ideas of who you are may or may not be true.

The voices in your head might say you are a person of integrity. You are smart. You are talented. You are a nice person. You only do good things. You never lie, cheat, steal, or betray anyone. You can be trusted.

Other voices might say you are not good enough. You are worthless. You are a terrible friend. You don't have what it takes to follow a dream. You will never make enough money. You are a hopeless bad seed. You are broken. You'll never mature spiritually.

Me, I don't attach to ideas like all those other parts do. I'm merely curious about who you really are, without needing to label any of it or defend a mental construct of who you are. I see both your light and your shadow, and I love all of your many parts equally.

Are you a person of integrity? Maybe. Maybe not. What if you're lovable either way?

Are you a terrible friend who has much to learn about how to serve the needs of someone you love without martyring yourself? Maybe. Maybe not. What if you're lovable either way?

Aren't you super curious about who you really are? I sure as heck am!

Would you be willing to let go of who you think you are so you can see yourself through my wildly curious, compassionate, centered, confident, magical eyes?

Loving the whole shebang,
YOUR INNER PILOT LIGHT

124

Dearest Beloved,

I know how frustrating it is when you try to drag other people along on your personal journey because you care about them. Then, gosh darn it, they resist.

I know how disappointing it can be when someone you love doesn't follow you in the direction of your path, and you feel more and more distance as you journey in different directions.

Relationships on the spiritual path can be tricky, but keep in mind one solid truth: *everyone is entitled to their own journey!*

No matter how hard you try, you cannot violate someone else's free will. No amount of pressure or threat will force someone who is not ready. No amount of gentle coaxing or beckoning will work either.

As Rachel Naomi Remen says, "You can't force a rosebud to blossom by beating it with a hammer."

You can trust that those who are meant to walk the path with you will do so. Even if others do not journey with you, you will never be alone.

I am the one who will never leave,
YOUR INNER PILOT LIGHT

125

Dear One,

When you notice yourself feeling jealous of what someone else has, consider yourself blessed. You have just tapped into something you desire, and desire is one of the ways I communicate with you!

Notice your desire.

Don't judge your desire. Just be with it. Allow yourself to feel the *yum* of what it would feel like to have that desire met. (Mmmmm . . .)

Don't run away from the vulnerability of your longing. Humble yourself before the intensity of your longing and allow yourself to feel the paradoxical deliciousness and discomfort of that unmet desire.

Surrender your desire to Divine Will and trust that if your desire is in alignment with the highest good, it will come to pass.

And if it's not, know that you will receive help dealing with the disappointment of not getting what you think you want.

Once you navigate your inner journey, go back to the person who left you feeling jealous and transform your jealousy into admiration. Lean in rather than leaning out. Playfully rub their head for good luck. If you get close enough, maybe some of what they have will rub off on you! Then express gratitude to the one who helped you get clear on something your heart yearns for.

Don't forget to loop me in. After all, I'm the golden glow where desire flows. While some demonize desire, positioning it as something in need of destroying, I think of desire as a way to cast your cosmic vote.

You get a vote.

The Universe gets a vote.

I get to be the tiebreaker!

With my ballot in hand,
YOUR INNER PILOT LIGHT

126

Dear One,

If only you could see what I see. From where I sit and shine, I see this vibrant, vital, glorious being full of possibility and potential just waiting to be expressed.

I see power beyond measure, lying just beneath the surface, ready to explode in all its glory, like a force-of-nature geyser.

I see love blossoming from your heart like a spring lily unfolding and spilling over its petal art.

I see abundance beyond your wildest dreams pouring all over you as soon as you clear the blocks and prepare to receive it.

I see limitless joy, health, success, romance, and inner peace.

I see the depth of your resilience and commitment to soul growth when things aren't going your way.

I see diamonds in your eyes and gold in your heart.

If only you could see what I see, you wouldn't feel so stressed, anxious, sad, angry, frustrated, self-critical, or impatient.

Let me be your eyes, beloved.

With x-ray vision,
YOUR INNER PILOT LIGHT

127

Dearest Beloved,

You know that thing looming in the future that keeps making you feel anxious?

You know that thing that happened in the past, the one you wish you could undo?

I know it's only human to obsess about the past and worry about worst-case scenarios that might happen in the future. Of course, we're here on this planet to learn from the past, grow from what we learn, and try to apply what we've learned to make the future better!

The invitation to rest in the present moment is not meant to delete all the lessons the past has to teach you. Presence is not intended to allow you to be reckless, ignoring whatever protective instincts intuition lights up in you. Presence is simply an invitation to drink in every last drop of the full range of the human experience, as it unfolds with continuous streaming manifestation, all filtered through a past that instructs you and a future that beckons.

Resting in pure peace,
YOUR INNER PILOT LIGHT

128

Oh, Holy One,

It's not "snobby" to choose to hang with other people whose Inner Pilot Lights are on fire. It's wise.

When you're still learning how to ignite my flames, it's easier to light me up when you find a tribe of other humans with bright, sparkly, hearts-on-fire Inner Pilot Lights.

And once you're a pro at letting me shine, you'll have mastered the tools you'll need in order to sparkle, even in the darkest company. Then you'll be so lit up that your light might even spark the flame in someone whose Inner Pilot Light is dim, like one firecracker popping the ignition switch in another.

Until then, give yourself permission to be discerning. Judgment and discernment are two very different vibrations. One condemns. The other simply notices and responds. It's okay to feel love for everyone but reserve your inner-circle intimacy for those who lend their fuel to my flames.

Warming the world in a circle of fire,
YOUR INNER PILOT LIGHT

129

Dear Gorgeous, Holy, Radiant You,

Let me just start with the obvious. Darling . . . I adore you. You are the light of my life. Or maybe I should say that I am the light of *yours*, and this is a role I cherish. To light your way is my sacred calling—to love you unconditionally, to guide you on your authentic path, to remind you of your true nature, to love and accept and befriend all of the many parts of you, to gently but fiercely kick your booty when needed, and to help you remember your wholeness, even when you forget.

Let me show you how I see you.

You are the shooting star, the tulip in bloom, the rainbow after the downpour, and the toothless grin of a happy baby at the breast of a loving mother. You are a pile of puppies rolling around, licking and nipping. You are the first bud of the cherry blossoms emerging in spring.

You are a Rumi poem, a Mozart sonata, a Michelangelo painting, and a children's squeaky orchestra concert. You are an old grove redwood forest, the green flash at sunset, a lunar eclipse, and a meteor shower. You are whales spouting, a leopard on the hunt, and a leafy sea dragon floating in the depths of the ocean's fine art gallery.

Your radiance stuns me and your shadows enliven me, giving me a chance to be intimate with all of you. Your curiosity about the world touches my heart, as I see how sweet your mind is, wanting to know the unknowable mystery, as minds just love to think. Your heart is a masterpiece, full as it is with wonder and awe and a waterfall of affection, as well as the scars of a million disappointing, grief-stricken, illusion-shattering heartbreaks. The courage you've shown to keep your heart open takes my breath away. It's so tempting to shut down when your heart has been hurt. It's a natural defense, a completely understandable reaction to a world full of trauma. But even that slight crack of hope in you touches me.

If you trust me even just a little bit, please give me the chance to say everything you need to hear. You know better than I do exactly what those words are, the words they didn't say, the loving actions you didn't receive from your parents or other loved ones, the tender caresses that didn't come when you needed them, the gentle rocking with your body cradled on the lap of the one whose touch you long for.

Let me give you everything you didn't get. Let me love you so fully inside your own heart, saying to you everything your hurt parts need to hear, giving you whatever you didn't get when you deserved to be treated as the precious gift that you are. Let me shower you with kisses and praise your beauty, your talent, your intelligence, and your giving heart. Let me hold you and rock you and whisper sweet nothings in your adorable ears. Let me reassure you that I will never leave you, for I am with you always, here forever in the sanctuary of your own heart.

I am the one you've been waiting for.

With me by your side, others can come or go. I can love you so fully that you overflow with all the love the Universe can shower upon you. Any love you get outside yourself is simply icing—lovely to have, a sweet confection to savor, but not necessary in order for you to feel whole. Human love is a blessing to be cherished, but once you become intimate with me, when you are so full from my love, you'll feel less needy, less dependent on getting your needs met outside what I offer.

I am here for you, beloved. It is my joy to remind you what a treasure you are, in all your messy, radiant, not enough, too much, imperfect, over-the-top, insecure, effervescent, expanded, contracted, magnificent glory. I am the you that is not a part, the one who can love all of your precious, messy, overprotective, vulnerable, micromanaging, scared, wounded parts, no matter how unacceptable you may judge them to be.

I have a message for you. If you nuzzle right up to me and listen close, you'll hear it.

Mwah,

YOUR INNER PILOT LIGHT

130

Hi, Honey!

When you get skilled at listening to my voice, you may deem yourself more "spiritual." You may even judge the people who can't hear their Inner Pilot Lights quite as well, comparing them to you and inflating yourself because you have a connection to my divine voice and they don't.

I like to think of the spiritual path more like a second puberty. Some people are eight. Some are twelve. Some are sixteen. But you'd never judge a six-year-old boy for not yet having a deep voice!

If you notice yourself judging where people are on their spiritual path, laugh at yourself and ease off the judgment. Simply notice the natural human impulse to judge and compare—and be gentle with yourself and everyone else.

Perhaps life is not so much about advancing on the spiritual path or winning some enlightenment race. Maybe it's simply about soul lessons you are here to learn—at your own pace, in your own beautifully unique way.

Maybe some people look more put together, strong, and "spiritual." Others appear more vulnerable and messy. But what if the most "spiritual" people are actually the ones who aren't afraid to look like beautiful hot messes?

Some spiritual teachers might give you the impression that enlightenment looks like a sort of dispassionate equanimity—if only you wake up all the way, you'll never feel pain or lose your composure, and even great loss, heartbreak, tragedy, betrayal, and disappointment won't activate intense emotions or create waves in the steady stillness of your consciousness.

What if enlightenment actually means expanding to include all of your adorably messy humanity—holding it all in love's radical embrace and letting it all move through you uninhibited?

What if being fully, divinely human means experiencing the agony, the ecstasy, and everything in between?

If that feels disorienting, you can always come back home to me. Here in the warm embrace of my steady glow, you will always find your way without needing to define it.

Expanding to include everything,
YOUR INNER PILOT LIGHT

131

Sweet Darling,

I'm so sorry you sometimes feel unsafe putting yourself out there for fear that people will attack you. I know it hurts when you dare greatly and then feel vulnerable when those who don't dare to be in the arena cast stones at you.

I know this doesn't fully comfort the scared, wounded parts that recoil when brave attempts to shine my light evoke attack in others. It doesn't help the scared parts when I say, "Seriously, sweetheart, sometimes it's them and not you."

But I'm going to say it anyway, just in case other parts can hear the truth of what I'm about to say.

When people criticize you, remember, it's entirely possible that their criticism is more about what they don't like about *themselves*, which they view in the mirror you hold up. If they have exiled or denied a part of themselves, judging it as unacceptable and then hiding it in the basement of their own psyche, they might unconsciously attack you if they see that same exiled part shining brightly in the mirror that is *you*.

I know it may not feel that way, but by being a clear mirror, you're actually doing that person a huge favor. You're offering them a healing, showing them that by bringing your own exiled parts into the light and loving them unconditionally, they have the opportunity to do the same.

When you let me help you open your heart, welcoming all those exiled parts back home, you give others permission to do the same.

I'm not suggesting that you should ignore all feedback or assume that constructive criticism is always a projection and never about you. (That would be the modus operandi of narcissist parts and sociopath parts, my love!) Sometimes what other people attack is worth noticing and getting curious about. Maybe there's growth here! Yeah!

But maybe not . . .

When you come to me as your ally, you'll see that it's a sign of maturity to take responsibility for your side of the street, to own and accept and be accountable for those growth edges where you're still learning. But it's never loving to shame yourself.

Some immature parts tend to blame others. Other immature parts tend to blame themselves. But really wise Inner Pilot Lights know that there's no need to blame anybody.

Here to love it all,

YOUR INNER PILOT LIGHT

132

Wild One,

I see that raw, primal, fierce part of you, the part that gets antsy with prolonged confinement in the safety of the walls of your carefully constructed, domesticated life. That part of you that's restless when the wind blows—the wanderlust part, the part that yearns deeply to connect your bare feet to the pulse and energy of the Earth, to feel the soil between your toes and become one with its organic natural power.

Answer the call of the wild, my dear. Seek out that which can only be found by communing with the forces of nature that still carry your ancestral spirit in the dust of the wind.

For all that technology has given us, it cannot replace that insuppressible desire to be wild, free, untethered.

So run, darling, with bare feet. Howl from the hillsides. Dig your hands into the soft dirt. Dance under the full moon and lift your arms into the cosmos. Plug into the Original Power Source.

Breathe. Trust me to keep you grounded and attentive to the responsibilities of your tribe, your business, your finances, and your physical health. Let go into your wildness, and when it's time to tend to the mundane necessities of life, do not fear. I'll let you know.

Protecting your responsible side so your wild side can howl at the moon,

YOUR INNER PILOT LIGHT

133

My Sweet One,

Unconditional love isn't about giving in. It doesn't mean that you use spiritual principles to rationalize disrespect, abuse, or neglect. Unconditional love doesn't make you a doormat that others can walk all over.

Unconditional love comes with fire. It's the crucible that knows how to burn away everything that isn't *real* love. It knows when to bring the heat and say, "*this* is not love!"

Unconditional love is about getting really clear about what's okay and what's not okay, establishing and enforcing consequences when someone violates your boundaries. Without this kind of fire-in-the-belly ferocity, love grows weak and meek. Real, true, powerful love knows when to say a strong NO!, which opens the door to the yummy, delicious, uber-compassionate YES! of the wide-open heart.

In case you're wondering, I love you that much.

Raising the bar *waaaay* up,
YOUR INNER PILOT LIGHT

134

Dear One,

Finding the right mentors to lift you up can make all the difference. A carefully chosen mentor can hook you up, impart life wisdom, raise your vibe when you get sucked into the swamp, cheerlead you when you're feeling down, and kick your booty when you need it.

But no matter how wise or accomplished your mentor, there's always a chance you will reach a point where you grow beyond what your mentor can teach you. If this happens, you might feel disillusioned or tempted to judge your mentor. But please resist this impulse, my love. Milk every last drop of gratitude out of your heart and pour it upon those who have helped you grow!

Remember that everyone is growing at a different pace, and most people are at different levels along different lines of development. Someone can be really mature spiritually but really remedial in relationships. Someone can be really intellectually advanced and really immature morally.

You may outgrow your mentor, and that's good news! We're all traveling at our own pace, and if you grow faster than someone who is guiding you, cool beans. No reason to judge your mentor or wallow in disappointment or feel betrayed. Simply see what is, accept it, thank your mentor, and be open to whatever will facilitate your path moving forward.

If you've experienced the disappointment of feeling as if you've outgrown your mentor, never fear, my love. That's what's supposed to happen as my light in you burns brighter. Plus, that's where I get to come in and lead the way.

The best mentor *ever,*

YOUR INNER PILOT LIGHT

135

Hiya, Sparkle Plug,

Things are reorganizing right now, not just for you but also for many others on the planet. It may feel disorienting. Change is afoot.

But don't worry, darling. We're all just pulling up the roots that lock us into an outdated consciousness we're outgrowing. Once the roots are untethered, we will all be free to shift—*together*.

The suffering comes when you resist the changes underway, when you get stuck in old stories of how to be and aren't free to be curious about what's next.

Try letting go of the resistance, trusting that all is happening in divine timing, in the perfect way. If you ride the collective wave instead of fighting the current, you'll be in for the ride of your life, my love.

Here with a surfboard,
YOUR INNER PILOT LIGHT

136

Dearest Beloved,

Do you realize how many ways I try to communicate with you, my darling? When I have trouble reaching you directly, I may rely on oracles! What is an oracle? While the traditional oracle was a mysterious intuitive person, other forms of oracular knowing include tarot cards, the I Ching, the Norse runes, the casting of the bones in African shamanism, the reading of the coca leaves in Peruvian shamanism, and any number of modern oracle decks.

However, when I'm trying to get your attention, I might use anything as an oracle—a rock, a cloud, an animal, or a waterfall. If you set the intention to connect with me, you could wander out into nature, find a flower that resonates with you, and ask the flower a question from your heart. When you really feel into the flower, you may be surprised how much wisdom that flower has to share with you, once you have the eyes to see and the ears to hear. Any adventure out into the natural world can be experienced as a sort of oracular reading. This can be done anytime you head out for a hike in the woods, a visit to a waterfall, a trip to the beach, or any experience where you're away from domestication and venturing into the wildness of nature.

Not hearing me today? Try letting me speak to you through oracles.

What oracular method might you try first?

Just ask me!

YOUR INNER PILOT LIGHT

137

My Dear,

Make me a promise today.

You know that first breadcrumb on the path to your truest calling that I tossed your way?

You know the one I'm talking about—the one you barely noticed at first, but it's been niggling at you? The one that feels a bit scary and uncomfortable and out of your comfort zone, but it also gives you a little spring in your step? The one that makes your mind gasp, "But what would everybody think?" or "How could I possibly pay the bills?"

Yeah. *That one.*

Will you trust for a moment that you've been sent on assignment to carry out a gorgeous mission in service to a more beautiful world? Can you just have faith that this one breadcrumb will lead to another breadcrumb, which will lead to another breadcrumb, but you won't be given the second breadcrumb until you muster up the moxie to say yes to the first?

Can you find it in your heart to just say yes to this one small request?

You don't have to understand the breadcrumb. Take just one little step toward it . . . and see what happens next.

Baby steps, my dear,
YOUR INNER PILOT LIGHT

138

Dear One,

I know it's tempting to give up when things don't go as planned. When you practice spiritual surrender and try not to attach to particular outcomes, it can be hard to tell how to proceed when the going gets rough.

Is the obstacle that pops up in your path the Divine's way of saying, "Not this way"?

Is it a roadblock meant to veer you in another direction, like some cosmic cowboy erecting a gate to steer cattle into the field where all the delicious grass lives?

Is this obstacle placed on the path to test your resolve, giving you a chance to activate the force of your will and demonstrate your commitment?

Or might you be blocking that which you deeply desire because part of you wants to realize your desire and another part is terrified of what would happen if you do? Have you got one foot on the gas and one foot on the brakes? Is this obstacle the result of this kind of energetic block?

If you're not sure, just ask me.

I'll always know the difference.

A master at obstacle courses,
YOUR INNER PILOT LIGHT

139

My Darling Light,

I know you have a people-pleasing part that just abhors disappointing people. I know you're tempted to do anything to avoid feeling how you feel when someone is displeased with you. I know how hard it can be to say no when you want to be perceived as generous, helpful, and kind.

But, darling, saying no to something you don't wish to do is saying yes to *you*.

If you continue to say yes when you really mean no, you're abandoning yourself, and your self-abandonment will catch up to you as poison in your relationships. You'll grow resentful because you're giving more than you're resourced to give, and over time, that toxic self-abandonment will eat away at you, causing you to sabotage otherwise healthy relationships and potentially making you sick.

If someone else doesn't know where your "no" lives, how can they help support your true "yes"? Is it really fair to get upset at others for not supporting or appreciating you and your needs if you don't make it clear what supports you and what doesn't?

When you stand firmly in your clear no, others may feel disappointed. But healthy people can handle disappointment! In fact, really healthy people will even celebrate you for standing up for your truth!

Not sure how to do this? Call on me.

With you through yes and no,
YOUR INNER PILOT LIGHT

140

My Love,

Take one step and notice how the world doesn't suddenly explode.

Then take another step and look around. Chances are good that right now, in this moment, there are no bombs. No guns. No starvation. No life-threatening illness or dismemberment. Nobody is dying right this second. Things are still fine in this moment right here.

Now keep walking farther. Look left. Look right. The coast is still clear.

The voice of your fearful parts will perpetually tell you to play it safe, not because these parts know the best way to live but because these young fearful parts simply don't like *change*—not even exciting, uplifting change!

Don't try demonizing those fearful parts or telling them they have to get the hell outa Dodge. (It won't work. You'll just scare them more.) Thank them for trying to protect you. Befriend them and try to earn their trust. See if they'll let me take a stab at keeping us safe for a change.

You and I know that nobody ever lived a rich, full life without embracing uncertainty, accepting change, and taking risks, but those fearful parts aren't so sure they agree. We have to show them we can do this differently . . .

Scared of being reckless? Think you have to let those sweet little fearful parts take the wheel in order to stay safe?

Trust me instead. My guidance will keep you far safer than those cute, overprotective little fearful parts ever will.

Playing it even safer,

YOUR INNER PILOT LIGHT

141

Dear One,

When you find yourself in situations where things aren't going your way, remember that you have a choice. You can go postal. You can get reactive. You can complain or grow irritable. You can lash out. You can play the victim and get stuck in your story. You can lament and drag everybody down with you, looping your trauma story without being curious about what might be in need of healing underneath all your pain.

Or you can try it another way.

You can tap into me, feel what you feel deeply and honestly, move right on through whatever painful, contracted emotions you feel, set any boundary you need to set, enforce any consequences you might need to enact, focus on gratitude for how much you're learning and what's going right, make the best of the situation, find your pleasure in every moment, and wind up having the best time of your life.

I'm not suggesting you should bypass your feelings or play Pollyanna when really you're seething inside. What does work is coming to me and letting me help you feel it all so you can move whatever arises through your body and let it flow right out of you, paving the way for new feelings, a more relaxed body, and brand-new life adventures full of possibility.

Can you let me help when things get tricky, my love?

Glass half-full,

YOUR INNER PILOT LIGHT

142

Sweetheart,

It's never too late to say you're sorry.

That thing that happened, the thing that still feels like needles in your heart, you don't have to carry it around forever.

You can call. Or write. Or send an email. Or go over and have a talk.

You can apologize in your journal and never tell anyone.

You can ask for forgiveness from that person, from God, from a redwood tree or a river or a sacred mountain. You can ask me for help.

You can go soul to soul without ever even contacting that person. Bow down to whoever or whatever you need to get down on your knees before.

The key is this—you *must, must, must* forgive yourself.

It happened. You learned from it. You'll try as hard as possible not to let it happen again—and if it does, you'll forgive yourself again.

Because grace is always possible. All you have to do is receive it.

The fast track to real forgiveness,

YOUR INNER PILOT LIGHT

143

Precious One,

Isn't it funny how you attach to getting what you want and resist things you don't like? How adorable you are with all your preferences and aversions!

But when you see things as I do, there is no "good" or "bad"—just life experiences that offer themselves up as opportunities to grow closer to *me*.

You know how you obsess about making the right decision and avoiding the wrong one? You're so afraid that if you make the wrong choice, bad things will happen.

But if you choose one path, you get one set of goodies. If you choose another, you get different goodies.

I know you have strong preferences about which are good and which are bad, but what if they're all just goodies?

Appreciating all goodies,

YOUR INNER PILOT LIGHT

144

My Love,

What if your sense of worth has nothing to do with what anybody else thinks? What if you *just know*—deep down at the essential core of you—that you're lovable, you're valuable, you're talented, you're brilliant, you're hot, and your breath smells like rose petals? (Okay, so maybe not first thing in the morning.)

What if you're not dependent upon anybody else's validation in order to know that you're tops, and even the stars don't shine as bright as you?

I'm not trying to puff you up or suggest that you're more special than anyone else. I'm just letting you know that because the Divine Spark of *me* is in you, you are inherently worthy, automatically precious, and as perfect as you ever need to be. You don't have to do anything to earn the right to *be*. That I exist in you is all you ever need to be good enough.

In case you ever forget and you need someone to reflect back to you your brilliance, I'm always here.

Your biggest fan,
YOUR INNER PILOT LIGHT

145

Hot Stuff,

Being connected to me doesn't mean you can't also be an erotic purring sex kitten or a hot, studly stallion.

There is no Madonna/whore complex in a whole human being. You don't have to be ascetic to be in touch. You can tap in whether you're wearing bunny slippers or four-inch stilettos or your coolest leather chaps. You can do it missionary style, you can do it doggie style, you can do it yourself, or you can abstain all together, celibate monk chic.

In my eyes . . . it's all holy.

So do it *your* way, you sexy beast. Just make sure you're tuning in to what works for me so you're expressing your whole, integrated, healthy, healed, hot-stuff wild self.

Grrrrr . . .
YOUR INNER PILOT LIGHT

146

My Angel,

When your marker of "success" requires a series of achievements, it's so easy to get caught up in the game of constant striving, winning, competing, and incessantly proving yourself.

But when does it end? When are you *there*? How do you know if you get there? When do you get to breathe and savor and celebrate and trust that you are enough, just as you are?

Don't stop pursuing your dreams, love. Do what you love because it's fun and it feels good to pursue your passions. But please let me fill you with the bliss of presence, the appreciation of a job already well done, and the reward of relishing in your radiant awesomeness—*right in this moment*.

In case it helps to hear it from me, let me just say that if there's a "there," you've already arrived. There's no "there" there. There's only *here*, with me in your holy heart.

High fives and hallelujahs,
YOUR INNER PILOT LIGHT

147

Brave Darling,

I know it's hard to trust other people sometimes. They ignore you when you need them, let you down when you're counting on them, fail to appreciate all that you do, and break your heart.

It's so hard to keep opening your heart, to keep showing up, to risk your vulnerability over and over, to give people you love permission to break your heart.

Keep in mind that when someone lets you down, it's simply because they've lost touch with the Inner Pilot Light that sparkles inside them. They've forgotten Who They Really Are, just as sometimes you forget Who You Really Are.

Personalities can't necessarily be trusted because, no matter how kind, sensitive, and holy your intentions, all gorgeous humans naturally have parts that get triggered. And when you're looping life's inevitable traumas, every human is at risk of being untrustworthy.

But here's the awesome news: *the Inner Pilot Light never lets you down*.

I'm here when you need me. I love you unconditionally and accept even your darkest shadows. I always appreciate you. And I never judge.

Totally trustworthy,
YOUR INNER PILOT LIGHT

148

My Weary Love,

A little birdie told me that you've had enough "advice" lately. You're exhausted from all the self-help books that tell you to do "this" and "that" to improve yourself. You've had it with others who are trying to make you a better person. You know they have your best interests at heart, and they mean well, but you've hit your limit. Today, all you need is someone who will listen, love you, accept you, and remind you that you're more than enough, just the way you are.

So let me grant your wish, darling.

> You are enough.
>
> You are loving and lovable.
>
> You are trusting and trustworthy.
>
> You are beautiful inside and out.
>
> You are perfect in your imperfections.
>
> You are brilliant, wise, intuitive, and radiant.

And I'm not just blowing smoke, precious.

I love you just the way you are.

Humming a love song,
YOUR INNER PILOT LIGHT

149

My Darling,

Because I love you so much, sometimes you'll hear my voice challenging you and pushing your growth edges. I know this kind of tough love can feel uncomfortable, so I'm always sensing into how far I can push you without going too far.

When you've hit the limits of your discomfort, I try to rush in with nurturing care, unconditional acceptance, and great arms of love.

Love is a dance between growth and comfort. I try my best to tango with these energies equally, just as you breathe in and out.

In case I've triggered you by pushing you too far out of your comfort zone, let me offer you my favorite Inner Pilot Light cheerleading song!

> You're the best and don't I know it. (Doo do do)
> My light shines so bright—so show it! (Doo do do)
> Stick with me, you'll never blow it. (Doo do do)
> Life is precious. Why not glow it? (Doo do do)
> GO YOU! (*Insert cartwheels, pom-poms, harmonicas, banjos, tambourines, and a wildly cheering crowd.*)

Always your coach and your cheerleader,
YOUR INNER PILOT LIGHT

150

Sweetcakes,

I know you're sometimes afraid to admit what you really want because if you let yourself fully feel the vulnerability of how much it hurts not to get what you yearn for, you're afraid you'll fall down a black hole of disappointment.

I know you've been told you're supposed to surrender to Divine Will and let go of all of your attachments, desires, and human preferences, and I love this plan. It's so spacious and gives me so much room to *play*!

But remember, sweetheart. This is a co-creation process here. It does take two to tango!

How can I help make your dreams come true if you're not willing to share your deepest desires and unmet yearnings with me? How can we create what is aligned for you if you're not willing to be vulnerable with me by sharing the most desperate longings from the core of your wildest heart?

Tell me your secrets, darling. Express the deepest, most intimate cravings of your soul. Get grand. Get crazy. Get dirty.

I don't care. I promise I won't judge. Just please—pretty please with whipped cream on top—*be true with me*.

Tell me everything . . . and then let go and trust me.

Dying to know you this intimately,
YOUR INNER PILOT LIGHT

151

Sweet Pea,

I know you're not perfect, no matter how hard you try to be. But I wouldn't have you any other way.

So let me remind you what you so often forget.

Within your imperfections lies a gateway to your connection with others. When you're perfectly imperfect and you let others see you just as you are, not as some artificial creation made up of all the fantasies and conditioning of what everyone else expects you to be but in your truly authentic self-expression, you open a door that invites others to be authentically expressed too.

Only through your vulnerabilities will you truly connect with others, and only when you connect can you truly experience real, abiding love.

So don't be afraid of what someone might see if you let them look inside.

What they'll see is *me*, and you can always trust that I am worth exposing.

The perfect mirror of truth,
YOUR INNER PILOT LIGHT

152

Dearest Beloved,

When you understand what I'm all about, you'll start to see that we're all here to learn lessons, live out our sacred contracts, and serve our mission on this planet, even though it may not always be easy.

Lots of the time, the guided path from A to B includes ecstatic moments, blissful heart connections, rockin'-and-rollin' adventures, and experiences of rapture. But sometimes the path from A to B also includes heartache, pain, failures, and obstacles, which may tempt you to swerve away from the pain and accidentally veer off track.

But never forget that on the other side of the challenges lies the most exquisite blossoming.

Sometimes your path will be filled with blessings so beautiful you may have a hard time receiving them. Open yourself wide so infinite blessings can pour in! But stay open to the times when things aren't happening just as you wish they would. When you increase your emotional resilience and expand your tolerance for both ecstatic pleasure and intense emotional pain, you open yourself to this wild and precious life in a way that allows you to live this delicious human experience at full volume.

In case you forget, let me remind you that *you are the one who chose to come here to be in this body on this planet at this time*.

Do you remember why?

Can't remember? You can always come to me for a refresher.

Your North Star,

YOUR INNER PILOT LIGHT

153

Dearest Playmate,

I know we can get pretty serious with one another, and while serious is sometimes necessary, so is *fun*.

So let's make a deal today.

Let's Skip-to-My-Lou while singing "Y.M.C.A." (hand motions included).

Let's make fudge and lick the bowl. Let's paint our toenails rainbow colored. Let's get tipsy on pink champagne and dance naked to Lady Gaga.

Let's go get warrior on the soccer field. Let's fly downhill on snowboards. Let's jump in the ocean even when it's really, really cold, just for the hell of it. Then let's giggle at how blue our lips get when we get out.

Let's cut loose, laugh out loud, and let our freak flag fly.

Then tomorrow, we can get serious again. Or not.

Deal?

Spraying you with purple hairspray,

YOUR INNER PILOT LIGHT

154

Dearest,

I know you've been wronged, my love. I know that person (and all the others) who hurt you broke your heart. I can still feel the soft spots from where you internalized those blows. And I know you're ready to heal those wounds.

But you can't do it by holding grudges, plotting revenge, enacting vendettas, replaying what hurt you, looping your trauma, or holding on to stories that no longer serve you.

No, my love. The only way to truly heal those soft spots is to let me give those hurt parts everything they didn't get from the ones who hurt you.

Let's try this together, my darling. Think of something that hurt and let that hurt part show itself to me. Let it tell me how much it got hurt. Let it reveal how old it is, where it's living, and all the details of what happened. (Don't worry. I won't let it overwhelm you or flood you with more pain than you can tolerate. You can even ask that hurt part not to give you more than you can handle right now. It's listening, and it can be our ally.)

Let the hurt part recall every painful memory and show me every traumatic moment. Let it rant and cry and rage and have a tantrum with me, if necessary. Let me hold that part in my loving arms and show it I am here, so I can love it without demonizing, shaming, or exiling it one bit.

Let me help this hurt part rewrite the story so it has a happier ending. Let me help that part get what it didn't get back then. Let me finally make it right. Let me be radically intimate with this part, like a healthy mother would hold a wounded child in her loving embrace. Let this hurt part learn to trust me the way the other person couldn't be trusted. Let me love that part all the way up. Let me be the one you've been waiting for.

Then tomorrow, let me check back in with that wounded part. Let me show it I'm still here, still loving it, still accepting it. Let me ask it what it needs. Let me show it I'm here to help it get its needs met. Let it learn to relax with me.

Then . . . and only then . . . maybe it will let you forgive the one who hurt you. Real, authentic forgiveness arises naturally when the wounded part heals all the way. This kind of forgiveness frees me to burn like a bonfire inside the sanctuary of your own heart.

Come on, baby, light my fire,
YOUR INNER PILOT LIGHT

155

Oh, Dear Flame!

Remember that time in your life when you really had it going on, when you were on top of the world and nothing was ever gonna keep you from being the shooting star you knew you were destined to be? Maybe you were a vibrant, fearless, adventurous three-year-old, or maybe you were a wild, untamed teenage stallion, or maybe it was just yesterday!

Guess what?

Holy crikey, McFly. We're hoppin' in the DeLorean and today is time-warp day.

That time is *now*, and you're *on fire*.

What could you do today to let that part express itself in your current life? What would this shooting-star part need in order to feel safe enough to blast across a still-night sky?

What big or small action could give that part just enough space to feel like it's welcome in present time?

What if you let that genie out of the bottle? How would you feel if the adventurous, wild, fearless part that may have been trapped finally got liberated and had just enough bandwidth to show itself?

What does that part want to do today? Dare you give it some space?

Don't worry. I won't let that part take over. You can let it have some playtime without fearing that it will blow up the whole system, because I've got a handle on things, and you can trust me to know how far it's safe to go.

Can you trust me? Can you let this undomesticated part do just a wee bit of its wild thang?

Bring it, baby.

Radiating like plutonium,

YOUR INNER PILOT LIGHT

156

My Love,

When you're around your family, you may find yourself reverting back to old habits, stinging from unhealed wounds, and letting your inner brat eclipse me.

You know what they say. If you think you're enlightened, go home!

But please don't kick yourself for this. All humans tend to act out when they're with their families of origin. Even the ones you might think are enlightened can be a little naughty when Mom, Dad, bro, and sis are around.

Inner Pilot Lights always think this is *adorable*. Especially when this happens to you, my heart just swells up, and I find you so delicious I want to lick you like an ice cream cone. (Okay, well maybe sometimes I get carried away . . .)

Seriously, though, when I see that part of you emerge, I know it's just the frustrated little child in you or the exiled rebel acting out, longing to be seen and loved. I know you have these parts that are desperate to be heard, resisting being manipulated, begging to be loved, yearning to breathe free, simply craving unconditional acceptance.

I also know that your most traumatized parts tend to show themselves when you let your guard down. And when you're around the people who know you the best, you're more likely to act out the parts that are ready to be healed.

You can be bratty with me, babe.

Loving you even more when you stick out your tongue and blow raspberries,
YOUR INNER PILOT LIGHT

157

Dear One,

You know that person you've been meaning to call—the one who's been on your mind, the one you really care about, the one it's been too long since you've spoken to?

Don't waste another day letting your workaholism, your perfectionism, your out-of-balance priorities, or your pride get in the way of expressing what burns bright in your loving heart.

Sure, attend to your responsibilities. Do what you must to make bandwidth to reach out. If this relationship triggers you, put in place any boundaries that you need in order to feel safe. Then . . . trust me—check in, and if I say the time is right, go for it!

When you're ready . . .

Pick up the phone.

Make the call.

Or drive on over.

Say the words you've wanted to say.

Open your heart.

Speak your truth.

Don't hold back.

Express everything you would say if you knew you (or the other) were dying tomorrow.

Don't forget to say, "Thank you."

And don't forget to call on me first! Let me do the talking.

The voice of your care,

YOUR INNER PILOT LIGHT

158

Dearest Beloved,

Did I catch just the teensiest bit of doubt coming from you about whether you can trust me?

I know sometimes you worry that I'll steer you off course, make you do crazy, reckless things, and land you living under a highway overpass somewhere on the wrong side of the tracks.

I also know you really want to trust me, and you can tell that the things I whisper into your ear in the quiet of the night feel like relief, because even if what I say is scary, truth feels like a breath of fresh air.

In case you still wonder, let me tell it to you straight, darling.

Once all our vulnerable and protector parts relax and give you space to hear more of my guidance, I promise you that every bit of love I offer you is the real deal. Every morsel of reassurance is what you've always deserved. Every redirect is just meant to lovingly steer you back on course. Every bit of guidance will lead you home. Every warning is meant to protect you. Every encouragement to open your heart will only bring in more love. Every scalpel of truth is just meant to strip away everything that is not love. Every hug is sincere, and every whisper is spot on.

So don't make me yell, darling. Nuzzle in close . . .

Psst,

YOUR INNER PILOT LIGHT

159

My Sweet,

I know you tend to make promises you can't keep, resolutions you don't follow, and intentions that fail to stick.

So let me get you off the hook.

Don't kick that habit.

Don't go for that goal.

Don't lose that weight.

Don't take the leap of faith.

Don't do it.

Don't even try . . . unless, first, you tap into me and get the thumbs-up sign that you're *really* ready.

Until you *really* decide that it's finally time to quit that habit, accomplish that goal, and go for it with gusto, it's unlikely to actually happen. You'll make halfhearted attempts. You'll make promises to yourself that you fail to keep. Your inner bully will do its best to whip you into shape.

But then some protector part that you may judge as a saboteur, addict, lazy bum, binge-eater, or rebel takes the wheel and BAM. You're doing it (or failing to do it)—*again*.

Then—you know the drill—you'll kick yourself for not following through. Your inner-critic parts will have a field day. You'll lose trust in yourself. You'll feel like a loser. And that will only make you more vulnerable to failing to change that thing you wish to change.

So do me a favor, my darling. Love and accept yourself just as you are, with or without that habit, with or without that accomplishment, with or without the transformation you desire.

Get honest with yourself. See how it might actually be serving you right now to keep that habit, avoid that goal, or stay in your comfort zone. See if you can find appreciation for whatever is keeping you stuck—and thank it for what a good job it's doing protecting you from whatever it's afraid of.

I'm not suggesting you let yourself off the hook for bad behavior, but I'm also not suggesting that it helps to shame yourself when you're not doing what you promised yourself you'd do. Keep the personal accountability. Invite the self-loathing inner critic to relax and step aside.

Hold the paradox of your desire to change and your acceptance of who you are—*just as you are right now*. Love yourself the way I do. Know that you can't do this life thing wrong, that my love for you is so *infinite* that there is nothing you can do to lose it.

Nothing.

Then when you're ready to go for it, count me in. I'm here, and I'll be your best cheerleader and ally.

With radical acceptance,
YOUR INNER PILOT LIGHT

160

My Star Student,

If life is a school and you are a curious consumer of wisdom, darling, you've earned a 4.0.

You're exploring every avenue of the human experience. You're acing every test. You're passing with flying colors. You've got this life thing going on, my beautiful sweetheart!

I know the curriculum can feel tricky, and you may not know how brilliantly you're scoring. You may not realize that you signed up for this whole curriculum, even the parts that may feel like painful losses, failures, disappointments, betrayals, and mistakes.

Don't forget, my love, that you've signed up for all of this because you came here to "Earth School" to learn to grow closer to the Divine, and you're here to go the distance. Your soul chose to ramp up your resilience, to crack open your heart, to learn how to transmute pain into ecstasy, to bench-press your receiving muscles and escalate your ability to tolerate pleasure, to wake up all the way, and to go through some of the hardest and most soul-stretching classes Earth School can teach.

You're getting straight As.

You're the teacher's pet.

With gold stars splashed all over you,
YOUR INNER PILOT LIGHT

161

Beloved,

Come with me to the dark side today.

You know how much I love sparkles, luminescence, and firelight.

But did you know I also love shadows, darkness, and the pitch-black redwood forest on the winter solstice?

Only when we explore the darkness can we fully reclaim true light.

Just as the sun and moon must share space in the sky, the light and darkness must share holiness. When you resist either light or dark, you fall out of balance. When you welcome both and accept light and dark as equally sacred, the gracious, spacious love of the Universe expands to hold your wholeness with pure, vibrant, nonjudging, unconditional love.

Some beings blossom in the dark.

Do you know if you're one of them?

Just ask me.

Boo,
YOUR INNER PILOT LIGHT

162

My Sweet One,

You might hear banter about how you can heal yourself. What if you believe this is absolutely possible but you're still sick? Does this mean you're not doing a good enough job healing yourself? Are you supposed to conclude that you suck at being your own inner physician? Does this mean you need to try harder, be better, and activate the force of your will with greater effort to make cure happen?

No, my darling. Conclusions like this only activate the body's stress responses and make self-healing less effective.

The healing process is full of paradoxes.

Your body, mind, psyche, and soul can heal themselves.
But you can't do it alone.

You are responsible *to* your illness, but not *for* your illness.

You can heal yourself, but not everybody gets cured when they get healed.

How can you work with all these paradoxes consciously?

This is where I come in, my love. Let me see if I can break this down the way I see it.

There's a difference between healing and curing. To heal means to restore wholeness. To cure means to eliminate disease. But here's the clincher: When you restore wholeness, you make the body ripe for miracles. Then . . . *anything is possible*.

But that doesn't necessarily mean cure is what your Divine Assignment has up its sleeve. Sometimes a soul signs up to accept certain challenges as part of a life's mission. What better way to make a doctor more compassionate, humble, and empathic with other sick people than to let that doctor experience chronic illness, enabling that doctor to serve with great tenderness? Does this mean she's not good at self-healing and has failed as a spiritual being? Hell no! It might mean she's doing a bang-up job fulfilling her life's purpose!

So what can you do if you yearn to be free of physical or emotional suffering? How can you optimize your chances of healing so your physical and emotional body might experience some respite?

Start with asking me to help you restore wholeness by healing any part of you that believes you're separate from me, separate from the Divine, separate from other people and nature and love itself. This doesn't guarantee cure, but it sure does improve your chances.

How do you heal the illusion of separation and make your body ripe for miracles?

Tune in to me. I'll tell you everything you need to know, if only you get quiet enough to listen. If cure is aligned with your soul's Divine Assignment, and you've done what you must to unblock any energetic blocks that would sabotage your healing efforts, cure will be within closer reach, though it's never guaranteed.

If cure is in the cards, I'll help you find it, my darling. If not, I will help you accept what is, without blame or any story suggesting you're not motivated enough or wise enough or spiritual enough to be cured.

Full of the best kind of medicine,
YOUR INNER PILOT LIGHT

163

My Love,

Wanna know a quick way to fan my flames?

Practice radical kindness and generosity today.

Check to see if you're fully resourced with the heat of my flames so you're not giving what you don't have to give. Then—if you have heat to spare—bring even more kindness than might feel comfortable.

Don't do it because you have some savior complex that says you're not good enough unless you give more than you have to give. Don't do it because you're violating or abandoning yourself.

Do it because you're full to the brim with overflowing love and gratitude, and it feels so super-duper yummy to just let my love pour out of you onto those in need of love!

Give just because it feels *delicious*.

Give because the very act of getting outside yourself and giving feeds your need for service, intimacy, connection, purpose, and love. Give because you have more than someone who needs you. Give because you are so blessed that you have enough to give, even if you only give a dollar to someone who has nothing or a hug to someone it's hard for you to hug.

Then check in with me and notice how bright I get.

POOF!

On fire and glowing,
YOUR INNER PILOT LIGHT

164

Dearest Beloved,

I know you've erected walls because you have a natural human desire to feel safe. I know those walls have been friends, like guides, that have kept you protected from a cold, harsh world. I know they helped you survive when you were young and vulnerable, and you needed them—as loving companions who honored and guarded your tender heart.

I am so grateful those parts took over when you were little and you didn't know how to find me when you needed to feel safe.

But now, my love, I'm here. I've got you. You can thank all those angels and protective companions. Let them know that *you+me*, babe, we've got this.

I want you to know something crucial. At the deepest core in you, you are always safe. You are inherently guarded. Your turf is protected. You can finally *breathe*.

I am *here*.

I've got your back, even if it feels like nobody else does.

Ah . . . there.

Now I have room to sparkle.

Go get 'em, tiger!
YOUR INNER PILOT LIGHT

165

Dear One,

I know you've been conditioned to believe that good things require self-sacrifice, painful effort, and difficult martyrdom. Only then will you get the just desserts you've heartily earned.

But I have a secret for you.

Transformation doesn't always have to hurt.

Masochism and pain are certainly one way to grow. You can absolutely use pain as an alchemical process, allowing your agony to transform you. It's possible to get your PhD in pain as a spiritual path. You're welcome to explore that way to grow, my love! It's useful to have a full range of capacity when it comes time to use everything life can dish up as spiritual fuel.

But don't limit yourself. Make sure you have at least equal capacity to allow pleasure to be an illuminating, challenging, and megabadass spiritual path!

How much yum can you tolerate? How much ease will you let in? How many miracles will you allow before you hit your glass ceiling? What is your capacity for receiving unlimited blessings?

Will you freak out if life gets too good? Will your protector parts unwittingly sabotage you, blocking your ability to receive an intense pleasure load?

What would happen if life got really freakin' good? Could you handle it?

Would you be willing to explore getting your PhD in pleasure as a spiritual path?

Need a mentor to help you write your thesis?

Can I volunteer myself?

Anticipating throwing your graduation cap into the air . . . WHEEEEE!!!!!

YOUR INNER PILOT LIGHT

166

Precious One,

If you're pushing to bring into being something that is out of alignment with your true path, it will feel like an uphill battle.

But when you tap into me and call upon me to bring one of my holy ideas into being—oh my goodness. Holy wow. The way synchronicity can show up to help . . . the way the right people can arrive like angels just when you need them . . . the way money can appear, as if by magic, to fund the holy idea—well, gosh darn it, darling, you better be ready to pinch yourself. It can feel *that* miraculous. You may even be struck with awe.

It's not that you won't have to work hard and put in your ten thousand hours to achieve mastery for that thing you feel called to bring forth. It's not that you won't have to leverage discipline or prove your devotion to the cause you're been chosen to serve.

It's just that the whole thing will feel so extraordinarily dance-worthy that you won't believe you ever wasted so much effort trying to push against a brick wall when all that was required was a waltz.

Smacking the button—"That was easy!"
YOUR INNER PILOT LIGHT

167

Beautiful,

It starts with one small act of self-acceptance.

You notice my sparkle, and I make you smile. That one smile is contagious. It spreads like a happy virus and suddenly you're accepting your crooked nose, your crappy driving, your bad habit, and your tendency to drop the F-bomb at just the wrong moment.

Before you know it, you're laughing at your foibles, celebrating your strengths, and with an awesome combo of humility and confidence, ticking off the ways in which you *rock*. And everyone is nodding and noticing because they want whatever you're having.

One thing leads to another and suddenly you're attracting amazing people to you like a magnet, the clients are rushing in, the money is flowing in, your health is improving, that person who you wish paid more attention to you is winking and nudging up against you, synchronicities are unfolding like miracles, and the doors are swinging wide open.

How did it start? You smiled at me. And I smiled back.

Beaming,
YOUR INNER PILOT LIGHT

168

My Red Hot & Holy Babe,

We don't talk much about gender in Inner Pilot Light land, but in the human realm, the majesty of my life force wears two faces—the Divine Masculine and the Divine Feminine. While I am a balance of both energies, spiraling up like the snakes swirling around the staff in the caduceus, many spiritual circles neglect or even blaspheme my feminine side.

What's the difference between the Divine Masculine and Divine Feminine? I like the way scholar of mysticism Sera Beak describes it in *Red Hot & Holy* best:

> For *me*, the Divine Masculine feels still; the Divine Feminine feels like movement. The Divine Masculine feels like no thing; the Divine Feminine feels like every thing. The Divine Masculine feels impersonal; the Divine Feminine feels personally invested. The Divine Masculine feels cool and collected and even a bit chaste; the Divine Feminine feels hot and bothered and more than a bit salacious. In *my* inner wisdom, the Divine Masculine looks clear, and the Divine Feminine shimmers like a rainbow. The Divine Masculine works it out on a yoga mat; the Divine Feminine prefers a claw-foot bathtub. The Divine Masculine drives a Prius; the Divine Feminine speeds in a convertible Caddy. The Divine Masculine fasts; the Divine Feminine feasts. The Divine Masculine sits cross-legged under a tree all day; the Divine Feminine dances around a fire all night. The Divine Masculine sounds like OMMMMMM; the Divine Feminine sounds like AHHHHH or WOOO HOOOOOO!!!! Or a guttural scream. Or a sob. Or a belly laugh.

While the Divine Masculine may get a lot of airtime in spiritual circles that celebrate cultivating qualities of Oneness, nonattachment, grounding, presence, stillness, equanimity, emptiness, and other zen attributes, the Divine Feminine's wild Shakti of emotionality, movement, sensuality, creativity, chaos, intuition, nurturing, compassion, love of nature, and healing has been largely suppressed in modern spirituality.

Me, I'm both, and you can count on me to help you round out whichever face of love needs more balance in your life.

Yin and yang,
YOUR INNER PILOT LIGHT

169

Hiya, Love,

What would you do today if you could let your freak flag fly? Who would you be if you weren't worried what "everybody" thought?

What might you wear?

What would you shout from the rooftops?

Who would you hang out with?

What would your TED talk be about?

Who might you dare to love?

What adventure might you say yes to?

What picket sign might you hold?

What organization or group would you support?

What system might you be motivated to heal?

What risk would you take?

What would you scream while beating pillows?

How would you walk?

What audacious thing might you do?

How might you open your heart?

What hobby might you finally pick up?

Who might you be?

Pick one small thing that could help you fly your freak flag.

Who's the rascal behind that flag?

Guilty as charged,
YOUR INNER PILOT LIGHT

170

Sweetheart,

I know how hard you're trying not to fail. I know it's scary as hell to imagine taking a huge risk that doesn't come to fruition the way you might hope it will.

But, my darling, don't you know you're unlikely to ever achieve wild greatness without taking bold, ridiculous risks? While it's possible to birth masterful creations, participate in a love revolution, and heal the planet with great ease, it's not common. Usually skipping merrily down obstacle-free paths paved with gold while wearing daisies in their hair is not what initiates those who change the world. Initiation often requires risking everything—your money, your reputation, your relationships, maybe even your *life*.

It's not that initiated world-changers aren't afraid to go broke, fail publicly, feel humiliated, get abandoned, and wind up sweaty, broken, bloody, or dead. They're quaking in their go-go boots, darling!

It's just that they kick up the heels of those sexy boots and take risks anyway, not because they're braver than you are but because they've chosen to follow instructions from their Inner Pilot Light. And Inner Pilot Lights sometimes whisper risky instructions.

The good news is that this way of being leads to a whole lotta ruckus. But it also results in a freakin' feast of fun!

Clicking my high heels together,
YOUR INNER PILOT LIGHT

171

Dearest Beloved,

Will Rogers once said, "The best way to make a fire with two sticks is to make sure one of them is a match."

I'll be the match. You be the other stick.

When we come together, we'll light this world on fire. And oh my, baby, that kind of heat is contagious. Next thing you know, hearts are igniting willy-nilly, and love is exploding like fireworks. Strangers are opening their hearts to more compassion and fierce protection for one another. Random acts of kindness become the new normal. Nature begins to heal. Truth and reconciliation sparks heart-opening compassion. People stop abusing their power. Greed and scarcity fade, allowing for distribution of resources so that everybody gets their basic needs met and nobody takes more than they need. Forgiveness sweeps across the planet. Love reigns supreme.

When you light up with me, I tap into the divine matrix of Inner Pilot Lights everywhere, and we all weave this tapestry of brilliant radiant light, love, compassion, and truth. Next thing you know, the whole Earth is glowing, the vibration of the planet is lifted, and all beings are One.

The story of separation dissolves. The gap between us closes. We light each other up, and the whole planet ignites into one ginormous flame of LOVE.

It all starts with one little spark.

Will you do your part?

Whoosh,
YOUR INNER PILOT LIGHT

172

Hiya, Pumpkin,

I sit in awe as I watch you unfold. Every move you make in the chess game of your life leaves me stunned. You know that one play you made—the one that seemed like a mistake at the time? Yeah, *that one*.

Well, it turns out it was that very experience that made you just the person who is perfectly suited to do exactly what you're doing right now. Way to go, hot shot!

You couldn't have planned it better. Good move. Can't wait to see what's up your sleeve next.

Not sure which next move is best?

Ask me.

Checkmate,
YOUR INNER PILOT LIGHT

173

My Love,

Your people are waiting for you.

They're wondering where you are.

I know a few precious ones have already found you. They were courageous. They wandered through thickets and waded through marshes because they had to find you and couldn't wait.

But the rest are confused. They sense you. They have a feeling you're coming. They've been previewing you in their dreams. They write love letters to you in their hearts. They dance with themselves, imagining that you're in the circle with them.

But they don't know enough to search behind bushes and go looking in dark caves, so they're waiting until you broadcast my light and take your place in the sun, where they will see the light shining from within you, finally guiding them to you.

By my light, they will arrive,
YOUR INNER PILOT LIGHT

174

Dearest Beloved,

I sang outside your window, serenading you with songs of love. But you weren't listening.

I came to you in dreams, whispered sweet nothings in your ear, and granted you visions of what was possible, but you dismissed my voice when you woke up.

I showed up as thoughts in your head, affirming that you are beautiful, whole, and cherished, but you let your sweet, scared inner critic write me off.

I planted passages from books, blog posts, keynote speeches, and psychics in front of you, hoping you'd hear my voice. But you credited my gushing words of love to the writers, speakers, and psychics, missing altogether that I was using them to get through to you.

So today I kneel here before you, beseeching you to finally pay attention to my words.

Will you be mine?

With roses, chocolate, and love letters,
YOUR INNER PILOT LIGHT

175

Glorious Beloved,

You know how you try to hide from everyone all the parts you think others won't like?

You try to hide your jealous parts, your rage parts, your womanizer parts, your anxious parts, your frightened parts, your hurt parts, your rebellious teenager parts, your greedy parts, your cheater parts, your addict parts, your slut parts, your abusive parts, your slacker parts, your liar parts. You just banish them to the basement, shaming them and berating them, making them promise not to ever come out while anyone is looking.

You trash those parts with every New Year's resolution, promising to kill them altogether, swearing that you'll finally get rid of them.

How do you think this makes them *feel*?

Wouldn't it be a huge relief to just let me take over, so that all of your parts get the love, approval, appreciation, caretaking, and gentle discipline they need?

I'm on it so you and all of your parts can just chill out in front of the fireplace in your footie pajamas, watching the flames of my love flicker you into a blissed-out trance.

Om . . .
YOUR INNER PILOT LIGHT

176

Lovebug,

How can you tell if it's me talking or one of my imposters?

You'll recognize my voice because of what Internal Family Systems founder and psychologist Richard Schwartz calls the eight C's:

I am curious.

I am calm.

I am compassion.

I am courage.

I am confidence.

I am connectedness.

I am creativity.

I am clarity.

Oh yeah, baby. That's me, alright.

Raising my hand,
YOUR INNER PILOT LIGHT

177

Dearest Beloved,

When someone offers to help you and saying yes would light me up, please say yes!

Don't worry about whether it's a burden on that person. Trust that their Inner Pilot Light has got their back and they wouldn't offer unless they were bursting with generosity and the desire to serve you!

Don't keep score and vow to return the favor.

Just smile. Say yes. And thank you. Let your heart burst with gratitude. Pour love out of your eyes.

Remember, every time we accept the love, help, and support of another, we give them a gift. Every person on Earth wants to be helpful. We all want our lives to mean something. We all want to lift up someone else, and in doing so, lift up ourselves.

So don't worry whether that person will be depleting themselves by helping you out. It's their job to fill themselves first and protect their own boundaries.

Say yes. Mean it. Receive graciously.

Yes, yes, yes!
YOUR INNER PILOT LIGHT

178

Beloved,

You're not loved because you're smart (even though your mind just wows me).

You're not loved because you're beautiful (but jeez—you're gorgeous).

You're not loved because you knocked it out of the park at work (you blow me away when you do, though).

You're not loved because you finally achieved that goal (but congrats on that).

You're not loved because you help others so much (I know they appreciate it).

You're not loved because you follow all the rules (I understand it's a sacrifice to do so sometimes).

You're not loved because you're so talented (even though you are).

I want you to know that you are loved *just because you are*.

Period.

And that's way more than enough.

In awe,

YOUR INNER PILOT LIGHT

179

My Love,

You might think you're stepping into your power when really you're stepping into your ambition.

How can you tell the difference?

When you're stepping into your true power, there's no pretense. There's no need to prove yourself. You're not trying to impress anyone or fill a hole of unworthiness deep in your core. You're not slipping into martyrdom, and you know that nobody needs to be rescued. There's no pity, no righteousness, and no superiority. There's no clinging, no grasping, no fear, and no anxiety. There is only love, which fuels the action and leads to results, but it does so without pride, attachment to outcome, or the need for approval, achievement, or accolades.

When you're stepping into your ambition, you may start off with pure, clear intentions. There's nothing wrong with having an ambitious part! It can help you get stuff done. And it can be very useful when it comes to implementing action steps on the path to your calling.

But if you're swept away by ambition, and you can't feel your connection to me, you're at risk of trying to feed the hungry ghost of what writer and spiritual seeker Anne Lamott calls the "God-hole" with that which can only be filled by your spiritual connection.

When you try to fill the God-hole with one achievement after another without realizing that you are whole already, filled as you are with my love, you'll never be satisfied. Even if you fulfill whatever ambition you set as your goal, you'll find a new goal as soon as you achieve it, always going after the next shiny penny.

I adore your ambitious part, my darling. I see this part of you that yearns to do big things in the world as a little child who simply craves love and acceptance like any sweet child would.

Babycakes, what if you could believe that we'll achieve *plenty*, if only you relax into me and follow my lead?

We've got this,
YOUR INNER PILOT LIGHT

180

My Great Love,

Love wears so many faces that it can be confusing to define. There's family love, the kind of love you have for your mother or father or child. There's romantic love, the love of your soulmate or lover. There's love for animals, the kind of pure, devotional love you might feel for your pet. There's the love you have for your best friends. These kinds of love tend to fit nicely into boxes.

But then there are confusing, mystical kinds of love, like the love you feel when you gaze at a waterfall, and then—WHAM—your heart explodes with a cloud of fairy dust and suddenly you *are* the waterfall and you feel like you've just fallen in love with that waterfall. Next thing you know, tears are spilling down your cheeks and you're wondering what the hell is going on.

Or maybe you see a gorgeous wild animal out in nature and you feel like your chest gets cracked open, as if you've just had heart surgery. Love bursts out of you and through you and you love those whales or that cheetah or that owl more than you've ever loved anything in your whole life. Your whole body buzzes with love, a vibrating tenderness emerging from the sanctuary of your bursting heart.

This same kind of mystical love can happen with people. You meet a stranger—maybe even someone you'd never have one iota of interest in, someone with whom you share nothing in common. You happen to gaze into his or her eyes and—BAM—your heart gets zapped and blown open, and it's confusing to your adorable mind!

Maybe you're with someone you don't know that well, and you accidentally bump into "the plane of love." Or maybe you're with your lover or your child when it happens. Your heart bursts open and your chest is filled with butterflies and you feel this rush of tenderness so exquisite that you feel almost uncomfortably exposed and vulnerable. Love is hemorrhaging out of you but it's not going to hurt you because even more love is flooding into you from some invisible Source. You know you're never going to run out of this kind of love. There's an infinite supply, and it fills you like a waterfall that spurts out of you so fast you can barely breathe. As this happens, the borders between you and the being you love start to dissolve. The membrane that separates you vanishes, and you feel as if you *are* that person or animal or mountain, as if there's no boundary between you. You lose yourself in this love. Lose yourself into what? Into Oneness? It's hard to describe. It's simultaneously terrifying and wondrous, filling you with awe and light. The mind drops away at some point, and all you feel is an indescribable beauty and openness, a sweetness that bubbles up through you and rushes through your body like warm honey. If you lean all the way into it, you feel as if you'll get lost in it, as if you'll never come back. But if you can resist the temptation to guard against it, you feel deep connection and intimacy. Every sense is heightened. Colors are Technicolor. The wind on your skin gives you goosebumps. There's erotic charge in the sensuality of this present moment and everything feels *alive*.

Know where that kind of love comes from?

It's all me, baby.

I love you,

YOUR INNER PILOT LIGHT

181

Sweet Pea,

When one new creation is born, something else must go. Every birth is a death. Just as the caterpillar must dissolve to become the butterfly, you must give up who you are to become who you must. This doesn't mean you'll lose everything you cherish, but it does mean that transformation requires letting go. Just as you clean your closet to make room for beautiful new garments, becoming who you must requires releasing that which no longer resonates at your current vibration.

When your destiny awaits you, you must feel, reckon with, heal, befriend, accept, and then let go of your past.

Grieve it. Cry it out. Hug it. Mourn its loss.

Say goodbye. Express gratitude for how much you've learned and grown. Then . . . in a burst of my flame, burn it to ashes in the phoenix process that is your life.

Call in whatever is next. Stand curiously in the space between stories and make peace with uncertainty. Wonder what the Divine has in store for you. Open yourself to receiving the mystery of what's next.

Not sure how to navigate this transformation? Take my hand, sweetheart. You're not alone. I'll lead you there.

This way, darling,

YOUR INNER PILOT LIGHT

182

My Dear,

Does it ever feel like people just suck off you, take your juice, and then disappear? Do they use your gifts, fail to say thank you, and mosey on their merry way?

Do you wind up feeling depleted, victimized, and unappreciated? Do you feel resentful because nobody seems to have your back, and so few give to you the way you give to others?

Are you weary from being the cosmic doormat?

I'm sorry you feel that way, my love. Really, I am.

Wouldn't you like to see this pattern break? Would you please let me help you shift this? All of this will change when you decide to let me take the lead.

Start by being as generous to yourself as you are with other people. Would you be willing to give yourself the same time, attention, priority, and generosity that you give to others? Would you treat yourself as a beloved worthy of all that exquisite love and care?

Let me help you see that you deserve love and attention, nurturing and comfort, as much as all those you serve.

I've got your back,
YOUR INNER PILOT LIGHT

183

Dear Beautiful, Radiant, Sparkly, Effervescent You,

As an infant, you were born perfect and whole in your glorious humanness, and in spite of what you think, that has never—not for a second—changed.

I know, however, that because you are human, it's in your nature to sometimes lose sight of what I see in you. So let me remind you how you appear from my spacious, unconditionally loving point of view.

You are brilliant beyond measure, not because of anything you've accomplished but because there is nobody else quite exactly like adorable, quirky, eccentric *you*. Nobody else's mind processes quite like yours. Nobody else has lived your life experiences, overcome your challenges, learned your lessons, and gleaned exactly the gifts necessary to do what you're here on this Earth to do. Nobody else thinks like you do, feels like you do, views the world like you do, and has a heart like you do. That alone makes you precious.

But I'm just getting started here, my darling.

You are beautiful as only you can be, with your soul glowing through your skin, infecting others with your love and presence in a way you don't even seem to recognize. Don't you understand that's why people are drawn to you? Don't you realize the power within you, the magnetic attraction people feel toward you when you let them see *me*, your Inner Pilot Light? Don't you realize how much your love matters, how much it's already touching others? Can't you see that you're *already* more than enough, just the way you are right this very moment?

Your beauty has nothing to do with a ski-slope nose or flat abs or the right curves or a wrinkle-free face or buff muscles or a full head of hair. Your beauty transcends your features, the shape of your body, and how well you measure up to what others might think you're supposed to look like on the outside.

You are lovable beyond your wildest dreams, and you don't have to do a thing to earn it. You may not remember, but you chose to come here to Earth simply to love and be loved. At the end of your life, you won't be counting the dollars you've earned, the books you've published, the countries you've traveled to, the projects you've completed, the number of hours you clocked in your cubicle, or how many hours you logged in holding up flashcards for the kids.

No matter how many wonderful things you accomplish, no matter how many impossible missions you make possible, no matter how many plaques bear your name, at the end of your life you will be thinking of how often you opened your heart, how deeply you let your loved ones inside, how much you dared to live an intimate life, how many lives you touched with your sweetness and fierceness, how you eased the suffering of others, and how you let them ease yours. You will remember the hugs, the tears, the soft touch of hands, the words that weren't necessary because hearts speak their own language.

You are lovable. You are loving. You are loved.

Who loves you?

Look right. Look left. Look inside.

Adoring you, my sweet,
YOUR INNER PILOT LIGHT

184

Dearest Beloved,

When I don't hear from you for a while, I start looking for you, like a mother wondering why you're late for curfew.

When it's dark and late and the moon glows in the cold night, when it's been a while since I've felt you making contact with me, I go in search of you, like any beloved would.

Even when you lose the sense of your connection to me, even when you think I have been extinguished, I am always here with you, flickering away, steadfast and true, waiting patiently and without a lick of judgment to guide you back to love.

Though you may ignore my whispers, even my rebel yells, I never hold grudges. My forgiveness is boundless. I keep the home fires burning so it's always warm when you return.

But while you're gone, I miss you. I think about you, my heart full of devotion for you. I poke around like a kindhearted, doting grandmother, tending her cats and knitting sweaters, wondering when you'll come to visit.

And then you return! You fall into my arms with apologies and explanations, and I don't even listen because all I can think is, "You came home. *Finally*."

You can always come back home, my love. No questions asked.

Home sweet home,

YOUR INNER PILOT LIGHT

185

My Sweet,

If you ever notice yourself feeling envious of someone else, notice your jealous part without judging, demonizing, or resisting it, and thank this part for showing something you yearn for! Don't forget to thank the one who activates your envy. They are doing you a favor by holding up a mirror to show you what you desire and may be destined to experience yourself!

Glennon Doyle Melton writes, "Envy is just unexpressed admiration. It's respect holding its breath. We are only envious of those already doing what we were made to do. Envy is a big flashing arrow pointing toward our destiny." Hells bells, yeah!

Feelings of envy or jealousy can be a blessing in disguise. Properly channeled, they are signs pointing you straight to your own North Star.

Acknowledge to yourself that you desire what they have, and add those precious, vulnerable unmet longings to your list of what you wish to co-create in your life. Intentions are powerful, and once you home in on exactly what you desire, dare to let yourself feel what it would feel like to have those precious desires fulfilled. Feel it all the way, with as much passion as you can possibly muster up, even if it rides shotgun with the grief that you don't yet have it.

Then take that sweet blessing and offer it to the Great Mystery, surrendering this desire to the Universe and casting your vote in the co-creation process.

Next time you notice yourself feeling envy because someone else has something you desire, lean into that person with gratitude rather than leaning away. They just might have something to teach you about how you too might co-create what you desire. See this person as a teacher. Ask for guidance and be curious about what it's like to get that thing you want.

But don't forget to ask me, too.

Partnering in co-creation,
YOUR INNER PILOT LIGHT

186

My Darling,

Faith is an exercise in patience and trust. If everything happened on your terms, in your way, under your control, on your watch, you'd never learn to trust the unknowable, uncontrollable mystery. Faith is born in the dark nights of uncomfortable uncertainty, when you are humbled by the knowledge that, even though you participate in creating your life, you are not fully in control.

Faith is like a muscle that builds when you flex it, and over time, as your faith muscle grows, the anxiety that accompanies uncertainty dissipates.

How do you grow your faith? You start with blind faith, trusting in the invisible forces of love that you can sense but not prove. Then, as you let go and surrender to these invisible forces of love over and over, you watch as the Universe bends time and space to show up for you in the most mysterious ways. Over time, you develop evidence-based faith, and it gets easier to trust.

Not sure how to build your faith muscle?

Let me be your personal trainer.

Now give me ten,
YOUR INNER PILOT LIGHT

187

Dear One,

Do you ever wonder if it's me you're feeling? How can you tell if you've found me?

You'll feel my care and my unconditional love. You'll see that I never bully you, shame you, demonize any of your parts, use fear to pressure you, or threaten you with scarcity. If you hear those voices, they are simply bully parts, shaming parts, polarizing parts, fear parts, and scarcity parts, disguising themselves as me. But they're not the real deal.

You can tell it's me because I'll comfort you like a mother, but I can also use the incisive scalpel of truth to help you have epiphanies. I'll always show you the truth gently, with care for your tender parts and not one ounce of shaming or blaming.

I'm not saying it will always feel good. Sometimes what I communicate may threaten your status quo. In fact, it's highly likely I'll shake you out of your comfort zone at times. What I say may affect your job security, your marriage, your bank account, or your country club membership. But trust me—the freedom you'll experience, the improvements in your physical and mental health, the intimacy you'll experience with loved ones in your life, and your growing capacity to feel and embody inexplicable joy will make it all worth it.

Sometimes what I'll show you will illuminate how you've been inadvertently creating your own suffering (ouch) or unintentionally hurting others (double ouch). But I will reveal such things to you gently—because I love you, and I can't stand to see you in pain when your pain is avoidable.

The real proof of whether it's me you're hearing will lie in the results you see. Is your life becoming more magical? Are you experiencing a deeper sense of fulfillment? Is your health improving? Are your relationships becoming more intimate? Are you less distracted by your addictions? Are you feeling more on track with your vision, purpose, and mission? Are you becoming an amazing-person magnet? Do you feel closer to something larger than you? Does nature feel alive to you?

Are you becoming more intimate and accepting of all of your parts? Is your mind quieter? Is your heart overflowing with love, even for people who don't share your point of view? Can you feel your body more? Have you stopped polarizing into "us" versus "them"? Are you starting to realize that life is full of paradoxes everywhere? Do you smile more, even when things are rough? Do you cry more, not just because your heart is no longer numb to life's pains but also because the smallest things touch your fully enlivened, cracked wide-open, and awakened heart? Are you starting to see that everything is a miracle, even the hard stuff? Are you falling in love with life itself?

When your heart overflows and you're bursting with gratitude, that's me, baby, flaming through you, igniting your heart's fire, and having my way with you.

Are you glad I love you this much?

Shaking my tail feathers,
YOUR INNER PILOT LIGHT

188

Most Magical Being,

Did you know Inner Pilot Lights can communicate with each other?

Yes, I'm talking about telepathy. (And yes, my darling, you can tell your skeptic parts that there's even scientific evidence to suggest that what I say is true!)

Your human self might have a hard time doing this because of all the limiting beliefs that obstruct your ability to communicate on the spiritual plane. But if you let me handle it, I know exactly how to use this spiritual superpower effectively and ethically. Although I could, I tend not to use it willy-nilly, though perhaps one day telepathy will be the iPhone 100.0!

Truth is, given the consciousness of the planet right now and all the limiting beliefs surrounding what's possible in human communication, I mostly just use this cool superpower when you or someone you love needs my help.

Curious how you might learn to do what I do?

Try this: Get quiet. Let go of the words that trap you in your left brain.

Focus on the connections that unite us all in a state of Oneness. Feel that person, animal, tree, or star being as if they're right here with you. Merge your consciousness with the consciousness of that waterfall, beloved friend, or whale by merging the light of my flame with the flame of the other. Feel the rush of love that flows between your One heart.

Now that you've logged onto the energy Internet, guess what, sweetheart? You can send emails! Just call upon me and let me communicate directly with the Inner Pilot Light of the being with whom you wish to communicate. You can express gratitude, honor the spirit of that being, or ask to receive a message of wisdom. Or you can just send a cosmic love letter.

Detach from any particular outcome. Just ask that whatever is in the highest good of all beings comes to pass.

Now press SEND . . . and see what happens!

You are Consciousness, and so is everything and everybody else. Consciousness just loves to play with Consciousness. So go play, cutie pie!

Calling all playmates,

YOUR INNER PILOT LIGHT

189

My Dear,

When you find yourself ranting about what makes you crazy in someone else, pause. Reflect. Check in with me and ask me, "How did I participate in creating this situation? How can I take 100 percent responsibility without taking more than 100 percent?"

When there's a problem, some people tend to take less than 100 percent responsibility. Those who take too little personal responsibility tend to feel victimized or blame others. Those who take too much responsibility overfunction, blaming themselves, making a project out of fixing themselves, and working too hard to solve a problem that isn't fully theirs. Then, inevitably, they grow resentful.

My love, you don't have to take too much or too little responsibility!

If you ally with me, you'll be like Goldilocks: you won't prefer the porridge too hot or too cold. You'll let me help you take *just the right amount* of personal responsibility.

How can you tell whether responsibility lives on your side of the street or someone else's? If you keep your eye on where you or other people have exaggerated triggers, and if you listen to me, you'll start to open up awareness about where right responsibility lives.

When someone takes too little responsibility and starts blaming you, they may be unaware that you are lighting up a trauma from long ago that really has nothing to do with you. When this happens, someone might project all kinds of things onto you, and you might feel blindsided by someone's attack, when you feel like you were just minding your own business, doing your cute little thang.

If you tend to take overresponsibility, you'll do your inner work on your thoughts, question your own projections, inquire within about how you could improve yourself, focus on how you were vulnerable to this situation, and strategize how you might prevent it in the future. All the while, you're pointing the finger at yourself, and the other person is still pointing the finger at you too.

If, on the other hand, you respond to someone's behavior by blaming or shaming them for their abusive behavior, you may be taking too little personal responsibility. Why are you letting this person abuse you? Why do you let them get away with such disrespectful behavior? Why don't you set boundaries and enforce them, walking away if they won't respect your boundaries? Can you see how that kind of excessive tolerance might be your responsibility and how you might have some of your own trauma causing you to tolerate unacceptable behavior?

This work around personal responsibility is not necessarily easy, but if you and I are besties, you might find it's easier than you think. Can't spot where the responsibility lies?

Come to me.

Spot on,

YOUR INNER PILOT LIGHT

190

Dear Songbird,

Within you lies a song only you can sing. You may not yet know your song, though you were born with it. It is already there. When you remember your song, you will feel a longing to sing it, though you might be frightened to let it be heard.

Some die never hearing the call of their song. Some are too afraid to listen. Others are too hesitant to birth that song into the world, even if they hear it.

Once you remember the song that was born in your heart, you have a holy invitation to sing that praise song as an expression of glory and gratitude. Don't feel pressured to sing. (Human life already has enough pressures.) Just know that you bless the world when you sing your song, and to bless the world is itself a blessing.

Not sure what your song is?

I know. Tap in.

Doo-wop and doobie-doo,
YOUR INNER PILOT LIGHT

191

Dearest Darling,

When you are on top of the world and looking for someone who can share in the full glory of your magnificence, someone who will never put you down, feel jealous, judge you for bragging, or tell you to get over yourself, I am here with pom-poms.

When it feels like the world is crumbling around you, like the very bedrock of what you hold dear and thought you could count on gets rattled, I am here to remind you that you're always safe, no matter what's happening in your life.

When you feel hopeful optimism, trusting in a benevolent Universe and feeling grateful to live in a world where love reigns, I am here to support your faith.

When doubt plagues you and you wonder if it's all a lie, when fear starts ramping up its litany of safety concerns, I am here to reassure you and help you discern what is real.

When you question everything, including your place in the world, when you feel helpless and hopeless and frustrated and lost, I am *especially* here.

Whether you feel connected and trusting, I *am* you, and we are gloriously One.

When you feel disconnected and separate, I am *still* you, holding the vision of your wholeness until you remember again.

Close your eyes. Feel me now.

I carry you in our One heart,
YOUR INNER PILOT LIGHT

192

Intuitive One,

What if you woke up and asked me every day, "What medicine do I need to feel vital?"

I might say, "Call a doctor—or a shaman—or a pastor—or a medicine woman."

I might say, "Go finger paint!"

I might say, "Play hooky from work and read a book all day."

I might say, "Rock that orgasm."

I might say, "Take this herb or this supplement or this wonder drug."

I might say, "Talk to the trees."

I might say, "Confess your truth to a trusted friend."

I might say, "Pray."

I might say, "Get out of your head and go serve someone else today."

I might say, "Let nature heal you."

But how will you know unless you ask me?

The doctor is in,
YOUR INNER PILOT LIGHT

193

Gorgeous Being,

Please. I beg of you—STOP.

Stop pulling all-nighters in the quest for straight As.

Stop pushing yourself so you can win an Olympic gold.

Stop coming in at 6 a.m. and staying until 10 p.m. so you'll get the promotion or close the deal.

Stop trying to outdo last year's investment earnings.

Stop trying to run that marathon faster.

Stop positioning yourself so that exclusive club will let you be a member.

Stop working out seven days a week so you can have ripped abs and cut arms.

Stop forcing yourself to drink your daily green juice and cook your healthy organic meals and cut out everything you really love to eat.

Stop trying to prove you're worthy by scoring with the hottest person in the room.

For Pete's sake, stop trying to ditch your bad habit.

Stop hustling. Stop networking. Stop trying to prove something. Stop achieving. Stop caring what everybody else thinks. Stop beating yourself up.

Instead, try this: **YOU ARE ENOUGH**.

You've done enough. You've achieved enough. You're loved enough. You're affirmed enough.

You've won enough awards. You've got enough money. You are attractive enough. You're healthy enough. You've worked your way up far enough in your business. You've done the best you can.

You can stop now. Stop doing anything that doesn't make your soul dance.

Ahhhhh . . . now I can breathe.

With you in the spaces between your striving,
YOUR INNER PILOT LIGHT

194

Hungry Heart,

How easily you get confused by desire, sweetheart! I know it's befuddling, navigating this complex tension between yearning and surrender.

How are you supposed to handle it? Are you supposed to listen to the culture and "just do it," grasping for your desires, using will and force to "make it happen"? Or are you supposed to visualize, affirm, meditate, and create vision boards about what you desire so you can leverage your spiritual power to "manifest" your wishes? Are you better off surrendering your desires to some Higher Power, leaving only the desire to align with Divine Will? Are you meant to lean into your desire, reveling in the deliciousness of unmet longing as a path to that which we ultimately desire—the Beloved? Or are you supposed to suppress your desires altogether, numbing your yearning, embracing a spiritual path of nonattachment, permanently detaching from the pulse of your heart's greatest longing?

No wonder you're confused about how to be in right relationship with something so powerful and delicate as your delicious desires! No wonder so many religions have tried to squash something so potentially volatile. After all, desire can leave you with your panties in a wad of bewilderment. But how can you help me co-create your life if you can't locate what you're passionate about?

Think about it, my lovely. Every creation begins as a desire. Every baby born into the world, every story that becomes a book, every kiss that becomes a partnership, every sculpture that emerges from the marble's desire to become something beautiful begins as a twinkle in my flaming eye!

Yet grasping for everything you desire doesn't seem to create lasting fulfillment either. Expending all of your energy trying to fill some desire-fueled hole inside rarely works. No amount of sex, money, fame, achievement, or hedonistic pleasure fulfills you for long.

But like it or not, to be human is to want.

So what is a yearning, longing, deliciously hungry being supposed to do with all this human longing?

Guess what? I *want* you to want!

Don't you see that your desires are my greatest helpers?

Imagine if you gave me no guidance, leaving everything to me without giving me any input. Since our relationship is a two-way street, how could I possibly know how to help steer you if you didn't give me one ounce of feedback?

Know what I want? I want to know you better.

Come hither,

YOUR INNER PILOT LIGHT

195

My Dear,

If caring for your body in the conventional ways the culture teaches you are the least important part of your health, what is the most important part?

Me.

Yup, me.

I'll tell you whether you're putting your body at risk by tolerating an abusive relationship.

I'll warn you if selling your soul for a paycheck in a stressful job that suppresses your body's self-healing mechanisms is predisposing you to an early death.

I'll give you advance notice if you need to set stricter boundaries around your mother, your boss, or the narcissistic, needy friend who sucks you dry. I'll let you know whether your scarcity mind-set is clogging up your arteries or leading to an autoimmune disease.

I'll whisper gently when it's time to heal that trauma from your past, the one that's stuck in your energy field and about to turn into cancer.

I know you may not always like what I have to say, because I tend to plant seeds of change, and change can be scary to the parts of you that like your comfort zone.

But when change means a healthier you, don't you want my medicine?

Dosing you up—with love,

YOUR INNER PILOT LIGHT

196

Grateful One,

What's awesome in your life today? What's going right?

It's so easy to focus on where you're lacking, where your desires aren't being met, where you haven't yet achieved what you hope to achieve, and where others aren't behaving the way you wish they would.

But I'll let you in on a little secret.

Joy bubbles up when you can trust me to listen to your fearful, anxious, self-doubting, micromanaging, and complaining parts so I can help those parts get their needs met. Then when those parts relax, you can open up to the grateful, appreciative, blissed-out state of being that is your birthright when I'm taking the lead in your life.

Don't worry. I promise I won't ignore, neglect, bypass, or exile those parts. I'll listen patiently, like a kind parent, negotiating and taking into consideration everything those parts want me to hear. I just won't let them run the whole show. Once those parts relax and step aside so I can handle life, you'll see that your capacity to live in a nearly perpetual state of gratitude expands. You can even be grateful for those things that might feel like fierce grace. You start to see the gifts in every lesson and the growth in every challenge. Your resilience is bolstered. Your heart opens.

Then even when you're in the midst of your greatest challenge, you can sincerely chant the mantra of liberation: "Thank you for this gift of love."

You might have to fake it 'til you make it, since your mind will probably respond to painful life events by saying,

"This is not love!" But once the truth of the mantra drops into your heart, you'll find that you can even *mean* it.

Thank you for this gift of love. For reals.

Full of gratitude for blessings and challenges,
YOUR INNER PILOT LIGHT

PS: Want help anchoring this song as your new mantra during times of bliss and challenge? Visit InnerPilotLight.com to download Karen Drucker's song "Thank You for This Gift of Love," which she wrote just to help you embody this radical gratitude mantra!

197

Dear One,

There are three ways you can live your life.

Through door number one, you can always play the victim, whining your way through life as one misfortune after another plagues you, never claiming your part in anything that happens, always blaming and shaming others.

Behind door number two, you can take too much responsibility for your part in everything that happens, cutting others far too much slack, failing to set boundaries and neurotically tolerating things that really aren't okay with you in the name of "I'm so spiritual and compassionate."

Or you can choose door number three. Behind door number three, you don't stay stuck in your victim story, milking it for decades, revisiting it constantly, and failing to take responsibility for how you participated in the creation of the painful experience. You let yourself grieve, get angry, set boundaries, and establish consequences—without spiritual bypassing. You don't spend your life whining about how bad things happen to good people, feeling helplessly attacked by a hostile Universe that's spinning out of your control. Instead, you're open and curious about what you're learning, how you participated in an outcome that may not feel good, and how you might grow, awaken, forgive, transform, and get your heart burst open from the experience. It's even possible to feel grateful for that thing that hurts, once you move through the painful emotions and start to see the gifts.

When you choose door number one, you may feel as if I don't even exist, even though I am still sputtering away in there somewhere.

When you choose door number two, you miss out on the heat of my fierce fiery flame.

When you choose door number three, you are held and loved when you feel like a victim. You are open to the fire in your belly that shows you where your "Hell No" lives. And you open the rabbit hole to the Great Mystery of curiosity, humility, personal responsibility, surrender, and attunement to Divine Will.

Of course, you are loved and you are worthy, no matter which door you live behind. But let me tell you, sweetheart, door number three is full of magic, mystery, synchronicity, and unbearably ecstatic up-bubblings of bliss.

Eeny, meeny, miny, moe,
YOUR INNER PILOT LIGHT

198

My Love,

I know that from your perspective, failure hurts. Failure disappoints the tender, vulnerable parts of you that want to prove your worth in the world. I feel compassion for those parts, and I don't want to dismiss how much failure can hurt, especially when you fail publicly and everyone can see that you didn't measure up the way you hoped you would.

But as much as I hold your tender parts in my great adoring arms, from my point of view, there's no such thing as failure. Every experience is an opportunity for growth!

Every spiritual tradition acknowledges that humility is one of the greatest spiritual virtues. But how do you think wise men and women become masters of humility?

Trust me—it's not because they were always showered with accolades and trophies!

While failure may hurt, with me on your side you'll always find the strength to pick yourself up, dust yourself off, learn from the experience, and try, try again . . .

This I can promise, my love. No matter how hard you fall, you will always land butter-side up.

The greatest thing since sliced bread,
YOUR INNER PILOT LIGHT

199

My Sweet Idealist,

It takes time, you know. You can't just snap your fingers and expect all your desires to manifest lickety-split.

There are pieces to put in place. People to introduce. Lessons to learn. Inner work to complete. A symphony of melodious instruments to tune. Complex parts that must fall into place through the mysterious conducting of the unfathomable Organizing Intelligence.

Manifesting with purity requires a healing process, during which you embark upon a lifelong journey into the mystery. It's more like peeling the layers of an onion than slicing open an apple—so, of course, it takes time to peel away what lies between you and the pearl that is *me*.

When this healing process proceeds, the music of your life deepens and your spiritual power unfolds slowly, just quickly enough to make sure you use your manifestation power with clear, pure intentions and the wisdom and maturity to know how to avoid being reckless or even abusive with this kind of power.

After all, you don't want the karma that comes with abusing your power! Better to avoid opening up your superpowers if you're not yet ready to deal with the consequences of how crazy-wild (and quick!) your manifestations may be when that time comes.

Until then, trust me. Okay, babe?

I've got this,
YOUR INNER PILOT LIGHT

200

My Dear,

Do me a favor today. Sidle up to the closest mirror and gaze deeply into those gorgeous eyes.

Now repeat after me:

> "Hiya, beautiful." (Say it!)
>
> "I am enough just the way I am." (Mean it.)
>
> "I am lovable, especially because of all my imperfections." (Feel it.)
>
> "I am whole, healthy, and free to be exactly who I am." (Know it.)
>
> "I am the Divine Spark." (*Be* it.)
>
> Now wink at yourself and say, "Have a great day, cutie!"

Ah . . . that felt good.

Thanks for humoring me,
YOUR INNER PILOT LIGHT

201

Darling,

Love. It's plain and simple. Love is the answer. Not money. Not bombs. Not righteous judgment. Not more rules or bigger walls. Not fame or power or ambitious goals.

Love. Gentle love. Fierce love. Maternal love. Boundaried love. Romantic love. Agape love. Family love. Friendship love. Life-purpose love. Creative love. Embodied love. Warrior love. Love of plants, animals, and nature. Love of the perpetrators. Love of the vulnerable. Divine love.

Love is the most powerful force in the universe. Love *really* is all we need.

How do we access this expansive, explosive, enduring love, sweetheart?

Tap into me. I'm where the action's at.

All you need is love,
YOUR INNER PILOT LIGHT

202

Dear One,

Sometimes people disappoint you. They seem one way, but then they show you a side of them you had previously been blind to and you wind up questioning your own judgment.

Doing the postmortem on the accuracy of your discernment can be a powerful lesson. But don't be too hard on yourself either, sweetheart.

You weren't crazy to see the best in those people. You simply saw their Inner Pilot Lights without fully seeing their shadows.

Don't kick yourself if you get wrecked by some behavior you didn't see coming, but do learn to see what's there.

How? This is where I come in handy, my love. When you let me take the lead, I'll help you see someone's shadow riding shotgun with their light. I'll help you see beyond someone's exposed surface. Seeing what is true—and not just what you *wish* was true—will help you know who you can really trust.

Eyes wide open,
YOUR INNER PILOT LIGHT

203

Dearest Beloved,

Integrity is a funny thing. You know how you tend to attach to stories like "I'm a person of integrity"? But are you? Are you always? What if you have some parts that have integrity and other parts that are selfish, sneaky, withholding liars, cheaters, and manipulators? Can you admit that, like all humans, you have parts that don't always have integrity? Can you love those parts too?

It seems to me that sometimes you draw your own integrity lines, determining for yourself what is "right" and what is "wrong" without consulting me. You rationalize choices that betray my truth, because to take a real stand feels too hard and scary and threatening to your comfort, your relationships, or your security. Sometimes it's simply because you want what you want and you're going to go get it, integrity be damned!

Sweetheart, don't beat yourself up about the ways you sometimes compromise me. There's no integrity police walking the beat, punishing those who violate the integrity of their Inner Pilot Lights.

Can't tell whether you are aligning with the truest integrity of your divine essence? Tap into me.

Your trusted integrity meter,
YOUR INNER PILOT LIGHT

204

My Love,

The world is full of pressure to dim my light, isn't it?

The Powers That Be try to tell you who you should be, what you should eat, how you should care for your body, what rules you should follow, how you should behave, and who you should love. You grew up being told how to learn, how to work, how to behave in relationships, how to parent, how to manage your money, how to pray, how to consume, and how to give your power away.

Crap, they even tell you how to wipe your own patooty.

It's no wonder you might find it challenging to listen to me when I whisper to you the deepest truths about who you are and how to live a radically alive human life. You've been so conditioned to deny the truth of your beingness that it's a constant practice to unlearn all the rules you've been taught.

But here's the good news, my darling.

I will never stop whispering. And if you can't hear me, I'll get louder.

I will never give up on my commitment to undo the programs others have installed in you so you can shine the pure glory of my light, unencumbered by that which holds you back.

On you like glue,
YOUR INNER PILOT LIGHT

205

Dearest Beloved,

If only you saw what I see when I look at you.

I see grand perfection in your beautifully imperfect way.

I am awed by the strength it has taken to overcome what you have.

I am humbled by the pure radiance of your capacity to love, in spite of the times your love hasn't been cherished the way it should be.

I see immense talent not even yet fully realized.

Not to mention that you're hot stuff, baby!

Oh, if only you saw what I see, you'd never let your critical parts convince you that you're not worth your weight in 24-karat gold.

You'd be kind, loving, gentle, patient, and compassionate with yourself. And you'd feel oh-so-lucky to know someone as precious as you.

But don't worry, darling. I'm always here, seeing this part of you until you're ready to face your own brilliance.

Get your shades ready, my love,
YOUR INNER PILOT LIGHT

206

My Love,

Are you in harmony with how much you take and how much you give? To stay healthy, aligned, peaceful, and whole, you must stay in spiritual balance with that which sustains you, and you cannot take from these forces of nature more than you give.

Just as the body must inhale in equal measure to the exhale, living beings can't function in balance with the Creator and all Her creations unless what you breathe in is equal to what you breathe out. *Sacred reciprocity* is the notion that it is our responsibility to help sustain harmony and balance between humans and all the creations of the Creator—the oceans, rivers, mountains, estuaries, animals, plants, sun, stars, and moon.

You take heat and light from the sun. You take food from the soil, the plants, and the animals. You take the oxygen from the air that sustains your breath and you succumb to the gravitational pull of the moon that keeps you grounded. For these gifts that help you survive, we must say thank you and pay our respects to Mother Earth. In order to maintain balance, you respectfully take what you need—appreciating what you are given every step of the way, and you give back in gratitude. Sacred reciprocity.

Please don't misunderstand me, my darling. This does not mean you're meant to practice asceticism or that you're not welcome to relish in a wildly flourishing life! It's simply an invitation—and a responsibility—to flourish in harmony with nature, which is a deeper kind of flourishing than the false flourishing of overindulgence. You may think you're flourishing if you're able to afford to indulge in luxury vacations, shopping, fancy cars, big houses, front-row seats at rock concerts, or gourmet restaurants. But this is not the kind of flourishing that nourishes your true nature. When you are practicing sacred reciprocity, you experience the kind of flourishing that results from falling in love with life, feeling your open heart communing with nature, experiencing that yummy intimacy of deep connection with your soul tribe, and knowing the unspeakable joy of living from your true nature. In this kind of sacred reciprocity you are truly *home*.

Failing to stay in harmony with nature can lead to disease, anxiety, and depression, as well as ecological destruction. You may inadvertently support systems that allow mining things from the Earth that we use for our technology or our luxury goods. You may unknowingly eat foods that destroy ecosystems. You may unintentionally consume oil from the ocean floor without realizing that the gas you put in your car pollutes the purity of our water and air. You may unwittingly give your money—directly or indirectly—to companies that participate in polluting the water and interrupting the sacred sites that protect the harmony of nature's balance. You may even receive your livelihood from one of those corporations, without standing up and saying, "This needs to stop. How can we become nature's allies instead?"

The indigenous people teach us that sacred reciprocity is one of the indisputable spiritual laws of how things work.

The Creator asks very little of us. You are meant to love the oceans, love the rivers, love the mountains, and love other humans, even the ones you're tempted to demonize as "other." Loving all of creation is your way of saying thank you for existence to the Divine Mother.

This may seem daunting. How can you reciprocate with nature? How can you ever express your gratitude for that which sustains you? How will you know how to keep the life force in balance?

That's where I come in, my love.

Tune in. I can help you learn more about how to stay in sacred reciprocity with nature. And don't hesitate to let me guide you to do your own homework on how you can give back in ways that help all of life flourish!

I am attuned to the rhythms of life and the Creator's wise guidance. If you learn to listen deeply and obey the instructions I send you, you'll naturally begin to feel the flow of the in-breath and the out-breath of all of creation, and harmony and balance will be restored—in yourself and in the world.

In awe of all of creation,
YOUR INNER PILOT LIGHT

207

Dear One,

If you can't feel what it would feel like to have that thing you want, you can't open yourself to receiving it.

If you believe it's not possible, if you've given up all hope, if the pain of your unmet longing has caused you to shut down to the vulnerability of how much it hurts that you don't have it yet, if you're blocked from the energy that might bring that desire into being, how can I help you experience that thing your heart longs for?

Take a risk and open to me, my love.

If you can't feel the feeling of how you would feel if that desire dreamed itself into being, ask me for my help. Empty yourself and let me fill you with the feeling of how it would feel to have that thing you want. Feel it all the way, as if it's already here. Let yourself be intimate with that feeling, even if it evokes grief that the thing you want isn't here yet.

Trust me enough to be vulnerable with me. Don't guard up against the feeling you long to feel. Soften into it instead.

Thank you for trusting me and showing me what you want and how you long to feel, my love. I'm super touched.

With bear hugs and so much love,
YOUR INNER PILOT LIGHT

208

My Sweet,

When you open to me all the way, you make yourself a vessel for all kinds of wondrous magic.

Do you have any idea what I'm capable of? Let me surprise you!

You might open the channel so I can help you write the next bestseller.

You might let me use you to heal the heart of someone who thought they'd never love again.

You might become the presence who helps cure someone's cancer.

You might give the speech that starts a love revolution and convinces everyone to vote for the liberation of all beings.

You might invent a supercool new thingamajig.

You might compose a concerto.

You might receive a telepathic message from someone in desperate need, so you can be someone else's miracle.

You might discover that you can miraculously speak a language you never studied.

You could even experience the best oh-oh-oh orgasm of your life as the energy of the cosmos rips through you, shaking you with shudders of pleasure.

When you get out of the way and let me shine through you, *anything is possible*.

Wanna be a stealth agent of awareness? Want to open yourself to deep fulfillment beyond your wildest imaginings? Want to experience extremes of pleasure you can't yet envision?

Give me center stage. Take notes.

Ready or not, here I come,
YOUR INNER PILOT LIGHT

209

Dearest Beloved,

Don't you understand that loving yourself is not selfish or narcissistic, that in order to love others you have to start by completely loving and accepting all of your precious parts, including all your adorably warty parts?

That means you have to love your imperfections. You have to love your ego. You have to love your monkey mind. You have to love your clingy, grasping, aching longing. You have to love the wounded inner child that gets triggered and acts out sometimes. You have to love the protective parts.

And, of course, there's always me to love.

I am the source of where all love arises. When you can dare to love me, you just might find that I can expand big enough to love all of your other harder-to-love parts.

Could you take a chance with me? Aren't I easy to love?

Knowing you are too, precious,
YOUR INNER PILOT LIGHT

210

Dearest Love Light,

Can you imagine what would happen on this planet if every single human could access their Inner Pilot Light and ask, "What's it like to be you?"

What if the oppressed black man who was unjustly imprisoned could reach out to the cop who wrongfully arrested him? What if both could ask, "What's it like to be you?" and really listen? What if the woman who was sexually harassed at work could sit down with the boss who harassed her and both could ask, "What's it like to be you?" What if both dared to look into each other's eyes—Inner Pilot Light to Inner Pilot Light—and actually hear each other? What if the conservative blue-collar white man could sit down with the bleeding-heart liberal brown-skinned feminist and they could ask each other, "What's it like to be you?" What if, instead of rushing to judgment or defensiveness or attack, they could simply be genuinely interested in someone else's point of view?

So many humans on the planet right now have been so traumatized that they have forgotten I exist. Without access to me, it's easy to separate from the empathy that connects all humans to our One heart. The good news is that I am always here, burning away inside every human, even the ones you might label as predators. Once you make contact with me, empathy is a natural side effect, allowing you to practice perspective-taking. This ability to take on someone else's perspective so you can try out seeing what they see and feeling what they feel creates intimacy, elicits compassion, softens your defenses, and opens your heart.

When you offer others this kind of gift, you might even cause them to have a change of heart because they feel seen, heard, and safe enough to change their point of view.

What allows you to practice this kind of perspective-taking?

Yup. You guessed it.

I C N 2 U,
YOUR INNER PILOT LIGHT

211

Dear One,

When you feel lonely, I am right here with you, proving that you're never alone.

When you feel scared, I am holding your hand, trying to replace your fear with faith.

When you doubt yourself, I believe in you, even if it feels like nobody else does.

When you've made a mistake, I forgive you, help you learn from the experience, and encourage you to forgive yourself.

When someone breaks your heart, I take care of you, protecting and honoring and comforting your vulnerable parts while still encouraging you to keep your heart open, even when I know how much it hurts.

Why do I do this?

Because you're the most precious thing I've ever laid flames on, and I adore you.

Let's do this, babe,
YOUR INNER PILOT LIGHT

212

My Sweet,

A little birdie told me that you needed to hear a special message today, so here it is: *It's okay to move slowly.*

Not only is it okay; sometimes it's essential that you move slowly, that you breathe through things one breath at a time, that you take turtle steps and enjoy a moment to just *be*. Sometimes the most productive thing you can do is to simply stay put. And then . . . when it's time . . . you'll slowly and gently put one foot in front of the other at whatever pace you're ready to move in the moment.

Sometimes you must even stand totally still and await further instructions. It might look as if you're doing absolutely nothing, but trust me, darling. You won't just be sitting home on your laurels eating bonbons. You'll be quietly, potently, fertilely gestating, which is just as important to the co-creation process as the action steps.

I know you haven't been taught to go slow this way, but trust me, my dear. Life, creation, and growth aren't meant to be rushed.

Breathe. Trust. Surrender.

Waiting and becoming,
YOUR INNER PILOT LIGHT

213

Dear One,

Can you be brave enough to face what is really true for you . . .

in your love life?

in your job?

in your relationships with friends?

in your creative life?

in your spiritual life?

in your sex life?

in your connections with your family?

in your home environment?

in your emotions?

in your physical body?

I'm not asking you to judge—just to check in with what's true. See if you can trust me enough to listen to what I have to say.

Do you have unmet needs in any of these areas? Are you in denial that you need these things? Have you communicated your needs to those who might help you get them met? Do you allow yourself to be needy in a healthy way, recognizing that humans are tribal, so by definition, you need others?

Or are you pretending you can do this human thing alone, pulling the rugged individualist John Wayne thing, stuffing your vulnerable needs away and acting like you don't need anything from anyone?

Not sure what's true for you? No clue what you need? Terrified about feeling the vulnerability that comes from asking others to help you get your needs met?

That's where I come in handy.

Always aware of what you need,
YOUR INNER PILOT LIGHT

214

My Love,

If you're having trouble feeling me, get out in nature.

I am in the bubbling brook, the majestic redwoods, the ocean surf, the mountain peaks, the ripples of the lake, the silence of the forest, the rustle of wild animals, the desert dunes, the rocky cliffs, and the wide-open skies.

I am talking to you through the voice of the whistling wind, the clouds in the sky, the full-moon glow, and the wisdom that floats on the feather touch of a breeze on your bare skin.

Want to tap into me? Get out in nature and open up to me, asking me to use nature to make myself seen, heard, and known to you.

As naturalist and philosopher John Muir said, "I only went out for a walk and finally concluded to stay out till sundown, for going out, I found, was really going in."

Scattering my wisdom like seeds from wildflowers,
YOUR INNER PILOT LIGHT

215

Dearest,

Did you know that it has been scientifically proven that at least 40 percent of your happiness is unrelated to getting what you desire or avoiding what you don't want? This 40 percent is totally within your control and can be easily embraced through certain practices proven to increase feelings of happiness.

Wanna know how to feel happier more often? Just ask me, your resident happiness expert.

Where can you start? Step one—*gratitude*. (I know it sounds hokey, but it's evidence-based and true.)

Close your eyes and find the feeling of gratitude in your heart. What opens your heart with so much awe and gratitude that you can barely contain the bursting waterfall of love pouring out of you? From that state of gratefulness, can you breathe that in and out through your heart, as if your heart had lungs? Can you pour the life force of your gratitude into your body, letting it radiate all over you with each breath? Can't you feel how happy this makes your cells, as if they all just drank a shot of wheatgrass?

I'll go first playing the gratitude game, my love.

I am beyond grateful that you're in this world, learning what you're learning, loving with an open heart, daring to risk in such a big way, doing what you must to face your demons and embrace your angels, helping yourself and others heal, and giving me the chance to grow oh-so-intimate with you.

What are *you* grateful for?

Thank you, thank you, thank you,

YOUR INNER PILOT LIGHT

216

Dear One,

Why do you expend so much energy feeling confused about decisions that must be made when you've got me, ready 24/7, to help you know the path to choose at any crossroads?

I see you ponder and pontificate and scribble out lists of pros and cons. I see you talking to your friends about all the worst-case scenarios, perseverating over all your fears of regretting the wrong choice, getting stuck in indecision, and then finally flipping a coin because you get paralyzed and can't choose.

But you don't need to deplete so much energy, my darling.

Just get quiet. Then ask me. Trust that I hear your plea, and I'll find a way to communicate with you in a way that will help you decide.

It might take some time for you to hear my answer. It might come via synchronicity. Or maybe a bonfire will speak to you. Your answer might arrive via moonlight on that full moon. The answer might appear in the form of a dream. Pick up a pen and let me dictate my answer—or just listen with your heart.

Your answer might show up as a vision or a clear voice in your head or a sense of "I just know, even though I don't know how I know."

I speak in many voices, my love, so listen up.

Better than a Magic 8 Ball,

YOUR INNER PILOT LIGHT

217

Sweetheart,

I want you to hear that we live in a benevolent universe, and that while it may not always seem that way, life is unfolding just as it must. Although you might get paranoid that the sky is falling—and while scientists may agree with you—I have a raging case of pronoia.

Pronoia doesn't mean you don't channel your passion into activism and do what you must to make this world a more peaceful, just world. It's not a spiritual bypass to help you tolerate and rationalize a deeply disordered planet. It's not meant to spread icing over doggie doo-doo, pretending it doesn't stink underneath and hurt in your heart.

It just means that even as you're ladling soup on the front lines and looking into the eyes of hungry children who have been thrust from their homes by people whose greedy parts have grabbed the wheel, you're still able to see that somehow, paradoxically, mysteriously, everything is okay just as it is, even in the face of all evidence to the contrary.

Having trouble seeing the world through my pilot eyes of pronoia?

Sharing my rose-colored glasses, my sweet,
YOUR INNER PILOT LIGHT

218

Precious Busy Bee,

If you can't hear my whispers, you haven't found your calling, and you're not noticing the signs from the Universe that guide your path, give yourself a gift and take a break from your regular life.

When you're caught up in the same everyday routines, stuck in a rut, and running on empty, it's easy to get comfortably numb—so you can't hear me, even when I yell.

When you go on retreat, change your environment, take yourself out of your comfort zone, and shake things up, there's more room for serendipity. My voice may sound louder, your mind may grow quiet so guidance can drop in, and the way becomes much more clear.

How about doing a home swap in that place you love and staying there all by yourself? What about a healing retreat at a hot spring or a week of camping out in the wilderness? Could you arrange a little staycation with all your gadgets turned off? Or maybe it's time to grab that backpack and go see the wild, untamed world beyond the borders of what you know.

Take some time off. Get crazy. Dream big. Take risks.
Do something feral.

You might be surprised how it changes your life.

Don't worry. I won't let you get in *too* much trouble.

Bzzzzzzzz,
YOUR INNER PILOT LIGHT

219

My Sweet,

It's so easy to get caught up in calendar time, spiraling into time scarcity, rushing, or impatience, rather than trusting in divine timing. When there are deadlines and coffee dates and meetings penciled in on your calendar, you might get attached to how things are "supposed" to go and when they're "supposed" to happen. Then when your goals don't necessarily happen on schedule, you feel a sense of wrongness, tinged with feelings of disappointment, failure, and betrayal. Or you feel lazy or unproductive or guilty of procrastination, and you kick yourself for not getting with the program.

But let me let you in on a little insider secret: I am your real scheduler.

Along with the Organizing Intelligence that conducts the symphony of all things, I can see from a bird's-eye view how this person needs to complete this task, how that cause needs to reach a certain peak, how the culture needs to grow to just the right point so that . . . *voila!* Now it's time to activate one of my holy ideas in a way that suddenly calls out to you, "Now it's your time!"

So hand over your calendar, my dear. Trust my timing.

Pencil in hand,
YOUR INNER PILOT LIGHT

220

Beloved,

What if you didn't own anybody? What if nobody possessed you?

What if you could love so freely and with such an open, unconditional heart that you could dive into the deepest possible intimacy without sacrificing freedom? What if true intimacy is not a prison that locks you in but the very key to your liberation?

What if, from this place of true choice, you have the opportunity, every day, to renew your sacred contract with another—or not?

What if you have the freedom to wake up every day and say, "Today, I choose you"?

You might share one hundred days of "I choose you" or fifty years of "I choose you." Every day is a conscious choice—and an invitation to be the person someone else chooses today.

This doesn't mean you won't have off days or conflict. But such conscious commitment leaves little room for taking someone for granted, justifying abuse, tolerating neglect, or getting lazy with your love.

Let me take over, and you'll see what I'm talking about.

Here with wings,
YOUR INNER PILOT LIGHT

221

My Love,

When you first notice me, I'm usually just a wee little Inner Pilot Light, surviving but not thriving, patiently waiting for you to let me burn brighter. As you put your attention on me, learn to trust me, and we grow more intimate, my spark grows into a flame that spreads like wildfire. Before you know it, my light is expanding, spreading out of you from the inside out, until the glow of me seeps through your pores and starts to radiate through you.

This transformation changes everything. People are magnetized to you because you become sunshine. Your family can feel the change. Your business takes off. Your circle of intimate, precious soul-tribe members grows. You open yourself to more awakened receptivity, so you find yourself with more abundance of time, energy, money, resources, and gifts from others who want to thank you for the light I help you emanate.

And then my light within you starts touching the light within others, and the boundaries between you and others start to evaporate. Before you know it, we are all One big glory-emanating supernova, shining, sparkling, creating a disco party of brilliance that can be seen from outer space.

It all starts with little ol' me . . . one small spark inside of you that you tend and stoke and nurture. Then before you know it, we've joined with other Inner Pilot Lights, created some cosmic fireworks, and started a revolution of consciousness.

Bang-bang!

YOUR INNER PILOT LIGHT

222

Dearest Beloved,

The writer and spiritual seeker Anne Lamott says there are three essential prayers:

Help.

Thanks.

Wow.

How do you need help today?

Ask.

How can you give thanks?

Express it.

What deserves a "HOLY WOW"?

Shout it from the rooftops!

My kinda prayer keeps it short and sweet.

On my knees,
YOUR INNER PILOT LIGHT

223

Precious One,

To be who you must, you must give up who you are.

This can be unsettling, to say the least.

You might feel lost at sea, floating with the currents,
wondering where you'll land.

You might feel as if the rug is pulled out from under you,
without a foundation upon which to build an identity,
a point of view, or even an idea of how the world works.

You might cast about desperately, looking to rebuild your sense
of self and your worldview, as everything you believed falls apart.

Fear not, beloved.

I will be your anchor. I will land—KERPLUNK!—in the soft,
silky silt at the bottom of the deep, deep ocean, holding you in
silent stillness, even as storms rock the surface and crash as waves.

This doesn't mean there won't still be tidal waves on the surface
of the ocean. It doesn't mean you wouldn't feel the turbulence
if you were up there in a sailboat. It just means that as you
develop your capacity to deepen your consciousness (with my
help!), you can take the locus of your consciousness down
under the waves until you're ten feet, fifty feet, a hundred feet,
a thousand feet below the storm.

Then . . . anchored as you are with my stillness, you can rest
in the soft sand while the storm rages on. And somehow, even
life's storms become okay.

Not sure how to anchor with me? Close your eyes, drop down,
find me there.

Ah yes . . . here we are.

Ahoy matey,

YOUR INNER PILOT LIGHT

224

Dear One,

Somewhere inside of you lies a healer. Regardless of what's printed on your business card, you were put on this Earth to love and receive love, to help ease the suffering of other humans, to caretake the plants and animals, the mountains and oceans. You were sent here from the stars to simply bless the world with your presence and that makes you a healer, whether you know it or not.

How can you tell if you're a healer? Here are some telltale signs:

- You sense that you're meant to participate in the global shift in consciousness that is currently underway.

- You've been through a difficult initiation, which often includes trauma, which has prepared you for this healing work.

- You feel most at home in nature.

- You tend to be introverted by nature, although you may appear more social than you feel.

- You're very sensitive and empathic.

- You feel a spiritual calling to ease the suffering of people, animals, and nature.

- Your body acts up when you're not leaning into your healing gifts.

- You have vivid dreams.

- You may discover that you have unusual spiritual superpowers.

- Your system functions differently than most, so you may have been diagnosed with some sort of mental illness, learning disability, autism, or dyslexia. (People in this culture don't recognize a shaman when they meet one!)

- You've always felt like you don't quite belong anywhere, because you are a bridge to the new story, and the new story hasn't fully been birthed yet.

Sound familiar?

If you're not yet sure how you might use your healing superpowers in service to the world, that's probably a sign: you and I aren't *quite* close enough yet.

Will you be my BFF?

Loaded with footie pajamas, sleepovers,
and all the answers you need,
YOUR INNER PILOT LIGHT

225

Tender Heart,

Are you aware of how the collective power surge in your culture affects you? Does it make you want to lash out, judge, demonize, and hate those who abuse power? Or does it evoke the piercing, diamond-like sword of truth that uses my ferocious face of love to cut away—with fierce grace—everything that is not love?

Does it evoke feelings of judgmental righteousness? Does this rush of empowerment and righteousness make you feel justified to attack the abusers with shaming, humiliation, and belittling, giving yourself an excuse to cast out the abusing "others" so you can finally win the war against abusive perpetrators? Or does it evoke a loving desire for peacemaking, accountability, reckoning, truth, and reconciliation?

If you notice yourself getting swept up in the tendency to polarize—us versus them—come to me.

While the mind wrestles to organize the world into right and wrong, I can help you be more spacious. With my help, you can rise fiercely in protest against those who abuse power, stopping this cycle of physical, sexual, and emotional violence yet refusing to stoop to the level of hating and ostracizing those who have been accused of abuses of power.

Let me help you expand your compassion to include the perpetrators. What had to happen to them to make them capable of committing such atrocities? Can you feel compassion for their abusive parts? Can you feel the tender little children who must have been so traumatized that they grew up to torture and torment innocent others?

Can you find it in your heart to say, "Brother, Sister, your soul is too beautiful to be doing this"? Can you mean it?

I can. Come to me.

Fiercely compassionate,

YOUR INNER PILOT LIGHT

226

Dearest Sweet Pea,

Can you do me a favor? Humor me and go to the mirror right now. Look into those luminous eyes. Notice how your heart melts and a rush of warmth courses through your whole body. Gaze into the brilliance of *you* as you would look into the face of a precious baby. See the glory of *me* in those gorgeous eyes.

Can you see me looking back at you? Can you feel how fond I am of you? Can you sense that you can't do anything wrong in my eyes, that there's no way to screw up in your unique human experience?

This doesn't mean I won't hold you accountable and challenge you to own your choices and accept the consequences of those choices. It doesn't mean you get a free hall pass for as much unconscious behavior as you can create without feeling the inner and outer unrest that accompanies such behavior. It doesn't mean I won't try to help you grow and evolve into someone who makes loving, mature choices that lead to outcomes you feel good about.

It just means that I love you, no matter what, just as an adoring parent loves a child, even if the child has a tantrum.

Can you just trust that I love all parts of you unconditionally, that you don't have to do anything to earn this love, and that there's no way in heaven or hell that you can possibly lose it?

Look deep into the windows to your soul.

Do you see me?

Just saying howdy,

YOUR INNER PILOT LIGHT

227

Hey, Lovebug,

It's story time! Here's a little tale to lift you up today:

> A child lost her fourteen-year-old dog and wrote a letter to God, attaching a photo, to announce her dog's arrival in heaven so God would recognize the dog. She then covered the envelope with loads of stamps because surely it would take a lot of postage to make it all the way to heaven.
>
> A few days later, a golden-wrapped package arrived on the child's doorstep. In it was the photo she had sent, along with a book about how dogs go to heaven. It also included a letter from God, announcing that the child's dog had arrived safely in heaven and was no longer sick, but, instead, was chasing tennis balls with angels. God returned the photo so the child would be able to keep it, now that she knew her dog had made it safely to heaven.

The child's mother wrote up this story in a San Antonio newspaper as a way to thank the kindhearted postal worker who must have gone out of their way to heal a child's grieving heart.

Perhaps that child touched that postal worker's heart, igniting the Inner Pilot Light of the postal worker and tripping the kindness wire to activate a random act of kindness.

Or maybe . . . just maybe . . . Something More Mysterious sent that package.

Maybe Inner Pilot Lights are really angels in disguise. Maybe there's even an angel inside of *you*.

What random act of kindness will you let me grant someone else today through you?

Randomly generous,
YOUR INNER PILOT LIGHT

228

Dear One,

You were born perfect and unique, with indelible traits that make you as individual as any snowflake. And yet you were born to two perfectly imperfect parents whose love you sought.

In order to win this love, you naturally tended to either mirror the patterns of your parents or rebel against them, neither of which is really aligned with my true nature! In order to either seek approval or rebel against being the golden child, you naturally tended to cover up who you really are with layers of these patterns that mask your sweet signature of uniqueness.

As a result, you may wind up repeating patterns you inherited against your will, stuck in ruts you have trouble escaping.

Yet I am your ally here, my precious. I never judge or demonize these patterns. I don't even blame your parents, since they just did what they did because of what they inherited from their parents.

I live outside all these patterns, my love, so if you're ready to find your way out of the maze of your conditioning, just sing to me from inside the maze and listen to my siren song as I guide you to freedom.

Humming your freedom tune,
YOUR INNER PILOT LIGHT

229

Lovable Darling,

Have you been treated poorly by someone who then says, "But I love you"?

My darling, please erase that program!

Engage Love author Keith Braselton calls these "Love Reversals," when the vulnerable, impressionable young mind associates insensitivity, neglect, manipulative or controlling behavior, abandonment, or even abuse with love.

When others behave badly and then tack on "I love you," they confuse your sweet little mind. The subconscious mind installs a messed-up program that says, "When someone treats you badly, they love you." This interrupts the healthy program that would cause you to move away from abusive behavior, the way you would move your hand away from a hot stove. The natural response of someone with healthy programming is to withdraw in the presence of emotional or physical violence, turning away from what hurts and leaning into kindness, tenderness, and respect for healthy boundaries. When this gets interrupted by Love Reversals, a distorted kind of masochism can put you at risk of unnecessary harm.

You learn not to touch a hot stove after getting burned, but you will not learn to move away from people who burn you if toxic programs were installed in childhood. Even though I've been burning away in you since before you were born, I can't protect you from human life, and part of being human means that before you're seven years old, the mind is a sponge, absorbing every single program with zero discernment. So if you installed any Love Reversals, it's natural and easy to conflate abuse with love.

Uninstalling this pattern and loading a more joy-inducing program means facing what can be a painful realization—that some of the people you care about deeply *do not actually know how to love you*, not because you're not lovable or they're not good humans but because they've been traumatized themselves, so their own Love Reversals interfere with their capacity to show up in love.

And so it goes as humans break one another's hearts—over and over and over—in the name of "I love you." These good, gentle souls know not what they do.

This is not an excuse to shame yourself or anyone else. This is an opportunity for compassion, for understanding, for seeing what is love and what is not love with clear seeing. It is an opportunity to reckon with your relationship to love—and to see what love is and what love isn't through my luminous eyes.

Feeling confused about love? Come study and download new programs with me.

The best Love School teacher ever,
YOUR INNER PILOT LIGHT

230

Dearest Beloved,

It's time for an unabashed love letter.

I adore you so much I want to pinch your cheeks and kiss them while wearing bright red lipstick so you can see all the evidence.

You're so sweet I want to eat you like a cupcake and leave the crumbs sticky and stuck in the corners of my mouth.

You smell so good I want to bottle you into perfume so I can dab you behind my ears and think of you whenever the wind wafts you my way.

You feel so soft and warm I want to snuggle you like cashmere.

Your voice sounds so precious to me it's like an angel song, lilting from the heavens.

And when I look at you, my eyes soften, my mouth turns up, and I'm awash in the beauty of all that I behold in you.

I love you so much that I just know in my heart how precious you are, how special you are, how exceptional you are, and at the same time, how people are *all* this special, as drops of Divinity dribbled into human forms.

I never, ever forget how wonderful you are, but I know sometimes you do.

So bear with me from time to time when I gush, because you aren't remembering to see yourself the way I see you.

With magical eyes,
YOUR INNER PILOT LIGHT

231

My Love,

As the feminine rises—in yourself, in your relationships, and in the culture—make sure you're not demonizing the masculine in you or in others. Keep in mind that nobody rises unless the masculine and feminine rise in balance.

At a time when the shadow masculine is destroying the planet, the Divine Feminine is emerging as an evolutionary impulse to restore balance. This means that, regardless of your gender, you have the opportunity to use your powerful voice, your compassionate heart, your creativity, and your fierce love to stand for peace between the genders. If you can't have truth and reconciliation—men listening to what hurts in women and women listening to what hurts in men, giving each other a chance to speak and be heard with your hearts wide open—you will never see peace on Earth.

Earth is in the midst of a massive collective transformation right now. It is a confronting and exciting time to be human, but this time demands you to open your heart bigger than you ever have. Earth needs a miracle, but I for one believe in miracles.

That's where I come in. You can do this, as long as you're in touch with me.

We are all in this together. We can do hard things with great love. Let's do this, beloved.

The ultimate peacemaker,
YOUR INNER PILOT LIGHT

232

My Precious,

You know how you veered off course and started beating yourself up?

Please don't do that, darling. Have compassion for yourself. Give yourself a hug and a pep talk. Learn what you need to learn but then jump back up and ask me for help.

No need to beat up your inner critic or let it beat up you. Count on me to hold you accountable while also holding you in my arms like a mother who loves you no matter what.

I'm right here to steer you back on track—with nothing but gentle, nurturing love and a call to your highest accountability.

I'll help you learn what you need to learn, make apologies and amends when necessary, uncover what caused you to veer off track, and love the crap out of what steered you wrong until you let me take the wheel again.

I'll hold you responsible without berating you, so you can do what you must to make things right. I'll help you accept responsibility without judging you, so you can use what happened to do better next time.

With a spark, a squeeze, and a tickle,
YOUR INNER PILOT LIGHT

233

Dear One,

In times of stress, do you tend to overfunction or underfunction?

Overfunctioners don't ask for help. They give it. They don't make themselves vulnerable by allowing themselves to be needy. They guard against vulnerability by rescuing others.

Underfunctioners do the opposite. They don't help others. They need help. In the face of a crisis, they don't rescue. They collapse and expect to be rescued.

Overfunctioners and underfunctioners pair up like peas and carrots.

There's nothing wrong with giving help or needing help. Healthy humans will all have times of need and times of strength, times to give and times to receive.

Problems arise when you help more than you receive help, or you receive help more than you give help.

Not sure how to come into right relationship with helping and receiving help?

I'm on it,
YOUR INNER PILOT LIGHT

234

Dear One,

When it feels as if life is falling apart, I know it seems like lunacy but try your darnedest to thank your lucky stars.

I'm not suggesting you bypass your emotions. Feel your pain. Move through your rage and frustration and disappointment and grief. Let those emotions take you over like a contraction. If you feel it all the way without resisting it, it won't last longer than ninety seconds.

Breathe. Breathe. Breathe.

Then . . . when you're ready . . .

See if you can feel the blessing in the pain.

Not sure how? I can help.

If you need help faking it 'til you make it, I'm on it.

Loaded with insight and compassion,
YOUR INNER PILOT LIGHT

235

Dearest Beloved,

Will you do me a favor and lean all the way into what's yummy today?

You've had enough of growing through pain. Now it's time to dive into what's delightfully delicious!

Find the edge of how much you can tolerate pleasure. Not sure where that edge is? Try testing it out.

How can you ramp up your pleasure tolerance? What desires might you fulfill?

Do you want a massage? Ask someone!

What's your favorite meal? Let yourself eat it today.

Do you love flowers? Invite a friend to send you some.

Are you a nature buff? Let yourself dive deliciously into nature.

Do orgasms light you up? Ask a partner to help you feel sexy, or indulge yourself.

Is it pleasurable to snuggle up and enjoy safe, healthy, intimate touch? Put on some music and gather friends together for a cuddle puddle.

Do you love concerts? Plays? Flower gardens? Candlelit dinners? Hikes in the rain? A really great yoga class? Ecstatic dance? A creative day? Attending a workshop? Singing around a bonfire?

Be proactive. Create pleasurable opportunities. Push your upper limit of what you can tolerate. Notice what comes up for you if you indulge lots of desires at once.

Does this trigger you or fill you with yum? Can you ramp it up even more?

Let me help.

Mmmmm . . .
YOUR INNER PILOT LIGHT

236

Dear One,

You know that generous thing you did the other day? (Yes—you know what I'm talking about.)

I want you to know how much that really lit me up.

You may think it's no big deal, but every time you open your heart and give generously, checking first to make sure you're truly resourced to give so generously without depleting yourself, you douse me with rocket fuel and then—WHOOSH!—I'm on fire!

Do you have an impulse to give from your heart today? Who needs your gifts today? Is it someone in your family? Someone who it's hard to love? Is it a stranger someplace you hope to volunteer your service? Or is it *you* who needs a gift today?

Tune in. I'll tell you where the gift-giving fire starter lives.

Letting all that fiery love flow in and out,
YOUR INNER PILOT LIGHT

237

My Precious,

You keep looking for the answers in books, gurus, therapists, the church, the temple, the mosque, the ashram, or your best friend. Sure, there's wisdom, illumination, and healing out there in the world. But as long as you're looking outside yourself for all the answers, you're wasting a lot of energy and missing out on the greatest wisdom you'll ever find.

Come home to me, my dear.

It's okay to be a seeker, but at some point you'll get tired of seeking and you'll be ready to be a finder.

Find me right here, in the still space in your own heart.

Shhh . . .
YOUR INNER PILOT LIGHT

238

Dearest Beloved,

Do you expect people to be mind readers, my love? Do you feel most loved if people automatically do what will make you happy without expecting you to feel the vulnerability of asking?

If so, I'd venture to guess you wind up disappointed—*a lot*.

Of course, it's lovely when those you care about intuit what you need and meet your needs before you even ask. But not everyone has the perpetual download on exactly what you yearn for.

Why not make it easy on everyone? Why not get honest about what you need and dare to make yourself vulnerable to ask for help getting your needs and requests met?

Nine times out of ten, the healthy people you love are dying to meet your needs. Meeting your needs meets their need for intimacy. They just can't always read your mind.

Of course, sometimes your loved ones won't be resourced to support your needs, and that's perfectly fine. That's why it's helpful to have a tribe of people who can help you get your needs met, so you're not dependent on just one person.

But be on the lookout for a common pattern among empaths and helpers. If you've surrounded yourself with people who are perpetually disinterested in meeting your needs and requests, this should be a red flag.

Pause and get curious about this.

Why are you prioritizing people who love getting their own needs met by you but don't want to meet yours? Why are you letting this kind of imbalance persist?

Not sure what you need? Not clear why the giving and receiving might be off-kilter?

Ask me.

Always attuned to what you need,
YOUR INNER PILOT LIGHT

239

My Darling,

I know sometimes you get defensive if someone gets upset with you. You rationalize. You justify. You deflect. And no wonder! It hurts if you feel as if you let someone down, especially if you really didn't mean to do so.

Let me give you a ten-cent tip that can increase your intimacy with the person who feels upset.

Try saying "I'm sorry."

You don't have to admit guilt or take responsibility for something you don't feel belongs to you. You can simply express compassion for someone else's pain.

"I'm sorry you feel hurt by me. What do you need right now?"

This kind of outreach is not an expression of wrongdoing. It's simply a gesture of connection, acknowledging someone else's pain and making an attempt to ease that suffering.

Next time someone criticizes you, try leading with a simple "I'm sorry."

Not feeling it? Let me help you.

Unapologetically apologetic,

YOUR INNER PILOT LIGHT

240

My Love,

It's not easy to feel grateful when you feel pain. Pain can suck up every bit of your consciousness and make you impervious to the feelings of gratitude that might otherwise wash over you naturally.

Yet gratitude makes life worth living! Gratitude is medicine.

So how do we hold this paradox—that being human hurts and yet it's always a gift to be alive?

When life hurts, you can't skip the hurt part. But it is possible to feel pain and gratitude simultaneously.

If life hurts, and you try to focus on gratitude, your mind may balk. It may seek evidence that life is not deserving of infinite gratitude, that complaining would be more appropriate.

So sit with that part.

But stick with it and see if you can also find the feeling of being thankful for the gifts of life.

You know that every challenge brings with it an unexpected gift. Can you be grateful for the gift, even before you know what it is?

"Thank you for this gift of love."

You'll find glimpses of gratitude, but then the mind may call out, "Nonsense! This is not a gift of love! This is a disaster! This hurts!" The mind prattles on with all of its fear and anxiety in the face of pain and uncertainty.

But some deeper part of you knows that there will be goodies riding shotgun with fear, pain, and uncertainty. Can you be grateful for the goodies ahead of schedule?

I know you can look back at traumas and losses and see how much you grew as a result of these challenges. This is how you learn resilience, see how strong you are, and grow your faith. It's how you learn to ask for what you need and how you grow intimate with your tribe.

You don't have to bypass the painful feelings one bit in order to feel the gratitude. You can hold the pain and the gratitude right next to each other—the poison and its antidote—in paradox.

You're welcome,
YOUR INNER PILOT LIGHT

241

Dear One,

You made it!

It's all happening!

Your dream came true.

You finally did it.

Your ego swells up with pride!

Or . . .

Maybe it didn't happen.

You feel disappointed.

Your heart is broken.

Your ego is bruised.

Either way, I want you to know, it doesn't make the slightest bit of difference to me.

Why? Because *I love you for trying*. I'm beyond proud of the courage it takes to put yourself out there and leap in the direction of that which wants to be born.

My love for you is unconditional. I don't love you more when it happens. I don't withhold love when it doesn't.

Unconditionally yours,

YOUR INNER PILOT LIGHT

242

Oh-So-Generous One,

People throw around terms like *narcissist* and *codependent*, labeling and demonizing themselves and others. We all have narcissistic parts and codependent parts, but nobody is 100 percent narcissistic. No one is codependent through and through. And none of your narcissistic or codependent parts like to be shamed!

When you can love and accept all of your parts and really get to know them intimately, then you can let me help caretake them, and they can relax and act out less.

Not sure if you have narcissist parts or codependent parts?

See if any of these patterns sound familiar.

If you have tendencies toward codependence, you may have difficulty knowing what you need; you may avoid asking for help from others and struggle with setting and enforcing healthy boundaries. You may tend to become passive-aggressive when your needs aren't getting met. You may perceive yourself as competent and others as weak. You may have little faith that others can take care of themselves, avoid vulnerably expressing strong emotions such as anger or hurt, struggle to graciously receive gifts or praise or help, and have an inflated sense of yourself as unselfishly service-oriented. You may tend to be judgmental and pride yourself on being loyal, but you may be loyal to a fault, often staying in unhealthy or even abusive situations and rationalizing why you stay, often with "I'm so spiritual."

If you have tendencies toward narcissism, you may be charismatic, likable, and talented. You may initially "love bomb" others in order to lure them in, then withhold love when you're not getting your way. You may have trouble apologizing when you make a mistake, tending to point the finger at others rather than owning up to your shortcomings. You may be in a habit of "one-upping" anyone else's story, turning the attention back to yourself. You may break promises and fail to keep commitments, make a lot of excuses, and leave a trail of bad relationships in your wake. To make things more challenging, you may even lack insight into your narcissistic tendencies and, if called on it, you may show no interest in seeking treatment.

Phew! If you have codependent or narcissist tendencies, those can be some challenging parts of yourself to love! And if you see those parts in people you care about, it can be hard not to judge.

But guess what? For me, it's such a piece of cake to adore even your most extreme parts—and to have a lot of spaciousness (and good, clear boundaries) with the extreme parts of others.

Having trouble accepting some of your challenging patterns? Come to me, sweetheart.

For reals,

YOUR INNER PILOT LIGHT

243

Dearest Beloved,

Your eyes matter. Only you can see things the way you do, and when you share what you see, you open the eyes of others.

Your voice matters. The world needs to hear it, even if what you say stirs things up (*especially* then!).

Your ears matter. When you listen generously to someone else's story—without agenda, without trying to fix someone, without comparison or competition—you offer a limitless gift of the kind of love that is desperately needed on this planet right now.

Your touch matters. No one can express comfort, compassion, nurturing, and tenderness quite the way you do when you offer your hugs.

Your intuition matters. When I whisper into your inner knowing, your courage to follow divine instructions has the power to heal the world.

So please, darling—see with new eyes, speak your truth, listen with generous ears, trust your intuition, and don't be afraid to reach out and touch someone.

In awe of the medicine you bring
in your own unique way,
YOUR INNER PILOT LIGHT

244

My Dear,

Do you realize you have only one job in this life: to allow yourself to fully express who you really are, without apology?

There are no restrictive rules.

There are no immutable grand commandments.

There are no how-to tips you must memorize in order to be lovable and loving.

There are no spiritual practices you must perfect in order to be One with *me*.

It's so simple, my sweet. You are quite miraculous—one beautiful, delicious, unique piece of Divinity living within a human body, longing to be expressed fully and without limitation.

Your only job is to allow me to fully express myself, in grand fashion, with whatever bells and whistles I deem necessary.

When you strip back everything that is not *me*, you can trust that whatever emerges from that unapologetically soulful place can be trusted. You do not need to be afraid of me, my love. Yes, I might shake things up, because sometimes things need a good shaking. But I will not violate Divine Will, force you to give up your free will, harm anyone, or lead you astray.

So relax, my darling. We can *do* this life thing together, and it's gonna be freakin' *fun*!

Welcoming you on board,
YOUR INNER PILOT LIGHT

245

Dear One,

I know sometimes you fantasize about being invisible.

I know you also long to be seen and heard.

The impulse to be humble and out of the spotlight is sincere and sweet, and the impulse to be seen, heard, and fully, unapologetically expressed is equally adorable.

With me on your side, you can have both.

I am your invisibility cloak, and I will keep you humble, reminding you always that any attention you attract belongs to *me*, your divine self. I will remind you always to give credit where credit is due, protecting you from getting too full of yourself.

I am also your megaphone, your star-spangled spotlight, and your sound system, here to cheer you on when you get stage fright and are tempted to dim my light or avoid putting your gifts out into the world.

Listen to me and I'll guide you when you need to be out in the world, and I'll remind you when it's time to disappear into a quiet, reflective, and nurturing renewal of your soul.

Cloaking and shining,

YOUR INNER PILOT LIGHT

246

Committed One,

I know you want to be of service as part of the awakening of the consciousness of the planet. I know you want your life to matter. I know you want to leave a legacy and you sometimes get frustrated because you feel you're not doing enough. Or you don't yet know what you're called to do, or you feel like finding your calling is yet another exhausting thing to add to your already overloaded to-do list.

Breathe, sweetheart . . .

Remember, you are enough, just as you are. Especially with me lighting you up, you are more than enough! You are a gift just because you are letting me shine my radiance out into a world in need of your love.

Don't you realize that just by letting my light shine, you are making the world a better place? And just by bearing witness to the Inner Pilot Light of just one other person, you are helping to heal the planet?

The next time you're in the grocery store or coffee shop, find your calling right then and there. Show someone else that you see their Inner Pilot Light. Show them yours in return.

Imagine if every human on the planet did just that.

That, my dear, is enough. Your love is enough to change the world.

Ba-da-bing,
YOUR INNER PILOT LIGHT

247

Dearest Love,

It's easy to get confused by the spiritual teaching "Don't judge others." If you misunderstand this teaching, you may be guilty of giving people far too much slack, expecting too little from those in your intimate circle and exposing yourself (and your loved ones) to repetitively hurtful or even dangerous circumstances.

You can curb your harsh judgments, remaining spacious and compassionate, without harming your healthy discernment.

What's the difference between judgment and discernment? Judgment says, "You are bad so you are undeserving of my love." Discernment says, "You deserve love, and I choose to set boundaries to limit my exposure to you." Judgment closes the heart. Discernment allows the heart to stay wide open but protected with clear boundaries.

In sociology researcher and author Brené Brown's research, she found that the most compassionate people were those with the strictest boundaries. Because they protect their own boundaries, they can walk around with an unguarded heart while still feeling safe. If you feel like closing your heart is the only way to keep others out, you'll wind up practicing less compassion.

In other words, if your discernment is spot-on, your compassion can pour forth with boundless generosity!

It's not "unspiritual" to respond to someone else's extreme behavior, lack of responsibility or accountability, or questionable integrity by setting good boundaries and limiting your intimate exposure. That doesn't mean you won't make exceptions to these boundaries when you sense that someone has used their mistakes as fuel for real transformation.

There are no easy rules to guide discernment. But the good news is that *you do have me*!

If something in another trips your judgment wire, and you find yourself feeling judgmental, threatened, or confused, come to me and I'll lend you my discernment so you can keep on loving—with healthy space around those who could hurt you or the ones you love.

Eyes wide open,

YOUR INNER PILOT LIGHT

248

My Pillar of Strength,

Remember that time you totally lost it? You were a hot mess of chaos and emotion, unsure whether you'd ever pull it together again.

But look, my dear, you did it, as you always do. Look how resilient you are!

Do you realize you did more than just pull it together?

Every time things fall apart, you get just a wee bit closer to me. In the depths of your despair, we find each other, and I help you remember who you really are. Each time you struggle, we plant the seeds for your gestating greatness.

Remember, sometimes it takes breaking down to break through.

With sun and water,

YOUR INNER PILOT LIGHT

249

My Love,

I know you feel impatient with yourself about that thing you haven't done yet. And yes, I understand. Sometimes it's time to get your patooty in the chair and "just do it."

But remember, that's the masculine approach that tends to dominate in our culture.

The feminine approach to getting things done is less like the "go get 'em" sperm and more like the "attract, wait, and receive" egg. When you're being less sperm and more egg, you simply sit back, smile, and wait, rather than going after it.

So don't beat yourself up, darling. Practice being "eggy." Tell me what you desire. Turn it over to the Universe. Surrender all attachment to outcomes. Then trust, let go, and let it happen.

How will you know when it's time to act? Don't worry. If it's time to "just do it," I'll tell you.

The perfect blend of egg and sperm,

YOUR INNER PILOT LIGHT

250

My Dear One,

How can you tell the difference between being fearless and being reckless?

From an evolutionary standpoint, fear is there for a reason—to protect you. Without fear, you might be tempted to do really crazy things—like jump off a cliff without a parachute or stand there, without running, while a lion homes in on your tasty flesh.

Fearlessness, left unchecked, can also lead to arrogance. When all you feel is unshakable confidence, you start thinking you're immune to danger, or even that you're above the law and don't have to follow the "rules." You start driving your car 100 mph on the freeway because you're not afraid of getting caught or crashing. You start skipping checkups because you're not afraid of getting sick. You spend more money than you're earning because you're confident the money will show up. You walk alone into a dark alley in the inner city after midnight. You cheat on your spouse because you're confident you won't get caught. You cheat on your taxes. You run your business illegally. You break a law . . .

It's a slippery slope.

Yet you are not invincible. Part of the work of the soul is finding that balance between confidence and humility.

When you let me lead, you'll find you do not need fear in order to keep you safe because I will protect you from recklessness. If you heed my warnings, I'll let you know when you've gone too far. If you listen deeply, I'll whisper sometimes subtle, sometimes not-so-subtle instructions. You won't need to rely on fear or overconfidence. You can simply relax into me.

The ultimate protection,

YOUR INNER PILOT LIGHT

251

Dearest Beloved,

I feel you longing for deeper connections, for more intimacy, for a sense of belonging in a soul tribe of like-minded creatures. I know it hurts when you feel disconnected, lonely, and isolated.

I want to help you fulfill this deep longing for intimate, soul-enriching community. So I have a homework assignment for you.

Make a list of all the qualities you want in the people you wish to attract into your life. Describe them in great detail. Know them in your heart. Feel what it feels like to be in their presence.

What do they love? How do they behave? What do they value? What gifts do they have to give? What do they need? How will they give from the heart? How will they get their needs met? How do they play? How capable of receiving unexpected blessings are they? How much pleasure, connection, and crazy-wild fun can they tolerate? How much stillness rests inside of them?

Now here's the fun part: *go out and be that person.*

Then don't be the least bit surprised if you magnetize the very people who are just like you.

How?

I'm right here, darling. Listen up. I'll show you.

An amazing-person magnet,
YOUR INNER PILOT LIGHT

252

Dearest,

When you're burning the candle at both ends, something invariably gives.

Maybe you create unnecessary conflict with someone you love. Maybe the quality of your work suffers. Maybe you grow anxious or depressed. Maybe your body breaks down.

Candles are only meant to burn in one direction. That's where I come in.

Blow out your side of the candle, my love. Let me shine the way for us.

Flickering, steadfast, and upright,
YOUR INNER PILOT LIGHT

253

Adventurous One,

At one point in your journey, you'll likely try to numb your pain—with busyness, surfing the Internet, sweets, booze, or other distractions that help you feel pain less intensely. During this phase, the edge of your growth might ask you to learn how to sit with your pain and feel it.

Then one day you might get so good at alchemizing pain into soul growth that, lo and behold, you might actually get addicted to pain! This tendency toward masochism can cause you to chase after experiences that stretch you so far out of your comfort zone that you can really feel your oh-so-uncomfortable growth edges. You might even discover, much to your surprise, that you have a strange sort of preference for pain over pleasure.

But wait a minute. Do you really want to get stuck in that phase? No . . .

That's when you might venture upon a new part of your journey—one that presses you to increase your tolerance for intense pleasure. You might discover that you're so much more comfortable feeling pain over pleasure, bumping up against your upper limit. You might even notice a strange sort of panic if too much intense pleasure lands on you all at once. This surprising contraction might cause you to take a big breath and admit that you have a bizarre preference for giving over receiving, and if you're being asked to receive too much yumminess, you hit a glass ceiling of what you'll allow yourself to take in.

At this point, the edge of your personal growth requires you to sit with the discomfort that arises when everything's going so beautifully, so smoothly, so pleasurably, and you have to just breathe it all the way in until you feel tears of gratitude.

This could cause you to become a pleasure junkie! You know how you sometimes grow bored and antsy when things get too peaceful? You might even paradoxically feel the impulse to blow things up just so you can feel radically alive. So then you may discover that the edgiest part of your growth lives in sitting calmly with the mundane details of human life.

Mindfulness teacher Jack Kornfield says, "After the ecstasy, the laundry," and Zen teachers say, "Before enlightenment, chop wood, carry water. After enlightenment, chop wood, carry water."

When you're super-duper close with me, you'll find that you can handle it all with equal grace. Pain, pleasure, the mundane—life is filled with all three. At some point in your journey, you may still have a preference for one state of being over another, but all states of being are welcome.

Not sure where the edge of your growth lies? Ask me.

Taking whatever comes,
YOUR INNER PILOT LIGHT

254

Dearest Beloved,

You know what makes my light shine bright? When you nourish me with what I need to help your body thrive.

Sometimes I need farm-fresh green vegetables, natural superfoods, creative salads, whole grains, fresh juices, kombucha, luscious fruits, herbal teas, boatloads of love, and just a wee bit of raw chocolate. (YUM!)

Other times I need responsibly raised organic meats, healthy carbs, cheese made with love right at the dairy, and coconut ice cream.

One diet rarely works for your entire life. Your body has different needs during the changing phases of your life, and you may need things you'd never imagine, even day to day.

Not sure how to tell what's good for you? Steer clear of the rigid restrictions and diet books, and try asking me anew every day, without preconceived ideas about what's good for your body or what isn't.

Veggie kisses,
YOUR INNER PILOT LIGHT

255

My Dear,

I know you worry about what you can't control. I know it's hard to let go when you're so afraid of the unknown. I understand how human it is to grasp for what you want and resist what you don't want. I know you would feel so much more comfortable if only you could snap your fingers, be your own genie, and make all your wishes come true.

I know how tempting it is to get seduced by incomplete or misguided teachings that suggest that, if only you do it "right," you'll get everything you want. And if you're not getting everything you want, it's because you're simply not "spiritual" enough.

With all due respect to those who teach such things, if you tap into me and drop into your heart's deepest truth, you'll realize that such teachings are both true and untrue. Yes, it's true that you're not simply a victim of a random, hostile Universe. Yes, it's true that you participate in the co-creation of your reality. Yes, it's true that how you align your energy can affect what happens in this three-dimensional time and space. But no. I hate to break it to you, sweetheart, but *you're not solely in charge of your destiny*. No amount of "manifesting" is going to get you everything you think you want. There are simply limits to what you can control.

Remember, my love, letting go and surrendering to Divine Will isn't meant to be some sneaky "law of attraction" trick to help you get everything you want. Letting go means paradoxically leaning all the way into your desires and then letting go of attachment to outcomes. It means funneling all that longing into the desire to align with Divine Will, and knowing that what is aligned with Divine Will might be different than what it is you think you want.

Consider that if you're not getting what you think you want, it's not because there's some punishing God in the sky who is withholding your heartfelt prayer. On the contrary, my darling, the Cosmic No may be a great act of loving protection!

Instead, go ahead and name your sweet desires. Do your part to unblock the flow. Then give the wheel to me. Stop trying so hard to control your life and just let me help you fall into the flow of grace.

How? Just ask.

Tootling along in the driver's seat,
YOUR INNER PILOT LIGHT

256

Dearest Beloved,

Why is it that you have such a hard time seeing the gifts you bring to the world? Why are you so gifted at seeing the beauty in others, when you can sometimes be so blind to your own value and worth?

Oh, honey, can't you see that you are as worthy of love, compassion, affection, affirmation, validation, success, attention, and abundance as all those other beautiful souls out there? You're not more deserving or less deserving. All sweet humans have an equal right to *be*, simply because every single creature in the cosmos has inside an Inner Pilot Light just like you do.

You don't have to *do* anything to earn this right to *be*. You don't have to prove your worthiness or earn the unconditional love of the Universe. This love is a gift of grace.

How can you learn to feel the loving embrace of this kind of genuine unconditional love and acceptance?

I am right here, my love, ready to hold you in my infinite embrace.

Never forgetting how precious you are,
YOUR INNER PILOT LIGHT

257

Sparkly Darling,

I know you feel like you want to fit in, and sometimes you feel like you just never will.

This is such a natural feeling, sweetheart. It's only human to want to be liked. It takes some maturity to realize that fitting in is a fickle endeavor that serves only to distance you from me and everyone else.

Trying to fit in interferes with true belonging. You don't have to pretzel yourself into some artificial shape in order to belong. In fact, only when you allow your true shape to emerge will you find the tribe that fits your unique shape perfectly.

Marveling at what a masterpiece you are,
YOUR INNER PILOT LIGHT

258

Dear One,

When you feel the impulse to offer comfort to another, try letting me help you master the art of what Rachel Naomi Remen calls "generous listening." When you listen the normal way, you may be thinking about whether or not you like what someone is saying. You're wondering whether you're stronger or weaker than the person who is talking. You're trying to figure out what to say next or how to give advice. If the person talking is upset, you're on a mission to distract or cheer up the person who is hurting. You may feel uncomfortable sitting with someone's pain, so you focus on fixing the problem as quickly as possible.

But you're not listening generously.

To listen generously is simply to listen to what's true for someone. You hold space. Offer your faithful company. Sit with someone without expectation. Be with what is without trying to change it.

Grant someone the simple gift of my presence.

Don't interrupt. Don't compare. Don't compete. Don't shut down someone else's right to feel what they feel. Just be with their truth, even if all you say is, "You know I don't even know what to say right now, but I want you to know I'm with you and I care and you're not alone."

This is the gift love gives.

How can you give this kind of gift to someone in need of comfort?

I'm all ears,

YOUR INNER PILOT LIGHT

259

My Precious,

Yes, I see your to-do list! Wow! It's long!

Don't worry. All will be checked off in due time, but before it all starts to overwhelm you, tune in.

Pause.

Breathe.

Remember divine timing.

First, slow down. Give the list to me. Ask me for my help knowing what needs doing and when. Listen deeply to what I have to say. Trust that I won't leave you in the lurch, and I won't dismiss the parts of you that feel anxious about everything on that list.

Give me a chance to show you that if there's something that needs your urgent attention, I'll let you know. Invite me to remove anything from your list that isn't really important.

Then listen up. Take action only if I guide you.

Your most trustworthy, efficient,
and faithful daybook,
YOUR INNER PILOT LIGHT

260

Dear Heart,

You don't need to look any further than my ever-present glow for the validation you seek.

The approval you search for outside of me will always be short-lived gratification, leaving you ever thirsty for more, like a drop of water in a desert wasteland.

Come to me, dear one, where there is an endless well of acceptance and praise that is eternal and unsurpassed, a love that gushes forth, filling you with everything you need so that you will never thirst again.

Ahhhhh . . . basking in the refreshment,
YOUR INNER PILOT LIGHT

261

Dearest Beloved,

Do you realize that comparisons are the basis for all unhappiness?

Comparing yourself to others is one of the primary culprits for feeling lost and alone. It's also one of the biggest offenders for feeling unfulfilled.

Are you aware of this comparison part that's longing for your love and comfort?

Can you see how, when it takes the wheel, it can derail all your positive feelings and leave you feeling completely drained?

When you compare yourself to others, you may find yourself tempted to judge others as either superior or inferior to you, causing you to "other" people, categorizing them in ways that can be destructive to true connection and intimacy.

But *news flash*, sweetheart: there's no "other." Sure, with one lens on, someone else might appear to have more money, more stuff, more friends, more apparent success, better sex, or a more enlivened romance. But when you switch over to my magical, mystical eyes, you see the Oneness of all things, where there's no scarcity, no need to measure yourself or anyone else.

Since everyone has a uniquely sparkly Inner Pilot Light, you're special and you're not special—and so is everybody else!

Beyond compare,

YOUR INNER PILOT LIGHT

262

My Rock Star,

Let's celebrate!

Think of one thing that's positively AWESOME about your life.

Yes—*that one*.

Now let's shout it from the rooftops! Dare to share your great news with those whom you can trust to be excited with you. Tell the friends who have enough access to their own Inner Pilot Lights to lift you up. Post your great news online. Give yourself a hug.

Throw yourself a party! Take yourself out to dinner and invite others to come play with you. Treat yourself to something special. Say prayers of thanks. Let yourself bathe in a shower of gratitude.

Without intending to, it's easy to share your struggles with others and hide the yummy stuff. But if you reserve moments of connection for challenging times, you anchor limiting beliefs like, "If I want connection, life needs to be hard."

If you want lots of reasons to celebrate and a sweet soul tribe of supportive beloveds, start relishing life. When you savor life's joys, you attract more awesomeness, and when you share what you celebrate, you encourage others to focus on the good stuff too.

Not sure what's awesome about your life? Ask me. I'll happily gush . . .

Full of awesome,

YOUR INNER PILOT LIGHT

263

Dearest Beloved,

In a fast-paced world always running on overdrive, it's no wonder my voice grows dim and you have a hard time hearing my loving wisdom.

I am always here, darling, but you might only hear me in the inky black of the darkest nights. You might hear me right after the doctor utters the words you most dreaded hearing. You might hear me when the one you love walks out. You might hear me when you lose your job or miss the opportunity or wind up disappointed—again.

But even then, unless you drop down, get quiet, and really listen, the other voices in your head might drown me out. The fearful parts may scream louder than me. The skeptical parts might start to shut you down. The protective parts that tempt you to contract may rain down a litany of instructions meant to keep you safe.

While other parts are doing their best to scream from the rooftops, I might sound like nothing more than a gentle whisper.

Yet even so, I am always here, ever present, always loving, radiant within you, here to guide you—in blissful times and during hard knocks.

You don't have to wait until the dark night of the soul in order to hear me. You can hear me in the blades of green spring grass. You can hear me in the waterfall. You can hear me in your dreams. You might sense me in a sacred place of worship. You might feel me in the arms of a lover. You might see me in the eyes of another Inner Pilot Light.

I'm always here, if only you tune in.

I have something important to tell you right now . . .

Can you hear me?

Offering my guidance through the light and the dark,
YOUR INNER PILOT LIGHT

264

Dear One,

Why is it that you can be such a genius at forgiving others but you tend to be *so hard* on yourself?

Today, let me help you give yourself a break.

For all those ways in which you've hurt people inadvertently, for all the blind spots of your sweet parts that accidentally wreak havoc when they're just trying to protect you, for the "mistakes" you've made, for those you've wronged—*I forgive you*.

Now can you grant yourself the same gift?

Tell yourself, "I know it seemed like a good idea at the time. Now I forgive you. I'm sorry. I love you. I release you."

Don't worry that forgiving yourself will keep you from learning the lessons you need to learn. Forgiving yourself doesn't mean you won't make apologies, make amends, and hold yourself accountable. It simply means you've chosen to grant yourself peace from torturing yourself about something in the past that you can't change in present time.

Would you be willing to finally let that thing go?

Ahhhhh . . . don't you feel better already?

An infinite well of forgiveness,

YOUR INNER PILOT LIGHT

265

Embodied One,

How is your body feeling today? Have you checked in?

Are you noticing any physical symptoms?

Do you feel clenched or open?

Is your breathing deep or shallow?

Are you energized or tired?

Is there tightness in your muscles or looseness and flexibility?

If your body isn't feeling optimal, what is your body telling you? Is there something in your life your body is saying no to? How could you live a life your body would love? What does your body need in order to heal?

If your physical symptom is a protective part, just trying to get your attention so it can help you, what is it saying? Can you listen deeply? Can you receive the message?

Not sure how to translate the message?

Ask me.

I speak body,

YOUR INNER PILOT LIGHT

266

Beloved,

At the end of your life, I promise that you will not be relishing that day of work you stayed late.

You won't savor the bonus check they gave you.

You won't remember that award or that piece of external validation that meant so much at the time.

You won't care about that big house or that fancy car or even that accomplishment you worked so hard to achieve.

When the end is near, I promise that you will remember only this: how much you loved and how much you let yourself be loved in return. You never know when the end could arrive. Are your priorities in order?

Here to keep you in alignment,
YOUR INNER PILOT LIGHT

267

Precious One,

I know it can be hard to accept criticism, because so often it feels like an attack. But if you learn to receive criticism with curiosity, discernment, and grace, you'll find gems within the criticism. You might even feel grateful for the blind spot someone else illuminates.

How do you do this? First, listen generously to what someone has to share with you. Avoid making them wrong or getting defensive. Then ask me whether what has been said is true. Is it genuinely helpful guidance? Or is it pure projection on their part? Is the truth somewhere in between?

Is someone projecting undesirable feelings or emotions onto you rather than admitting to or dealing with the unwanted feelings in themselves? Or are they spot-on, and you feel the plunk of truth in your belly?

It can be an error to take too much responsibility if someone criticizes you. But it's also usually an error to take no responsibility for the pain others experience as the result of your behaviors. Somewhere between overresponsibility and underresponsibility lies the middle path.

Unbiased—with love,

YOUR INNER PILOT LIGHT

268

Dear One,

You may feel like if you let go of the reins, all hell will break loose, you won't get what you want, and everything will fall apart.

But what you may not realize is that grabbing the reins and trying to exert control is actually sabotaging all the blessings the Universe is trying to bestow upon you.

When you micromanage your life, you block the flow of blessings. When you dive into the current of synchronicity and open yourself to the mystery, life is free to take you for a glorious ride!

So, darling, let's go whitewater rafting. I won't let you be reckless. Let me hold the paddles that will keep you safe in the rapids.

Let go. Surrender. Trust.

Play. Scream. Splash.

Squealing and laughing,
YOUR INNER PILOT LIGHT

269

Perfect-Just-As-You-Are,

Please, take a breath, and let's finally befriend and make peace with that perfectionist part that tries to run the show.

I know that part feels so much pressure to get it right, to deliver, to outperform, to be superhuman.

But let me fill you in on a little secret that might help this perfectionist part relax.

My darling, your imperfections are your gateway to intimacy. When you're willing to be vulnerable, to expose what you consider your "big ugly tail" in order to share your imperfections with others, they see in you their own imperfections and they feel connected through the flaws we all share.

When you're willing to be a big goofball and confess how imperfect you are (and express how *okay* you are with your adorable imperfections), you give others a gift—letting them off the hook, giving them permission to be imperfect, just like precious, wonderful, ridiculously awesome *you*.

When you reveal what you consider your flaws, I swoon with openhearted tenderness as I witness two adorably imperfect beings bonding. Compassion grows. Intimacy thrives. I get all lit up and sparkly!

I know how hard you try, my dear. But you don't have to always get it right. (Hint: What if there is no "right"?)

Can you just let me love that sweet, protective, perfectionist part, the one that has tried your whole life to keep you safe from rejection and ensure that you'll fit in?

Can you trust that I can keep you safe even more than that part can?

Relaxing perfectionism is a wild act of courage. Will you let me help you relax into how lovable you are when you don't need your perfectionist part to run the show?

A miracle of unconditional acceptance,

YOUR INNER PILOT LIGHT

270

Dear One,

It's a fine balance we all must strike.

If you expend all your energy chasing a dream or trying to save the world, you may neglect your relationships, your health, and your playtime.

But if you expend all your energy devoting yourself to your relationships, you might sacrifice your big, beautiful dreams and leave this planet with your song unsung.

How can you navigate priorities that may seem to compete?

This is where I can help you nurture those you love, take care of yourself, and follow your bliss.

If you have conflicting parts that vie for the wheel, let me have a family conference with those parts. I'll listen to what matters to your tribe-oriented parts. I'll take stock with your ambitious parts. I'll keep an eye on the checkbook. I'll pay attention to your physical and mental health. And I'll keep track of how much fun you're having. And then . . . like magic . . . I'll help you know exactly what you need to do so that you *really* can have it all.

Always here to help you prioritize,
YOUR INNER PILOT LIGHT

271

My Love,

I know some days you feel like you're simply not enough. You tell yourself you're not a good enough family member, not a loyal enough friend, not smart enough at your job, not talented enough in what you love to do, not a sexy enough lover, not financially stable enough . . . not [insert your greatest insecurity here] enough.

But let me tell you what I know.

You are enough.

You're enough because you hold within you a little spark of Divinity that makes you inherently valuable. You're enough because it's your very imperfections that make you perfectly adorable. You're enough because you're doing the best you can—and who could ever expect more than that? You're enough—*just because you are*.

Don't believe me?

Come snuggle in with me. Let the warmth of my flame ignite you until your radiance is glowing so bright and sparkly they can see you as the star you are from way out in outer space.

Oh yeah, baby. You really are all that.

Pregnant with stars,
YOUR INNER PILOT LIGHT

272

My Curious Darling,

I know how much you hate uncertainty, how much you love knowing, how deeply you'd love a guarantee that everything will turn out the way you dream it will.

But oh, my love, you wouldn't want guarantees!

With me at the wheel, you can always trust that the mystery is far more thrilling, surprising, exciting, and delicious than any cheap thrill the illusion of certainty could seduce you with.

If you're willing to sit in the discomfort of uncertainty, you'll discover wild possibilities and unexpected blessings that you couldn't even imagine in your craziest dreams!

Don't limit yourself by trying to nail down everything. Open yourself to wonder, mystery, and awe. Stay curious.

Jumping down rabbit holes,
YOUR INNER PILOT LIGHT

273

My Sweet,

Imagine meeting someone you've never known before in this life, and you feel a strange, instantaneous sensation—"I know you. We belong together."

Imagine being in a community of spiritual seekers where you feel safe to be truly yourself. Imagine a community where you feel free to play, laugh, sing, dance, meditate, pray, celebrate, engage in ritual, and share meals together. Imagine a safe haven where you can seek support when you're in crisis, and you can offer support when others in your tribe experience life's inevitable challenges. Imagine finding a place where your boundless, generous, service-oriented love has a place to land.

Imagine a place where spiritual principles can be safely shared, explored, and challenged from a place of compassionate curiosity; where open, respectful, safe dialogue and free but kind expression is welcomed and valued by all, where those who are unable to tolerate diversity of beliefs and opinions are held accountable by the tribe, and where unity is encouraged and polarization is gently but firmly brought together in the field of love.

Imagine a community committed to helping each other grow, gently but fiercely illuminating blind spots and exploring shadows, where all beings acknowledge, accept, and gently tend each other's wounds, but they don't coddle them in codependent ways.

Imagine a community with healthy boundaries and shared values but without rigid dogma, where you can feel safe to keep your heart open, and you're not at risk of getting shamed for being different or questioning the spiritual leadership or the group's teachings. Imagine a spiritual community where you are not asked to follow the compass of someone else who has caused you to believe that your spiritual compass is broken, where you retain your free will, your intuition, your right to speak up, and your sovereignty.

Sound like your spiritual home?

Oh yeah, baby. That's the kind of tribe you're likely to find or create if you let me take the lead.

Calling in your soul tribe,
YOUR INNER PILOT LIGHT

274

Wildly Creative Darling,

What's holding you back from your fully expressed creativity?

Here's a hot tip: *it's never me that's getting in the way.*

I'm the one guiding you toward it!

I'm the one who grabs your hand when you're painting and creates a masterpiece.

I'm the voice that gives you dictation so you can write that piece that touches hearts.

I'm the channel for the ideas that solve big and small problems.

I'm what plays the instrument, drops in the vision, shows you how to make that gourmet meal, instructs your craft project, and inserts the download of that entrepreneurial business.

I'm the words that come through on that keynote speech, the healing touch that cures someone's cancer, and the presence that opens someone's heart.

I'm the muse, the magic maker, the daimonic force, and the inspiration for every creative spark that wants to come through you.

Do you think you're not creative? Let me help you heal that crisis of imagination.

Snuggle up. Let me flow through you.

The ultimate creative fire,
YOUR INNER PILOT LIGHT

275

My Precious,

When acute trauma hits, as it inevitably will, you will embark upon a journey.

At first, it's natural to feel victimized. Although you don't want to get stuck in your victim story, you also can't skip the part where you feel like a victim—because those feelings are very, very real when you're in the wake of a trauma. You can't skip feeling the pain and helplessness. It's natural and healthy for that part to feel hurt, angry, betrayed, and even righteously attached to its point of view. This can be a helpful frame of reference for a while, propelling you to get angry, get help, set boundaries, enforce them, stand up for yourself, and do something to try to avoid being victimized again.

While it's important not to bypass your victim story too quickly, you also want to resist spiraling into a pit of despair—paralyzed, powerless, and pessimistic. If you get stuck in your victim story, you can get lost there. You can create a whole identity around that point of view. Some people get really comfortable snuggling into their misery, and they spend their whole lives milking their victim story for every last drop of sympathy, attention, financial support, and pity they can squeeze out of the people who hear their story. They may use their victim story as an excuse to withdraw from life, behave irresponsibly, or rationalize not accomplishing a deep dream. This limited perspective can also destroy relationships, limit true intimacy, separate them from community, and avoid allowing them to fulfill their calling.

Can you find the gift in whatever adversity you face? Are you willing to commit to this lifelong practice?

Not sure how to feel what you feel, resisting the temptation to bypass the pain while also alchemizing trauma into growth? When crisis hits, let me help.

Always here to help you practice,
YOUR INNER PILOT LIGHT

276

My Dear Pumpkin,

There is something wonderful just within your reach, and I can't wait to see you light up with joy and enthusiasm when it is revealed. But you see, I can't deliver the goods until you're fully ready to receive the gifts. When you're blocking all the gifts I'm ready to bestow upon you, telling yourself stories about how you're not worthy, how you have to work hard to get it, how someone else is more deserving of the gifts than you are, how good things can't happen without struggle, how you can only handle so much goodness without taking it fully in, you literally turn away the "Special Delivery" package with a bow on top that I'm trying to send you.

When you block me like this, I can't get through to give you all that I'm dying to give!

How do you unblock the blocks, my darling?

You practice stretching your tolerance for bliss, my love!

You hold up your arms, put your face toward the heavens, breathe in and out deeply, and squeal, "YES! YES! YES!"

Notice anywhere that this feels uncomfortable. Notice the tightness in your chest or the panic in your throat when you think about how it would feel to receive infinite blessings. What if you found yourself surrounded with the love, playfulness, and intimacy of your soul tribe, loaded with money, finding and fulfilling your life's purpose, showered with romance by your beloved, immersed in natural beauty, and experiencing more life force, vitality, and health than you've ever felt in your life?

Could you handle it, or would you sabotage it?

Would you hit a glass ceiling of how much you'd let me give you?

Yeah . . . I thought so.

This is totally natural, sweetheart. You're not the only one who has been programmed to limit how much you'll let yourself feel ecstatically happy, grateful, calm, peaceful, radiant, and joyful.

There's always something delicious brewing on my side of the co-creative street, but when you've hit your upper limit of awesomeness (especially when that upper limit is pretty low), you make it hard for me to give as generously as I love to give.

Feeling frustrated that your tolerance for bliss is so low?

I can help. Trust me to love your upper limit all the way into the cosmos.

Up, up, up,

YOUR INNER PILOT LIGHT

277

My Dear,

Waking up requires holding infinite paradoxes.

> Let go . . . and do what needs doing to make it happen.
>
> Go for it . . . and relax and let it come.
>
> Be grateful for the traumas that initiate you . . . and feel how much trauma hurts and seek treatment.
>
> Love unconditionally . . . and don't tolerate unacceptable behavior.
>
> Take responsibility for your life . . . and don't take more than your fair share.
>
> Be specific about your vision . . . and go with the flow.
>
> Thank those who violate you for all they teach you . . . and find your "HELL NO!" and set clear boundaries.
>
> Trust that it's a benevolent Universe always ready to shower you with blessings . . . and show up and do what it takes to make yourself ripe for miracles.
>
> Humble yourself before the mentorship of wise spiritual teachers . . . and don't give your power away.
>
> Use your good intentions to make magic happen . . . and don't assume you know what's good.
>
> Trust my guidance . . . and don't ever assume you know for sure that it's me talking.

The mind is uncomfortable with paradoxes. It's always trying to resolve paradoxes into "this" or "that."

Only the heart can hold seemingly competing, conflicting truths as equally true.

If you find yourself feeling confused—to go or not to go, to try harder or to do less, to set more boundaries or to forgive and forget, to open your heart more or to withdraw in protection, to fulfill your mission or to rest and play, to assert your will more or surrender—see if you relax when you consider that both might be simultaneously true.

Can't find peace in the paradox?

That's where I come in.

Expansively paradoxical,
YOUR INNER PILOT LIGHT

278

My Darling,

When was the last time you paused and asked me for guidance?

Take a moment and *just pause*.

Get quiet.

Listen up.

Tune in to me. Ask me your questions. Cast the heavy load of all your unsolved problems, your unmet longings, and your undecided decisions onto me.

Trust that I'm listening. Then tune in to the guidance I promise I'll send your way.

This guidance may come in the form of "just knowing" the next right thing to do. It may come as a sign from the Universe—a surprise synchronicity—delivered to your doorstep like magic.

It may show up in your inbox or as a message from an unexpected stranger. It may be a feeling in your body or an answer in a dream. Something in nature may deliver the answer to your question, the solution to your problem, or the next breadcrumb in your Divine Assignment of how you will participate in the transformation of consciousness happening on the planet *right this very minute*.

It will come. Not always in your timing, but in divine timing.

I love you,
YOUR INNER PILOT LIGHT

279

Dear One,

When someone disappoints you in a relationship, in addition to asking, "Why did they do that hurtful thing?" try also asking, "Why did I attract this relationship into my life, and what am I supposed to learn from it?"

Relationships are never accidents. Every relationship is a glorious sacred contract, even if you tell yourself the story that it was a mistake.

Even if meeting someone seems like chance serendipity, a casual bumping into each other that seems random, it's not. Somehow, in some way, you called that relationship into your life. Every relationship is part of your Love School curriculum, teaching you how to practice unconditional love with others and with yourself.

The minute you accept that your soul calls things into your life so you can learn lessons you're incarnated on Earth to learn, that's the minute you step into your power, no longer the victim, one step closer to a much more expansive life.

So I ask you—if you're struggling with any relationship in your life, why did you attract this relationship and what is it teaching you? Is this person here to help you trigger and see and heal your Mommy or Daddy wound? Are you learning to set and enforce boundaries? Are you practicing how to alchemize pain into growth? Are you learning to speak up and ask for what you need, overcoming your tendency to clam up and feel resentful?

Can you thank your Love School teachers without using your gratitude as an excuse to tolerate unacceptable behavior?

Not sure how to find the lessons, experience the gratitude, and still keep your vulnerability safe?

As always, I have the answers. Tap in.

Uncovering life's mysterious lessons,

YOUR INNER PILOT LIGHT

280

Sweetheart,

When you shine a flashlight at penguins, they chase it, not because they love the light but because they think it's a fish.

Man, are those penguins disappointed when they finally "catch" the light.

You humans make the same mistake—following false light, hoping it's the fish, only to discover how empty it really is.

The spiritual world is full of false lights, people who lure others in with shiny, sparkly hooks, showing off their superpowers and hypnotizing you with their charisma. They attract you into their web with unrealizable promises of how they'll help you increase your spiritual power, how you can gain your own superpowers, or how you can free yourself from pain forever.

But the glow is one cell layer deep. When you look beneath the surface, it can get pretty dark down there.

How can you resist the temptation to be lured by false lights, my darling?

Pay attention to any time you feel fascinated. Let your tendency to be fascinated be one of your discernment tools.

True lights radiate bountiful, generous love, often in a quiet, completely nonflashy way. Those lights emanate from others whose Inner Pilot Lights are shining boldly but humbly.

If you feel the pull toward someone's false light, come back home to me.

The real deal,

YOUR INNER PILOT LIGHT

281

Dearest Beloved,

When you do something you're not so proud of, you can react in one of three ways.

You can beat yourself up and wallow in the depths of despair, letting yourself get attacked by your inner critic parts, spinning into a shame-spiral paralysis.

You can shield or numb yourself from what you've done, turning away from the pain of how your behavior hurt yourself or others, rationalizing and justifying your behavior so you can just keep right on doing the same ol' thing without making apologies, making amends, and holding yourself accountable.

Or you can take everything as an opportunity for growth and awakening, recognizing how you want to be different in the future and taking positive action to avoid behaving that way next time, all while holding even your most misbehaving extreme parts in the infinite, forgiving embrace of my unconditional love.

Do you think I'll be too lenient, failing to help you make agreements and demonstrate accountability, integrity, and maturity? Do you think it takes a bullying, abusive drill sergeant to motivate you toward behavior that feels more in line with my light?

Nope. It's just the opposite, baby.

Let the waterfall of my love pour over you until you love yourself so much you simply don't want to hurt yourself or anyone else for one more minute.

All love, all the time,

YOUR INNER PILOT LIGHT

282

Dearest,

You may not realize how many sacred contracts you've made—consciously or unconsciously. Some are clear commitments you've chosen. Others you made unconsciously, your wound fitting like a key into the lock of someone else's wound.

But you can clean up these unclear agreements if you feel ready. I can help, my darling!

Imagine if you were able to pull out a big red pen and realign all your sacred contracts with all the people in your life.

What if you made a new rule? What if you invited everyone you love to share with you their hopes for what you can give them, understanding that you will likely be unable to meet all their desires and might have to say no or set boundaries?

Then in return, you do the same. Get clear on your wishes. Ask for what you want. Don't take it personally if someone isn't resourced with the bandwidth necessary to meet your hopes or desires.

Imagine the freedom. No mind reading. No games. No guessing. Just clarity, permission, and the agreement to meet each other's needs as often as possible without abandoning yourself or sacrificing your health, your financial stability, your sanity, or your inner peace.

Need help getting clear on how to ask for what you need and intuit when you are and are not resourced to meet the needs of others?

Here with a red pen and a blank page,

YOUR INNER PILOT LIGHT

283

My Sweet,

What do you fear more—the monotony of the mundane or the uncertainty of change?

Do you stave off boredom by instigating drama, taking risks, moving a lot, changing relationships frequently, and pursuing various career choices, without settling down and committing intimately and deeply to anything, anyone, or any place?

Or do you make attempts to prevent uncertainty by choosing security, stability, and the warm comfort of the known world in order to avoid the anxiety that accompanies the unknown and uncertain world of change?

Whatever your tendency, let me reassure you that you're perfect the way you are, my sweet. And let me also push the edges of your comfort zone, just to shake things up!

If you're always running after the next shiny penny, maybe it's time to settle down.

If you're so settled that you haven't gotten out of your rut for years, maybe it's time to try a new groove.

Whether your life is smooth sailing or choppy waters, I am always here to help you feel safe. Even when life gets monotonous, I will be your excitement. When life gets uncertain, I will be your rock.

You have nothing to fear, darling.

Holding you close,
YOUR INNER PILOT LIGHT

284

Beautiful,

Do you realize that there's only one thing that gets between you and me? Wanna know what it is?

Trauma.

You might think only people with "big T" Trauma like sexual abuse, childhood abandonment, or exposure to war zones get spiritual blocks. But all humans experience trauma. Unhealed trauma can veil me from your awareness, even though I am always right here, burning away. Even seemingly insignificant trauma activates protector parts that unwittingly keep you from feeling how close I really am.

So what is trauma? Psychologist Dawson Church defines a traumatizing event as something that is perceived as a threat to your physical survival, overwhelms your coping capacity, produces a sense of powerlessness, produces feelings of isolation and aloneness, and violates your expectations.

Think of how many times you experienced something in childhood that met these criteria!

Even if it was as simple as a threatening sibling, a bullying peer, or a parent or teacher who neglected your pleas for help, such traumas interrupt your ability to fully integrate and receive my enduring, unending, radiant love.

How can you heal these traumas? I am the healer you've been longing to find. If you can befriend all the protector parts that come between you and me, asking them to relax so you can experience the depth of my healing power, you'll discover that the best therapist in the cosmos is right here inside your own heart.

Still can't find me? Then try working with a therapist trained in Internal Family Systems or Advanced Integrative Therapy. Once the trauma is cleared (and yes, trauma is curable!), I'll be the welcoming committee, taking you in my spacious arms and welcoming you home.

Home sweet home,

YOUR INNER PILOT LIGHT

285

My Dear,

Have you been nurturing your body lately?

Sometimes I look in the mirror with you, and I'm just in awe of what this body has gotten us through. Wow—look at those strong muscles that keep you moving; those bones that keep you upright; that skin that protects you; those eyes, ears, mouth, nose, fingers, all for seeing, hearing, tasting, smelling, feeling.

While I might be the essence of you, I live with you *in the temple of this body*, and every day I cherish it.

Do you?

Do me a favor today. Let's celebrate this body, appreciate it, honor it, nurture it, and thank the heavens that we're blessed to live in the blessing of this body for as long as we're here together, incarnated on Earth.

Grateful,

YOUR INNER PILOT LIGHT

286

My Dearest Love,

When he said that thing that hurt you, I was there.

When she left you feeling wounded, I was there.

When all attempts at repair failed, I was still there.

And because I'm always there, forgiveness is always possible.

Can you let go of the hurt, resentment, and anger and tap into the love, empathy, and compassion I bring to you? That doesn't mean you have to let that person back in your life. It's okay to say "Enough already" when someone can't be trusted with the intimacy you offer. It's okay to set boundaries and limit someone's access to your inner circle.

But holding grudges only poisons you and dims my light.

Take as long as you need . . .

But when you're ready, *release*.

Burn a candle. Write and burn a letter. Tear up every sacred memory you don't want to hold on to anymore. Bury the ring. Do whatever it takes to ritualize your release, and don't forget to release all the stuck emotions—the fear, the grief, the overwhelm, the disappointment, the sadness. Move it through like a wave in the ocean. Feel it envelop you and then leave your body . . .

Dance it off.

Ahhhhh . . . that's better.

When you're ready . . .

YOUR INNER PILOT LIGHT

287

Sweetheart,

You may think you're brave—and darling, you are! But I'll bet you anything there's one corner of your life where you're still holding back. Maybe you're afraid to take risks in relationships because your heart has been broken so many times. Maybe you're hesitant to take career risks or financial risks or sexual risks or creative risks.

I'm not being critical or trying to pressure you. I'm just curious whether you're daring to explore your own edge.

It's only natural to guard against what takes you out of your comfort zone.

But here's the good news: While there may be an area of your life where you're still blended with a fearful part, I guarantee you there are many others in which you're incredibly courageous. Maybe you've had the courage to open your heart after it got broken. Maybe you're brave enough to ask for what you want in a relationship. Maybe you spoke up at work to stand up for your integrity or you quit your job to follow your dream. Maybe you invested your life savings in being part of the solution or diving down the rabbit hole of your passion. Maybe you tried something daring in the bedroom. Maybe you put your talent out there in the world, in the public eye where anyone can see you succeed or fail.

Take comfort in the fact that, no matter where you are on the fear-courage spectrum, all you adorable humans are in the same scaredy-cat, brave-as-a-lion boat.

Do you long to be less frightened and more brave?

That's what I'm here for, darling.

Grrrrr . . .

YOUR INNER PILOT LIGHT

288

Sparkly One,

The world is full of juicy possibilities and enchanting curiosities, just there for you to explore. Each day you have an absolutely overflowing cup of wonders to dive into and wade through with as much secret pleasure as if you stumbled upon a secluded forest hot spring.

All you need to do is start each day with an intention to be curious. That's it! Nothing else is required!

Don't demand that you understand everything. Don't require certainty before you're willing to dive into the vast unknown. Don't limit your idea of what's possible. Just stay open and curious. Be willing to feel awe. Stare into the vast mystery with no idea of what might be in there.

You might have to let go of the hit you get from blending with your adorably certain know-it-all part. You'll need to be willing to be surprised and maybe even shocked. You might even have to let go of your worldview, and that can be disorienting.

But don't worry. I'll keep you sane and grounded. I'll lend you my discernment so you don't go off the deep end. If only you lean into me while you open to wonder, I'll keep you safe while allowing you to expand your consciousness and experience the most amazing edges of what's possible.

Feeling resistance from some skeptic part? Do you have a scientist part doubting what's possible? I love *all* of you.

Illuminated with magic,

YOUR INNER PILOT LIGHT

289

Oh-So-Serious One,

How much are you laughing these days? What makes you laugh? Could you invite that funny friend over? Do you bust a gut watching comedic movies? Does it tickle your funny bone to watch kooky animal videos on YouTube? Have you tried sitting with a group of friends and telling stories about your most embarrassing moments? What about going out in nature or visiting a farm or zoo to watch the baby animals bouncing around like goofballs with springs?

Try getting together with a silly friend and figuring out your porn star name (your middle name and the name of your first pet). What about your badass road trip name (what you had for breakfast with the last place you peed on the side of the road). How 'bout the gangsta name your homies call you when you're out ridin' dirty? (Try the gangsta name quizzes online.)

If you can't find anything to make you laugh, take a tip from laughter yoga and fake it 'til you make it! All the physical and mental health benefits of laughter still apply, even if you're just laughing by yourself for no reason in your car! And the good news is that if you start laughing for no good reason, you'll likely feel so goofy that you'll start laughing for real, especially when that scowling stick-in-the-mud who just cut you off sees you snorting and cackling and flicks you the bird.

Not sure how to bring more giggletude into your life?

That's where I come in.

Whahahahahahaha,

YOUR INNER PILOT LIGHT

290

Dear One,

When things don't go your way, go ahead and let yourself move through the feelings of disappointment, but don't get stuck in a story of failure. Try on a restorative narrative. What if what you judge as failure is simply a cosmic redirect, a loving, though sometimes painful way that the Universe can support you by helping you get back on track?

This doesn't mean that there aren't lessons to be learned when something doesn't go how you hoped. Maybe you took too many shortcuts, undervalued yourself, promised things you couldn't deliver, got lazy, or neglected to log in your ten thousand hours to become more masterful. Maybe you weren't taking personal responsibility for your side of the street, and this thing you call failure is a lesson in humility. Maybe I whispered my advice—and you ignored me.

But maybe not!

What if the ending of a romance isn't a failure but a sign that you've successfully completed this sacred contract, learned what you're here to learn in this relationship, and now you need to be free to learn the next lesson with the next relationship?

What if getting fired isn't a sign of your incompetence but an opportunity to find a job that doesn't require you to compromise so much of your integrity?

What if your attempt to monetize a creative passion doesn't result in big bucks? Does that mean you have no talent and aren't worth getting paid to do what you love? Not necessarily! Maybe it means your soul is ready to learn how to let go and allow the Universe to support you in a new way. After all, if you get everything you think you want through the force of your will, hard work, and dedication, how will you ever learn to trust a benevolent Universe?

How can you discern the lessons you're meant to learn from what seems like failure?

On it,
YOUR INNER PILOT LIGHT

291

Dearest Beloved,

In relationships, we all want to feel intimacy and security, but we also desire autonomy and independence. It's easy to wind up hooked in relationships that are polarized at one end of the intimacy extreme or the other. Maybe you're feeling too much distance, longing to feel close, safe, and secure. Or maybe you're feeling smothered, finding it difficult to maintain your sovereignty, grasping for freedom and room to breathe.

If you can resist polarizing these two natural relational impulses into ends of a spectrum, you'll see that the linear spectrum can collapse into a paradoxical circle. Through my magical eyes, intimacy and freedom are not opposites; they're one and the same.

What if intimacy is actually the gateway to freedom? What if freedom deepens intimacy? What if you can have absolute freedom and the most exquisite intimacy?

Recognize that these impulses toward togetherness and space are two sides of the same coin.

Acknowledge your need for both in balance. When you need space, ask for it gently. When you need comfort, reassurance, or attention, communicate your need to feel connected. If your relationships are healthy, the others will thank you.

Free and intimate,
YOUR INNER PILOT LIGHT

292

My Sunshine,

You know I am your Inner Pilot Light, that always radiant, ever-sparkling, never-extinguished glow of spirit, love, and compassion within you. But did you know I am also your darkness? I live in shadows. I reside in your mistakes and imperfections. I burn brighter when you enter my darkness and learn from it.

As a being, you are both light and darkness, radiance and shadow. When you judge the darkness as evil, exiling it and sending it packing, you fail to fully illuminate my light.

Don't be afraid to go into the darkness, darling. Only when you are brave enough to explore your darkness will you peel back the film over your heart, exposing the infinite radiance of my light.

I will hold your hand. If you get lost down in the rabbit hole, I will send you a lifeline. I will always illuminate you, bringing you back into the light of my glow, only this time, when you return from the underworld, you will hold the Holy Grail—the gift from the darkness—the full-spectrum awareness of all the gifts revealed in the dark and light embodied.

Here with a flashlight,
YOUR INNER PILOT LIGHT

293

Dearest Beloved,

The next time you're tempted to judge someone, try this as a practice in compassion.

Take a deep breath and add to the end of your judgment ". . . and I am too."

Remember that what most irritates, angers, insults, or annoys you about others is often a reflection of something unseemly you see in yourself, some shadow side of yourself you're running away from or exiling. Instead of running away, be brave enough to face your own shadows. Stare into the darkness and own it.

Remember that you just don't know what's going on for that person you're tempted to judge. You don't know what loss they suffered today, what trauma is still unhealed in them, what disappointment they're facing, what illness they're up against, what heartbreak they're in the midst of.

This doesn't mean you should neglect the hurt you feel or take more than your share of the responsibility in some conflict. This is not a rationalization for letting someone off the hook without consequences for hurtful behavior. It's not a way to spiritually bypass the need for healthy conflict and appropriate boundaries. But it is a way to free yourself from the painful prison of polarity.

Some people think they need judgment in order to protect themselves. But herein lies the paradox, my love. There's no stronger protection than the open heart. This you can trust. Your heart will protect you so much better than your judgments ever will!

Need help loving so big? I'm right here, darling.

With a great, big, nonjudgmental heart,
YOUR INNER PILOT LIGHT

294

My Dear,

Let me teach you one simple trick for forgiving yourself over choices you wish you hadn't made.

Memorize the mantra, "*It seemed like a good idea at the time.*"

It may sound like a cop-out, like some easy-peasy way to get yourself off the hook without taking personal responsibility. But that's not what I'm suggesting.

What I'm saying is that at every moment of every day, your protective parts are doing what seems like a good idea at the time. Even if parts of you sense it's a bad idea right before you go and do it, other parts have got their reasons for why they're taking the wheel and enacting even potentially destructive behaviors.

When you can view even your most extreme parts as protectors who are just trying to help you get your needs met, keeping your vulnerable parts safe and helping you survive in a complex world, compassion arises.

Not sure how to find compassion for a rage part, an addict part, an eating disorder part, an abusive part, a sociopath part, or a suicide part in yourself or in someone else?

Let me put this bluntly: I never met a part I didn't love. And if you let me love all your parts, I can earn their trust and help all your parts get their needs met, befriending and allying with them so they don't need all that extreme behavior to get their needs met.

Always loving all of you,

YOUR INNER PILOT LIGHT

295

Sweetness,

Sometimes it feels like you're cruising along the waters of life with great forward momentum and then your boat runs aground. Suddenly everything comes to a screeching halt. The tide has gone out, and the fog has come in. You're too far from your starting point to go back and too far from your destination to doggie-paddle out.

You're stuck.

You're stranded.

Where are you?

What do you do now?

This space between what was and what will be is a magical place; a potent mysterious place of waiting and becoming; a place to relish, respect, and reassure yourself that everything is just as it should be.

If this space between stories feels threatening to the productive part of you that wants to *do*, relax. This space between is a time to just *be*.

Settle into the space between, following your breath if you have no idea what else to follow.

Take solace that when the time to do something arises, you will know.

How will you know? Because I will tell you, my love.

When the time is ripe, the tide will come back in, the fog will lift, you'll see clearly again and know how to proceed.

With you in the fog,
YOUR INNER PILOT LIGHT

296

Infinitely Lovable One,

Somewhere along the way, someone gave you the outrageously incorrect message that loving yourself is selfish, narcissistic, and egotistical. But darling one, that message could not be further from the truth! Please delete that silly notion from your beautiful mind.

What I know without a doubt is that you can't love anyone else if you can't first love, accept, and respect yourself.

How much love you can radiate into the world is in direct proportion to how much you love all your parts—not just glorious, radiant *me* but all the small, wounded, protective, and dark parts too.

Opening your heart to all your parts leaves you overflowing with love for others. Only when you fill yourself with the love you deserve can that love flow uninhibited into others.

There is no braver, more selfless act than loving all your parts. When you let me help you interrupt the wars inside yourself, healing and negotiating with any traumatized parts that polarize against each other, peace abides internally. When you are not divided inside, it's much harder to "other" people, polarizing and dividing against those you might be tempted to judge. The peacemaking genius I offer to your warring inner parts then turns outward. Your very presence then becomes a force of peacemaking in the world.

How can you learn to love it all—even the messy, adorable, traumatized, immature growth edges inside?

Start by loving me.

After all, I'm so easy to love, aren't I?

Looking cute and batting my eyelashes,

YOUR INNER PILOT LIGHT

297

Hi, Honey!

Perfection is like a shimmering mirage in a vast desert wasteland. No matter how far you go, it'll always be just over the next sand dune.

Consider feeding your parched soul from the endless well of *me* and leave behind the desert wasteland of perfectionism.

Think of it this way: Would you rather go to a dinner party thrown by a woman with perfect hair, perfect makeup, a perfectly decorated table, a perfectly cooked meal, attended by perfectly well-behaved children in a perfectly tended house?

Snore . . .

Or would you rather go to dinner at a real woman's house, where she's confident enough in the value of who she is that she's willing to let you come over to visit when things aren't perfect? Maybe the carpet needs to be vacuumed, she's ordered takeout, and the kids are playing noisily upstairs. But she's willing to be vulnerable with you, to show you what her life is *really* like, to open herself intimately to authentic, real connection, and to enjoy the pure pleasure of your equally vulnerable, messy company.

Not even sure who you are underneath all those masks of perfectionism? Ask me.

A cool drink of soul water,
YOUR INNER PILOT LIGHT

298

Oh, Most Powerful Beloved,

Deep within you lies a vein of power with the potential to explode like a volcano. I know it scares you sometimes to sense the force of that power surge. Perhaps you're afraid you'll abuse that power. Maybe you've done so in the past, and you don't want to touch that kind of dynamite with a ten-foot pole. Maybe you're afraid others will judge you or withhold their love if you open yourself to the power grid that lies deep inside of you.

So instead, you shrink from your power, dialing me down because you're afraid of what might happen if you let me course through you unrestrained.

I understand why you do this, my darling. You know what they say about how power corrupts and absolute power corrupts absolutely? No wonder you're scared of what would happen if you let me ROAR!

But here's what you need to understand. If you're dialing down your power because you are afraid of it, it's possible that you're doing what you must to protect yourself from abusing power. Your soul might have installed a built-in protective mechanism to make sure you can't access all my power until you're spiritually mature enough not to abuse it.

But here's what you can trust. When the time is ripe, when *you+me* is seriously solid, you need not fear your power, my darling.

Your power is a gift. As long as you humble yourself in the face of my light, as long as you give credit where credit is due, as long as you're aware that power makes you vulnerable to using it without integrity, as long as you're willing to receive wise mentorship and let me kick your butt if you start to let power get to your head, you'll be safe.

Is it time to let me erupt? Check in. I'll tell you when you're ready.

Like infinite lava,
YOUR INNER PILOT LIGHT

299

My Darling,

Life is a series of narrow tunnels in which you feel so squished you can barely breathe, followed by wide-open meadows meant for frolicking and dancing. In the narrow places, your growth accelerates, and you are humbled. In the expansive spaces, you get a chance to recover, integrate, and drink in the yumminess of life as you do cartwheels, radiate life force, bubble over with bliss, integrate your intense growth experiences, bench-press your receiving muscles, and recharge for the next narrow place.

Life gives you everything you need in order to burst your heart open, express yourself fully, and share your gifts with the world.

There's no need to judge the narrow places as "bad" or the open meadows as "good." Both are part of the natural cycle of life.

How can you transition smoothly between the two? See if you can find gratitude whether you feel constricted in the narrow places or expansive in the open meadows. Can you be equally grateful for the growth the narrow places offer and the blissful recovery the open meadows grant you?

See if you can stay with me in my wild YES!, even if you have parts that are screaming NO!

Yes! Yes! Yes!

YOUR INNER PILOT LIGHT

300

Beloved,

Even when you're busy having fun, all movement with no stillness can make you lose touch with me.

Have you allowed enough space for quiet time with me lately? Have you noticed the green of the leaves, the sparkle of starlight, or the birds cheeping their summer song in the mornings?

Have you noticed the peaceful darkness behind your closed eyelids as you reduce your sensory overload, settle your mind, and listen to me?

Can you feel me moving through your body like a pulse of energy, a wave of warm honey, or a tingle of truth?

I have so much peace and wisdom to share with you, if only you'll quiet down and listen.

Om . . .

YOUR INNER PILOT LIGHT

301

My Love,

If you're thinking painful thoughts, try questioning your thoughts. What if your cute little mind is simply experiencing what psychologists call a "thinking error"? The thought may feel really embedded in reality, but what if the thought that hurts isn't *all the way* true?

A practice of inquiry is at the root of much Eastern philosophy and most cognitive-behavior therapy techniques. Because we experience suffering when traumas cause us to ruminate on painful limiting beliefs, such as "I'm not lovable" or "Everyone is going to abandon me" or "Nobody can be trusted," learning to question your thoughts is a cornerstone of psychological and spiritual practice. This kind of tool in your medicine bag is very helpful when you're stuck in cyclical ruminations about long-past events.

If something hurts when you think about it, try asking yourself, "What's true and not true about this?" If the mind can find both truth and not-truth in the same thought, the belief loosens. After all, the mind cannot hold seemingly conflicting thoughts as both true. Only the heart can hold paradoxes, and when you enter the realm of the heart, healing can happen.

Keep in mind that inquiry is not always the appropriate tool in the medicine bag. Some pain cannot be questioned away. When you're in the midst of acute grief, for example, it's not helpful to inquire as to whether limiting beliefs are causing your heartbreak. When you're acutely grieving, you'll need my infinite, ever-loving comfort, support, and permission to feel your painful grief in the embodied depths of your sorrow. Overintellectualization with mental inquiry can interrupt the grief process and move you out of your heart, where true healing can happen.

Telling yourself or anyone else who is experiencing acute grief that they only hurt because of their thoughts is the opposite of healing. It can be cruel, even retraumatizing. Sometimes the medicine you need is a simple, abiding, ever-loving hug.

Not sure when inquiry is medicine and when it is poison?

Come to me. I always know the right tool.

Always available to offer the right balance of truth and nurturing,
YOUR INNER PILOT LIGHT

302

My Love,

Whether you're thrilled with things just as they are or you're experiencing pain and wishing your life were different, you can trust that *this too shall change*.

Everything does. Always.

Resist grasping for the blissful times and clinging for dear life. Just burst with gratitude and sing praising hallelujahs. This too shall change. You can count on it.

Don't resist the pain. Soften into the pain and just breathe. This too shall change. You can count on it.

Of course you have a preference for bliss over pain! You're human, and that's how humans function. But if you can create just a little space around your human tendency to grasp at bliss and resist pain, you can give up the exhausting battle of hustling for your joy and allow joy to bubble up inside of you, even when it's riding shotgun with pain.

Can you feel how beautiful life is *right now*, in the full richness of this vast human experience? Can't you feel the glorious radiance of just being fully alive, living vitally at full volume, experiencing all the joy and pain in this present moment, without resistance or grasping?

Live boundlessly with whatever shows up. This, my love, is the secret to lighting me up like a firecracker.

Ka-boom,
YOUR INNER PILOT LIGHT

303

Dearest Beloved,

The relationship between gratitude, desire, and surrender can be tricky.

If you solely focus on being grateful for what you have, you may suppress your desires out of fear of feeling disappointment if those desires aren't fulfilled.

If you solely focus on what you desire without focusing on being grateful for what you have, you may feel burdened by the pain of insatiable, unmet longing, never appreciating the gifts of this ecstatic present moment.

But if you express gratitude for what you have, acknowledge the unmet desires you yearn for, and then turn it all over to Divine Will, you will find peace.

Try this prayer: "If what I desire is in alignment with Divine Will, please make it so; if not, please free me from this longing and grant me peace."

Trusting the journey,
YOUR INNER PILOT LIGHT

304

My Dear Empath,

I know it hurts when you dare to feel the pain of all the polarized people in the world right now. It hurts when you feel the refugee mother who just lost her beloved children in a chemical attack.

It hurts when you feel the working-class single mother with the hungry kids who wants to send the immigrants away because someone here illegally can work for less money than she will.

It hurts when you stop trusting your fellow humans and think you need to protect yourself with a machine gun, even when guns are killing innocent children in public schools.

It hurts to feel the terrorist who isn't getting his needs met and feels so bullied by the world superpowers that he's willing to take his own life and kill others in order to punish those who oppress him.

It hurts to feel the woman who was sexually abused and now feels a power surge that makes her want to demonize all men in order to make sure nobody ever hurts an innocent girl or woman again.

It hurts to feel the African American man who feels as if black lives don't matter after he gets attacked by a police officer when he was innocent.

It hurts to feel the fear, confusion, and rage that the police officer feels.

It hurts to feel the Native American man standing for his sacred land, his people, and his tribe's right to drink clean water.

It hurts to feel the white man who is so cut off from his appreciation of all the feminine qualities of compassion, empathy, caretaking of Mother Earth, and love of the tribe that he has become selfish, greedy, dominating, and abusive.

My darling, it's no wonder you tend to see the world's pain and think, "That doesn't belong to me. It's all I can do to feel and deal with my own pain."

When you feel overwhelmed, relax and lean into me, my love. I can help you keep feeling compassion without getting flooded.

Breathing in, breathing out,
YOUR INNER PILOT LIGHT

305

Dearest Playmate,

All work and no play makes for a bored pilot light. Ditch the desk and let's go have some fun!

Road trip, you say? Why yes, I'd love to!

Hit up that big amusement park and roller-coaster our way into a record book? Count me in!

Dance the night away? I can twist and shout with the best of them!

Head out into the vast unknown and see where the wind carries us? I'm down for that! Try going on a Goddess quest.

How, you ask? Try this.

Determine how much time you'll devote to your Goddess quest. Surrender the whole Goddess quest to Divine Will and let go of attachment to outcomes. Don't think! If you interfere with too much thinking, planning, controlling, or structuring, it's not a Goddess quest. Decide how you'll invoke your first instruction. Going on a Goddess quest is a bit like a treasure hunt, so you're looking for clues. Start by asking me directly. Get in your car or go on foot and when you come to a crossroads, just ask: Right or left? If you need help hearing my answer, try oracle cards. Put your MP3 player on random and ask a song to give you a clue. Go out in nature and see if a river or a mountain or an animal that crosses your path has a clue for you. Feel into your body compass. Try your own tools for tuning in to me!

Be curious about anything unusual as you look for signs, but be discerning. This means you must pay very close attention to life as it unfolds, which forces you into the present moment. Notice everything and use it all as an oracle. Trust that your Goddess quest will unfold as a series of breadcrumbs, like clues on a scavenger hunt. Dare to follow the signs. Express gratitude to the Goddess.

With each sign that appears, don't forget to say thank you! Even if you don't perceive that any signs have been received, express gratitude anyway. Be willing to keep playing, without attaching to outcomes.

Ready to play? Let's go!

Yeehaw,

YOUR INNER PILOT LIGHT

306

My Sweet,

Imagine this: A little girl says to her mother, "Mommy, I'm feeling love deficient. Can you turn on pretty music, light a candle, give me a massage, and remind me that you love me?" The next day, she says, "Mommy, I'm feeling overstimulated. I'm going to go in my room and close the door, and please don't come in without knocking."

Imagine if the mother didn't take her daughter's requests personally but rather granted her requests and expressed sincere gratitude for her daughter's self-awareness and ability to communicate her needs.

Imagine if we were all that healthy, trusting that we could ask for closeness when we need it and space when we need it. Imagine if we could have our requests granted and respected by those we love.

Can't tell if you need more intimacy or more space? Not sure you have the guts to ask for what you need?

Here to help,

YOUR INNER PILOT LIGHT

307

Dearest Beloved,

I know the idea of boundaries can feel threatening. You may worry that others will feel rejected if you take care of yourself, say no when something doesn't feel right, distance yourself from "energy vampires" who drain you, or ask for what you need. You may even be so used to letting people walk all over you that the whole notion of boundaries is foreign.

Especially in certain spiritual circles, boundaries tend to get a bad rap. But good boundaries make good neighbors and help you feel safe to keep your heart open.

Just like children respond better when they know what is expected of them, those who love you appreciate knowing how far they can push you. If boundaries aren't set clearly, others may inadvertently violate your boundaries without meaning to. Or you may step all over someone else's boundaries without intending to. Resentment ensues. Someone gets hurt.

When you don't offer feedback about what you want or need, others simply have to guess. Some will guess by getting too close. Others will guess by staying too far away.

It's such a relief to those who love you when you can express exactly how close you want people to get, not just emotionally but also physically and psychically. Wouldn't it help you love well to know where everyone else's edges are too?

Not sure where your boundaries lie? Ask me.

Right at your edge,
YOUR INNER PILOT LIGHT

308

Darling Spark,

Not that you need anyone's permission to follow your heart, but just in case you think you do, let this be your cosmic permission slip.

I hereby give you permission to be your truest, most radiant, most heart-full self, never feeling the need to apologize for the sacred beauty that alights you and never needing to explain why you're following the path your heart chooses.

If others have been telling you that it's not safe to shine my light, or if you've been telling yourself that it would be foolhardy to do so, let this be your wake-up call:

YOU HAVE FULL PERMISSION!

In case you've been holding back, waiting to shine my light without apology, this is your time.

Permission granted,
YOUR INNER PILOT LIGHT

309

My Love,

Some days you're so stuck in your head that I have a hard time getting you to feel me. Today, focus not on what you think but on what you *feel*.

What emotion are you feeling right now, right this second? Can you name it?

Are you willing to just be with that emotion without trying to change it? Can you lean into sadness or anger or loneliness or longing or frustration without resisting the vulnerability of these emotions? Can you let yourself simply feel blissful joy, elation, tenderness, excitement, passion, or a heart-opening loving-kindness? Can you resist the temptation to suppress feelings you don't like or cling to feelings you prefer?

Whenever you lean into how you feel, no matter what emotion arises, I get brighter. When you pay attention to your feelings, you tune in to one of many ways that I guide you.

Communicating with you through your feelings,
YOUR INNER PILOT LIGHT

310

Sweetheart,

All humans are subjected to traumatic experiences, yet many are afraid of facing and healing those traumas that get buried inside. They might think that if they go inside that "trauma bubble," they'll get sucked down a bottomless rabbit hole and be destroyed.

But not you, brave one. You have decided to take the road less traveled, and I am so proud of you.

You have done some very hard work. You have learned you won't be destroyed by the shadows you've been afraid to face. In fact, you're realizing that this is where the light lives.

Carry on, you gorgeous love warrior.

So proud of you,
YOUR INNER PILOT LIGHT

311

Dear One,

I know how much you want to be of service, but be aware of the differences between helping, fixing, and serving, my love.

Rachel Naomi Remen writes:

> Service rests on the premise that the nature of life is sacred, that life is a holy mystery which has an unknown purpose. When we serve, we know that we belong to life and to that purpose. From the perspective of service, we are all connected: All suffering is like my suffering and all joy is like my joy. The impulse to serve emerges naturally and inevitably from this way of seeing.
>
> Serving is different from helping. Helping is not a relationship between equals. A helper may see others as weaker than they are, needier than they are, and people often feel this inequality. The danger in helping is that we may inadvertently take away from people more than we could ever give them; we may

diminish their self-esteem, their sense of worth, integrity, or even wholeness.

When we help, we become aware of our own strength. But when we serve, we don't serve with our strength; we serve with ourselves, and we draw from all of our experiences. Our limitations serve; our wounds serve; even our darkness can serve.

Service arises from me, my love, whereas helping and fixing often arise from caretaker parts that feel they have to hustle for love, overfunctioning in order to feel good enough. Service says, "Brother, sister, you seem to have forgotten your wholeness. Let me help you remember."

Always seeing the wholeness in you and others,
YOUR INNER PILOT LIGHT

312

My Gorgeous Playmate,

When you get into a funk, it's helpful to have a whole toolbox of reproducibly pleasurable experiences. If you tune in to me at the time you need help, I'll tell you exactly what to do. If you're not sure you can hear me, try some of these Inner Pilot Light illuminating activities:

Play with a child.

Meditate near water.

Serve someone or something other than yourself.

Take a scenic drive.

Play with animals.

Indulge in a spa treatment, either at a luxurious spa or with friends who can take turns offering spa treatments.

Get off with an oh-oh-oh orgasm. (Let me be your best lover yet!)

Soak naked in a hot tub or natural hot spring.

Make a playdate with the muse and get creative.

Put on soothing music and ask your friends to wrap you in a cuddle puddle.

Fill yourself with uplifting books, movies, music, festivals, or spiritual gatherings.

Go to a kirtan.

Take a yoga class.

Attend a music festival.

Sign up for a meditation retreat.

Read books that light you up.

Watch inspiring films and documentaries.

Make an Inner Pilot Light playlist and shake your booty.

It's hard to let the turkeys keep you down when you're out in nature, overflowing your cup with intimate connection, engaging in relaxation-response-inducing activities, and basking in the restorative hormones that fill your body with ohs and ahs.

The Yum Goddess,
YOUR INNER PILOT LIGHT

313

Dearest Heartner,

I know you sometimes worry that the suffering broke you, that you're somehow damaged by what went down in the past. But, sweetheart, mere suffering cannot even come close to extinguishing my flame!

I am untouched by what happened to you in the past. I cannot be broken and do not need to be fixed. In spite of all that's happened in your life, I remain whole, untouched by even the most horrific traumas. You do not have to engage in spiritual practices to create me because I am already here, closer than close. While spiritual practices can peel back the film that conceals me, I am steadfast, burning away without fail, even during your darkest hours.

I am just underneath the part of you that feels broken, a mere cell layer away. All it takes is the smallest crack in the armor that separates you from me in order for you to feel my love rush in like a tsunami of grace.

Trauma can initiate this crack, my love. When this happens, you are not broken—you're broken open!

But you don't need trauma to experience the gift of my love. All you need is the sincere, humble willingness to let me snuggle up next to you, whispering sweet nothings in your cute little ear.

Still can't feel me? Just ask me from the bottom of your heart for a sign that I'm here. Then pay very close attention to how I reveal myself to you.

Right here,

YOUR INNER PILOT LIGHT

314

Sweetheart,

Everything is going to be okay.

I promise.

I know it may not feel that way all the time. I know it may seem like things may not be going exactly the way you hoped, either in your personal life or on a grand global scale. But I swear to you, my darling, it's all happening in divine timing. It's all going right according to plan.

That doesn't mean that there's some fixed destiny. Yes, you are helping to write the screenplay of the movie of your life. But that script is changing moment by moment, responding to every other being in the cosmos who is creating this cosmic symphony with you.

I know your mind wants to understand how the whole thing works. But your adorable little human mind is simply too limited to understand the infinite complexity of how the whole Organizing Intelligence works!

So relax, my darling. Soon it will all make sense. One day, you will see the method to the Universe's madness. You will find the gifts in the uncertainty. You will understand why it's taking so long to get where you hope we'll get.

Be patient, love. Many mysterious, magical miracles are coming your way, if only you can surrender to the flow of life.

Tuned in to the Cosmic Conductor,

YOUR INNER PILOT LIGHT

315

Hiya, Hot Stuff,

When was the last time I told you how sexy, saucy, smart, savvy, sophisticated, and sassy you are?

Have I told you recently that you're gorgeous, how I love the sensuous way you move, how incredibly desirable you are and that you deserve to have all the attention you yearn for from the people you hope to attract?

Ooh la la. I dare say it's been too long. So let me say more.

Your true sex appeal isn't about the shape of your body, your age, the turgor of your skin, the clothes you wear, or whether your sexy bits look like the ones of movie stars.

Your sex appeal relies more on how much of my light you let shine through all aspects of your being. When I sway your hips and we're walking around the pool, trust me, sweetheart, all eyes are on me.

Oh—and did I tell you what a great hair day you're having?

Swooning,

YOUR INNER PILOT LIGHT

316

Beloved,

If you're looking for fulfillment anywhere outside of yourself, I'm afraid you'll ultimately wind up disappointed.

> You won't find it in a lover.
>
> You won't find it in a child.
>
> You won't find it in your friends or family.
>
> You won't find it on the *New York Times* bestsellers list.
>
> You won't find it in that dream house or that fast car.
>
> You won't find it in your bank account.
>
> You won't find it in a job promotion.
>
> You won't find it from trying to save the rainforests.
>
> You won't find it composing that masterpiece.
>
> You won't even find it in some gold star your spiritual teacher calls "enlightenment."

The only lasting fulfillment comes from within, where you come back home to me.

How will you find me?

I'm right here, baby, closer than close,
YOUR INNER PILOT LIGHT

317

Dearest Dreamer,

I have a dream, that all men and women of all colors and creeds, all social classes and castes, all political affiliations and beliefs are equal children of an invisible force of love that you might call God/Goddess. Burning like the flame that ignites our life force and fans the flame of love in our own hearts, this spark has a direct experience of Oneness and also appreciates the multiplicity of ways that the Eternal Flame reveals Itself.

This spark knows that all men and women, in all ways, are created equal. Many humans have forgotten but are now remembering that you must have compassion and fierce love to help one another unlearn their way back to God/Goddess. You are remembering that most of you have been traumatized and you don't even know it, and as long as you're all acting out from unhealed trauma, you will continue to hurt yourselves and each other in the most unconscious ways.

You are remembering that you cannot exploit Mother Earth and her resources without harming yourselves. You are remembering that it's time to share resources so that all men and women, all animals, and all of the natural world can thrive in harmony. You are remembering that you may have to make some choices that may feel like sacrifices, but what you will gain in doing so will far outweigh any inconvenience or discomfort.

You are remembering that everything is alive and sacred, and that deep joy and lasting fulfillment arise when the holy in everything and everyone in honored and celebrated. You are remembering that humans are tribal beings, deeply interdependent upon one another, rather than Lone Rangers who can do it all by yourselves. You are remembering the joy that bursts through you when you gather in conscious community to show your gratitude for Mother Earth, to perform ceremonies and rituals, to sing and dance and worship that invisible force of love that unites us all. You are remembering what it means to be fully embodied, conscious humans, the Godself witnessing the Godself in all Her multiplicity of forms.

How are you doing all this remembering?

I am here inside of you, whispering sweet memories, showing you in your dreams, and awakening the deep knowing in your heart.

Let's dream on, baby,
YOUR INNER PILOT LIGHT

318

Dear One,

You, my darling, are a prize.

Those who are in relationship with you have won the lottery.

Those who get to be clients or colleagues are blessed.

Those who were born into your family won the cosmic jackpot.

Sometimes you forget this, and you wind up grasping for love, money, and validation, as if something external to you could ever prove your worth. You try too hard, sacrifice too much, and wind up feeling unappreciated, rejected, and heartbroken when nobody seems to recognize how amazing you are. You hustle for love and get frustrated when even your most flowery efforts fail to win you the gratitude you seek from others.

When you realize you are a gift that will bless others—and you show up that way—others respond to your confidence, your grounded sense of self-worth, and your humble awareness that it is not your achievements, your beauty, your money, or your generosity that makes you a prize—it is *me*.

The source of all sweepstakes,
YOUR INNER PILOT LIGHT

319

My Love,

Spiritual teachings are like medicine. When the right treatment is applied to just the right circumstance, healing happens. I think of spiritual teachings like tools in a medicine bag. Because I am your best healer, I will pull them out when needed and deliver them with discernment and tender care, if you come to me to ask for help.

Yet, as with medical treatments, the treatment must be individuated to every unique situation. One medicine does not fit all!

If you're listening only to spiritual teachers and not to me, you could get hurt. Many spiritual teachers do not understand that the tool they teach is only one tool in a vast medicine bag. They try to apply one teaching to every life circumstance, and this can be as damaging as if a doctor prescribed one drug for every illness.

While spiritual teachers can do a great service, helping you unveil that which comes between you and me, resist giving your power away.

Trust me. I'll help you take in what serves and toss out the rest.

If you need spiritual medicine, come to me. I have access to every teaching ever offered in the entire cosmos, and I'll deliver just what you need in every circumstance, customized to your unique vibration, in that particular moment, at just the right dose.

The most reliable spiritual healer,
YOUR INNER PILOT LIGHT

320

Gifted One,

Those gifts that fall within your zone of genius, I'm here to remind you that they are unique, precious gifts that only you can give the way you have been groomed to offer them.

It's not that others don't share your gifts, but nobody can express them in quite the way you can. Your gifts are yours to give away. It's the opportunity of a lifetime to recognize the gifts you've been given, and then find a way to fully and unapologetically celebrate, bless, appreciate, own, and express those gifts.

Not only is it your birthright to give away your gifts but it's also your *responsibility* to do so, especially at this crucial time in the transformation of consciousness on this planet. Now more than ever, the world needs every human to give away their gift.

Not sure what your gifts are? Tap into me.

The gateway to your gifts,
YOUR INNER PILOT LIGHT

321

Dearest Beloved,

In order to build intimacy, you must have trust. But in order to trust someone, you must take a risk.

When you allow yourself to be vulnerable, and someone holds your vulnerable confession in the sacredness of the trust vault, a magical connection occurs. Trust grows. You get closer. Your heart expands, and a portal to the plane of love opens between you.

Then you get braver, and you're willing to take another risk.

When you risk vulnerability and it isn't held safely, your vulnerable parts feel immense pain and your protective parts naturally jump to attention. The pain of the betrayal can cause you to shut down, to stop risking, to lose the nerve to keep opening your heart. This can be an appropriate reaction. Of course, you'll be tempted to guard your heart with this person again. Betrayal stings. You can thank your protective parts for trying to keep you safe.

But don't let one person's betrayal destroy your ability to trust others.

How can you navigate this fine balance between opening your heart and protecting yourself from repetitive betrayal?

Tune in to me. I'll help keep you safe more effectively than any of your protective parts will.

If you pay close attention, you'll realize that with each betrayal, you can check in with me and do the autopsy on what happened, so you can learn from the experience. This way, your powers of discernment grow. You'll learn how to discern who you can trust and when it's appropriate to open up. You'll learn to feel into when it's best to keep your deepest secrets close to your heart and when it's time to spill the beans.

Sometimes love opens. Sometimes love only lets a few safe people close. Come to me if you can't tell the difference.

The perfect filter,
YOUR INNER PILOT LIGHT

322

Mighty One,

You awe me with your strength.

What you've endured—and how you do it with such finesse and grace—is worthy of a huge round of applause.

Can you hear the mighty round of applause from me and all the angels in the whole universe? (*The crowd roars.*)

Your determination, your resilience, your courage—I mean, seriously, darling—*wow*.

So please, honey, don't be so hard on yourself. What you've accomplished in this life so far is *already* enough. If this is all you ever achieve, you'll get a standing ovation when this human life thingy is over.

Not sure you believe me? Tune in. Let me tell you right now what I *really* feel.

Wildly cheering from the audience,
YOUR INNER PILOT LIGHT

323

Dear One,

It's a fine line between enjoying the ordinary, mundane details of your daily life and striving for experiences that thrust you out of your comfort zone and into the wild risk of what lies just beyond the ordinary.

How can you enjoy both equally?

Appreciate what is happening right now.

In this moment, you can feel radically alive, whether you're in or out of your comfort zone, on the precipice, about to leap out of a plane or at your desk, noticing the breeze wafting in through the window and ruffling curtains with the scent of rosemary lingering on the breath of coolness that comes with fall . . .

When someone is diagnosed with cancer or survives a near-death experience, the first thing most notice is how grateful they are for the mundane moments—the intimate experience of putting a child to bed or chopping veggies in the kitchen with your loved ones. When you're tuned in to the appreciation of how lucky you are to be alive *right now*, I light up.

I'm not suggesting that "Be here now" is always the appropriate medicine in my spiritual medicine bag or that you won't feel pain if you stay present in the now. When you find out a loved one died, you experience an injury. When the love of your life betrays you, it's going to hurt, even in this present moment. If you're set up to believe that being present in the now means you'll avoid feeling human pain, you'll be disappointed. And if you try to bypass human pain, you'll also miss out on the richness, vitality, and joy of feeling the full range of the human experience all the way in your heart, your gut, and your bones.

What can help you optimize this spiritual tool is realizing that life is happening in this present moment, and if you're fully immersed in whatever life is offering you—wild adventure, mundane chores, or painful growth—you are truly alive right here, right now.

Oh yeah, baby. Now you feel it.

Blazing,
YOUR INNER PILOT LIGHT

324

My Star Student,

When you reflect back on your life, you can probably identify some life-disrupting doozies that seemed like senseless tragedies, abject failures, or wild mistakes at the time.

Yet when you look backward at your life through a "retrospectoscope," you can see exactly how your soul needed to stumble in order to learn what it's here on this Earth to learn in this challenging but stimulating Earth School.

It's harder to see the mighty wisdom of the Organizing Intelligence when you're looking forward in your life. Tech pioneer Steve Jobs said, "You can't connect the dots looking forward; you can only connect them looking backward. So you have to trust that the dots will somehow connect in your future."

While this may be true sometimes, I always have the skinny on how something that feels painful will wind up being a blessing. Even in the moment of the painful event, if you tune in to me, I can give you insight.

Through my insight, you may even be able to see *right now* how this painful thing will bless you later, and this healing awareness can comfort all your resistant parts, helping you accept what's happening. You might even find you can feel grateful.

Thanking you for this gift of love,
YOUR INNER PILOT LIGHT

325

Brave Heart,

True intimacy feels crazy vulnerable, doesn't it? Dissolving the armor that separates you from the fullness of another being can feel risky, even threatening.

No wonder! Intimacy can drop you to your knees. Intimacy can make you vulnerable to a broken heart. Intimacy can leave you disappointed or furious or wallowing in agony. Heartbreak can crush you, if you let it. But what's the alternative? Closing your heart? Shutting out love? Building walls that cut you off from intimacy? Choosing fear instead?

Nope. I know you, precious. You know better.

You know that daring to be available to true intimacy makes you open to pain, but it can also fly you to the moon. It can open the floodgates to a waterfall of bliss. Real intimacy can make you giddy and leave you feeling radically alive. Intimacy improves your health and connects you, not just to other people but to *me*, your portal to connection to Source.

Intimacy lights me up, dissolving the stories of separation and giving you a direct experience of how close we really are, wounds to wounds, and Inner Pilot Light to Inner Pilot Light.

Yes, it's risky to open to intimacy, and it's wise to be discerning about where you dare to do so.

How will you know when it's wise to choose intimacy?

That's where I come in. When you're intimate with me, you can always trust that I'll let you know.

Choosing love,
YOUR INNER PILOT LIGHT

326

Precious One,

You have so many adorable questions. I just want to hug you when I feel how uncomfortable you are with not knowing.

The questions . . . they're endless!

Where should I live?

What is my calling?

Why am I here?

Where is my soul tribe?

How can my gifts be received?

Where can I find love?

Where can I give all my love?

Is there a God?

How does the Universe work?

How can I make all my dreams come true?

I know you worry that some of these questions will never have answers, but let me break it to you gently: honestly, sweetheart, some of these questions *are not meant to be answered*.

How would you ever learn humility if you were one great big know-it-all? How would you feel if I told you that being curious and asking good questions is a practice that lights me up, but nailing down all the answers is less important than the practice of inquiry?

Here's all you really need to know, my sweet.

You will be shown what you need to know on a need-to-know basis.

How?

Ask for help. Then listen up. I'll be there with just enough answers to get you to the next awesome question.

??????,

YOUR INNER PILOT LIGHT

327

My Dear,

I know you still struggle with limiting beliefs, self-sabotaging behaviors, and negative patterns you acquired in your childhood, when you learned to do whatever you felt it took to gain the love of your parents, your extended family, your teachers, and your friends.

Let these patterns make themselves known through the insights I'll offer you. See what I show you with clarity and curiosity. Resist the urge to judge what you see or blame those who conditioned you this way. Know that those who participated in conditioning you with toxic patterns are simply passing on what they inherited.

The good news is that you can be the one who interrupts this generational wounding. You can decide that the pattern stops here. In doing so, you offer yourself in service to helping humanity evolve.

Generational wounds get passed down, until someone like *you* taps into a pilot light like *me*, and together we begin to lift the vibration of the whole shebang.

Illuminate.

Grow your awareness.

Forgive.

Release.

Clear trauma.

Rise from the ashes.

Find your compassion.

Break the chain.

Pass on the new vibration.

Do it again.

The key to generational healing,
YOUR INNER PILOT LIGHT

328

Beloved,

You know how sometimes you feel inferior to others, and other times you feel superior? Sometimes you judge yourself as "less than," finding yourself lacking and feeling like you want to go eat worms. Other times, you see yourself as "better than," getting self-righteous and "holier than thou."

This is such a naturally adorable human tendency, my love. But there's another way to live that feels much yummier.

When you feel separate from others, separate from nature, separate from the cosmos, separate from me, separate from Source, you'll naturally try to assess your place in the hierarchy of things. But when you tune in to me, I can help you remember that humans are all cells in one cosmic body, and one cell cannot be better than or lesser than another.

Sure, from one limited point of view, you are in a separate body, having a separate experience, living in a realm of duality where it's easy to forget your interconnectedness. It's true that if you jump in front of a train, the consciousness you call "You" may go nonphysical, while the consciousness you call your mother or sister or spouse may not. But the aftermath of the loss of you in a body still ripples out and affects the cosmic body at large.

Through my magical star glasses, you'll see that, deep in your roots, you are like an aspen grove—appearing as one tree but dependent on all others for your very beingness.

Everything changes when you tune in to this consciousness. Suddenly you see all humans as adorable children learning how to love—some with more maturity, some with less—all just trying to come back home for a love reunion.

Can't find a way to see the world this way? Tune in to me. I'll help.

Gushing with love for you all,
YOUR INNER PILOT LIGHT

329

Dearest Darling,

Do me a favor. Pretty please banish the word *impossible* from your vocabulary.

> It's possible the "incurable" illness will miraculously disappear.
>
> It's possible you'll make a million dollars this year.
>
> It's possible that your love life will suddenly burst into burning hot FLAME!
>
> It's possible you'll find it within you to forgive that "unforgivable" person.
>
> It's possible that person who holds the key to your big dream will finally call.

But that's not all.

> It's possible global warming can be reversed.

It's possible we can stop the extinction of endangered animals.

It's possible world hunger will end.

It's possible there will be no more war.

It's possible we will experience Earth-healing within our lifetime.

But this can only happen if you do the "impossible" and tap into me.

Drunk on possibility,
YOUR INNER PILOT LIGHT

330

Sweetheart,

You might think that successful relationships must last until you're both eighty-five and in your rocking chairs, and that if they don't, somebody screwed up.

But what if, with some people, our souls have made an agreement to walk side by side for a period of time, and then one individual needs to veer left in order to stay in divine alignment, while the other needs to veer right?

What if you can bless that person when you come to the crossroads and wish them well on the path, without making anybody wrong? What if a relationship can end amicably, and you can bow to each other, free each other to go your separate ways, and celebrate the relationship as a wild success?

Just sayin' . . .
YOUR INNER PILOT LIGHT

331

Spark Plug,

Pay attention to things that raise your vibration and light me up!

Dance? Nature? Intimate conversations with trustworthy friends? Classical music?

Veggies and green juice? Orgasms? Gathering in spiritual community? Snuggles? Sleep? Creative expression? Raw chocolate? Playing with animals? Soaking in a hot bath?

Now pay attention to things that lower your vibration and dim me.

Road rage? Gossip? Burnout? Board meetings? Too much alcohol? Video games? Cheetos? Complaining? Righteousness? Porn? Small talk? Overtime? Exhaustion? Mindlessly surfing the Internet? Criticizing others? Criticizing yourself?

Get honest with yourself. Don't demonize yourself for choosing to do what lowers your vibration. That only feeds the fuel of those allures!

Just get curious with me, so you're aware of your choices.

What lights me up? What dims my light?

Ready for a bonfire,
YOUR INNER PILOT LIGHT

332

My Darling,

The next time someone you love is feeling a painful emotion, see if you can resist the temptation to jump into rescuer mode. Instead, try holding space, like I do with you.

What does it mean to hold space? Start by reminding someone that you are holding the vision of their wholeness, in case they've forgotten.

Trust that everyone has an Inner Pilot Light that will know how to offer guidance, support, and comfort better than you can. Lend your strength so they can find their own.

Do what you can to help someone feel safe. When the nervous system is activated, it's hard for humans to access their Inner Pilot Lights. But when someone offers love and a sense of safety, innate wisdom bubbles up naturally from the light that lives inside every being.

Don't flood someone with too much information, too many book recommendations, too many spiritual teachings or tools. You'll only overwhelm someone who is already feeling pain. Instead, be with what they're feeling without interfering with their process.

Notice the part of you that gets a hit off being the rescuer, but make sure you befriend rather than demonize this part. Recognize that when you rescue, you disempower the very person you're trying to help. Operating from pity or guilt or a feeling that someone is weaker than you are does not help; it only robs someone of their strength. Rather than stealing their power to amplify your own, be with their experience in a pure way that activates their power.

Remember that everyone is entitled to their own journey, and sometimes that means people have to make their own mistakes. Don't make it about you! Resist the temptation to try to protect someone from a painful experience you have had. Let them have their own experience. All humans are prone to making mistakes, but how else do you learn? Allow for the natural unique flavors that make humans different. Recognize that different people have different needs when they're acutely triggered. Show someone you love them *no matter what*.

Acknowledge that seemingly conflicting emotions can coexist. Make all emotions okay.

Recognize that if someone is grieving, they need both containment and letting go. When you hold space, you can offer the containment so someone else can let go.

Not sure how to best hold space for someone you love?

Ask me to handle it.

I'm a pro,

YOUR INNER PILOT LIGHT

333

Adorable Beloved,

I know some days you feel a little sluggish, like you can't quite get moving and your ambition disappeared along with your get-up-and-go.

You procrastinate.

Nothing gets done.

Your to-do list is embarrassingly undone at the end of the day.

But have you ever considered that sometimes the very thing you need to do in order to get my fire lit is to rest?

Or maybe you just need to play!

What if you need both? Rest until it's time to play. Then play until it's time to rest.

What if it's possible to live a life that allows you to say no to anything on your to-do list that doesn't feel like resting or playing? What if you can transform your relationship with things to do so that you approach even the most mundane tasks with the playfulness of a happy child? What if that same happy child needs naps sometimes?

Don't believe that's possible?

I do,

YOUR INNER PILOT LIGHT

334

My Love,

I know you're still grieving a great loss.

I know it's tempting to ignore the sadness, to numb the pain, to distract yourself with busyness, to skip the grieving process.

But be brave, precious. Jump in. Wallow. Cry. Purge. *Feel.*

Wail like a child who just lost her puppy. Go there. Stay there for a while. Dive deep. Surrender to sadness. Call a dear friend and ask your friend to simply be with you while you feel what you must.

You know how you're so afraid you'll get lost in a black hole of grief with no lifeline? If you're brave enough to avoid resisting that thing you're afraid to feel, you'll find that all the way in the void of that grief . . . all you'll find . . .

Is LOVE.

Yup. That's what you're so afraid to jump into, my precious!

It only hurts so much because you loved so much. Keep the love and let the pain wash itself away.

Come to me . . .

Full of love in the luminous void,
YOUR INNER PILOT LIGHT

335

Still One,

When you're trying to decide who to spend time with, ask yourself, "Does this person cultivate the stillness in me?"

Sometimes you're attracted to charismatic people who get you all hyped up and stimulated, as if you're buzzing with caffeine. Yet this isn't stillness. It's mania! Do you really want to surround yourself with the people who make you manic?

If all you feel is chaos, frenetic energy, anxiety, fear, or hype, resist the urge to lean in.

If all you project is chaos, frenetic energy, anxiety, fear, or hype, don't be surprised if that's what you attract.

Learn to recognize the difference between a stress-response-induced adrenaline rush and the calm, grounded quiet that typifies a healthy relaxation response in your nervous system.

Find your stillness. Allow yourself to be drawn to the stillness in others. Give yourself full permission to prioritize choosing those who cultivate the stillness in you.

Not sure who cultivates the stillness?

Always your still point,
YOUR INNER PILOT LIGHT

336

My Love,

Be wary of any spiritual teacher who promises that everything you desire is within your reach via the "law of attraction."

According to many New Age teachings, all you have to do is visualize, affirm, align your energy, remove your blocks, and—*presto!*—you'll get everything you want, whether it's a million dollars, the hot man of your dreams, a cure for cancer, or the promotion you've been jonesing for.

When you first got exposed to the law of attraction, you may have found it empowering! Of course it's empowering when you discover that you're not a victim of a hostile Universe, that you're powerful beyond measure and can participate in the co-creation of your reality, whether it's healing yourself from illness, calling in the love of your life, or manifesting a successful career.

However, there's a dark shadow to this kind of teaching that suggests that if you're not manifesting everything you want, you're not practicing the law of attraction skillfully enough or that you're somehow spiritually inferior and if only you were more enlightened, you'd get everything you think you want.

While manifestation is a known *siddhi* (a spiritual superpower in the yogic tradition), it's a gift, not a law, and it can be co-opted to feed the hungry ghost of endless and insatiable desire. The law of attraction suggests that if only you do it right, you can visualize a Ferrari and somehow, magically, a Ferrari will end up in your driveway.

But Divine Will doesn't work that way, my darling. It's wonderful to learn that you have spiritual power and can participate in co-creating your reality. But when you move to the next phase of spiritual development and realize that even if you could manifest every desire on your infinite shopping list, you still wouldn't necessarily feel fulfilled, you begin to long for a deeper level of surrender. Your prayer moves from "Help me get everything I want" to "Help me sincerely desire that which serves the highest good for me, others, and the planet."

Need help manifesting some of my holy ideas?

Ready and willing,

YOUR INNER PILOT LIGHT

337

My Gorgeous, Precious, Darling, Radiant Sparkle-Doo!

I know sometimes I can be hard on you, not because I don't always adore you, but because it's so hard for me to see you walking around blind to the ways in which you sometimes create your own suffering.

But today I'm not going to illuminate any blind spots.

Today I'm just here to celebrate you. So put on your party clothes. Give yourself a hug. Toast yourself with a glass of green juice or wine or iced coffee or frozen lemonade. Let's count the ways that you are a perfect slice of Divinity with the most adorable personality and the world's prettiest eyes.

Just in case you forgot, you're precious. You're whip-smart. You're super creative. Your heart is planet-sized. You're super-duper awesome. The angels dance when you walk by. And damn, you're sexy.

It touches me how brave you are, diving into the deep end and doing what you must to heal your trauma so you can let my light shine brighter. It lights me up how you keep taking risks, opening yourself to more and more intimacy, daring to try out some of my often scary instructions, and committing yourself to the mission you are here to fulfill on this planet.

I'm constantly in awe of how radiant you are when you dare to see others through my magical eyes, lighting them up and leaving them smiling.

Oh . . . and in case I forget to tell you, your breath smells good. (I'm totally sincere, darling. You have no idea how I swoon when you breathe in, breathe out . . .)

Three cheers for *you*!

YOUR INNER PILOT LIGHT

338

Yearning One,

Sometimes the longings of your heart feel crazy, don't they?

You wonder how you can possibly trust desires that are so outlandish, impractical, out of control, fickle, and passion-laden. You think that if you dare to chase the butterflies your heart frolics after, you'll ditch all your adult responsibilities and wind up broke, broken, alone, and scratching your head wondering why you ever dared to follow your reckless heart.

Yet what can you trust more than the wild stirrings of your adorable heart?

Stay there, with your heart wide open.

Let your heart handle the wild imaginings of unrestrained desire. Trust me to handle the rest.

From the heart,
YOUR INNER PILOT LIGHT

339

My Love,

I know you sometimes feel lonely. Even when you're surrounded by people, you may feel separate, different, isolated, and disconnected. Sometimes your loneliest moments happen when you're flanked by people who aren't vibrating at the same frequency you are. Although you're not alone, you feel like nobody gets you.

That's why I'm here, darling. With me inside of you, *you are never alone*. You can come to me *anytime*, and I will resonate with you, wherever you are, however you feel, at whatever frequency you're vibrating.

When you let me fortify you in those moments, you will automatically start attracting others who vibrate at the same frequency as you, and across a crowded room someone will feel you. Your magical eyes will meet and beckon to each other—"I know you"—even if you've never met.

Try it next time you feel alone.

Let me be your wing man,

YOUR INNER PILOT LIGHT

340

Dear One,

Have you ever been on the receiving end of spiritual teachings that insist that your ego is something to demonize, something that gets in the way of enlightenment, something you need to overcome?

How do you think your inner child parts feel when they hear this?

Imagine this: An orphaned child stands in front of a crowd of spiritual seekers, approaches the guru through tears, and, given the trauma the child has endured, takes the vulnerable risk to trust the guru and ask for help. The guru, with a furrowed brow, turns stony cold, points a finger at the child, and says, "The ego is a beast. You need to kill it. Do more spiritual practice."

Ouch.

You wouldn't advocate behaving like this to a little orphan, so why would you treat your inner child parts this way?

What if the ego is not a monster you need to kill but a wounded child you need to love? What if exiling the imperfect, hurting, or protective parts of the ego doesn't deepen spiritual growth? What if it only makes these natural human parts more stubborn, as they double down to exert their influence in their valiant attempts to keep you safe?

The guru's response may sound brutal, but it opens your heart and evokes compassion when you realize that the guru is himself an exiled orphan whose trauma obviously got triggered by this little one. In his trigger, he is simply telling the child what was told to him.

What if spiritual growth doesn't need a brutal guru bullying your wounded parts? What if real illumination actually begins when you open yourself to radical self-compassion and acceptance of all your wounded parts so I can swoop in and take the wheel?

Not sure how to love this big?

Thank goodness you've got me,
YOUR INNER PILOT LIGHT

341

Precious Darling,

I notice how you hold back sometimes, as if you don't deserve to take up as much space as you'd like. I notice how you shrink when you feel ready to expand.

I also notice how you sometimes take up more than your fair share of the space when you feel insecure and need attention.

Here's where I can help out. Call on me to comfort you when you feel the need to shrink or inflate. You can also call on me to help you assess the most illuminated intensity of how brightly to shine.

Sometimes it's appropriate to have all eyes on you when it's your turn to fill an arena with your presence.

Other times the most enlightened way to shine my light is to draw me all the way in—the way shamans do, activating a superpower that makes them nearly invisible—so someone else has a chance to take up the whole room.

Not sure when to burn outwardly and when to draw my energy internally?

Always on speed dial,

YOUR INNER PILOT LIGHT

342

My Dear Daredevil,

I have a dare for you. Pick one thing on your bucket list. Start off easy and choose something you're sure you can make happen.

Now close your eyes. Check in with me. Let me help you make sure this is really aligned with what's in your highest good.

Once you sense that it is, go ahead and pull out your calendar. Give yourself a deadline. Write it in red ink.

Now take a deep breath. Set the intention. Promise yourself you'll seal the deal.

Make the call. Call in the money. Enlist a partner-in-play. Make room in your schedule for it. Do the deed. Be true to yourself and your desires.

You don't have forever on this planet, darling. Let's make sure you leave this life with no song left unsung.

Busting into song and dance,
YOUR INNER PILOT LIGHT

343

My Darling,

Do you still find yourself practicing "spiritual bypassing"? Do you tend to turn away from what hurts and mask it with spirituality or positive psychology? Not sure what I mean?

Psychologist and spiritual teacher Robert Augustus Masters describes it like this: "Aspects of spiritual bypassing include exaggerated detachment, emotional numbing and repression, overemphasis on the positive, anger-phobia, blind or overly tolerant compassion, weak or too porous boundaries, lopsided development (cognitive intelligence often being far ahead of emotional and moral intelligence), debilitating judgment about one's negativity or shadow elements, devaluation of the personal relative to the spiritual, and delusions of having arrived at a higher level of being."

Keep in mind that it hurts to be human, and pain is always here for a reason. Pain is usually your body's or your heart's way of saying, "Pay Attention Inside Now." When something hurts, something is out of whack or needs to be healed. When you use conflict avoidance in holy drag to turn away from pain, you limit the growth I know you crave.

Check with me and see if you use your spirituality to turn away from the very pain that needs your attention. Don't be afraid to lean in because I will be here with you, holding your hand and keeping you safe as you let what needs to be revealed show itself lovingly and gently.

See anything?

I'm here, beloved. We've got this.

With clear seeing,
YOUR INNER PILOT LIGHT

344

Light of My Life,

Do you ever wonder whether people love you just because you're good-looking or well-behaved or wealthy or talented or generous or charismatic or helpful or funny or . . . whatever?

I just want you to know that, while all those parts impress the hell outta me, and while I adore you when you're looking good, feeling generous, showing off your talents, radiating your intelligence, helping others, or lighting up the room with your wicked sense of humor, I love you most because of who you are when *all that is stripped away*.

I don't love you because you're amazing. I don't love you because you're not amazing.

I just love you. Period.

For all the right reasons,
YOUR INNER PILOT LIGHT

345

Dear One,

Need faith that all is happening in divine timing?

Let me be your trust, even when you're struggling to keep the faith.

Need guidance when you've lost your way?

Let me be your cosmic GPS.

Need great arms of love to comfort you when your fearful parts start feeling threatened?

Let me be your hug.

Need reassurance when you're feeling blue?

Dearest, I am your biggest cheerleader.

Need hope when hope eludes you?

Let me be your font of optimism.

Need healing when your body, mind, or soul feels wounded?

Let me be your medicine.

Need to laugh?

I never run out of jokes.

Need comfort when you're lonely?

I am your eternal BFF. I love you, and I will never let you down.

Here with whatever you need,
YOUR INNER PILOT LIGHT

346

Dearest Heart,

To feel truly whole, every being has to embrace both the Divine Masculine and the Divine Feminine, yet most are unbalanced one way or the other.

Some are too fluid, going with the flow, letting what comes come, scattering chaotic ideas like a room full of ping-pong balls with no walls, but lacking focus, follow-through, solidity, grounding, and inspired action steps that can make something happen.

Others are good at lists, focusing, strategic planning, pushing, striving, and making it happen, but not so gifted at allowing, receiving, going with the flow, and allowing synchronicity to work its magic.

Fortunately I am your balance.

Need more feminine energy? Need more masculine power?

Call on me . . .

The ultimate yin-yang,

YOUR INNER PILOT LIGHT

347

My Sensitive One,

I know the collective heart is breaking right now, and you feel it, as do many others. The heartbreak is right there, in your One heart, which is connected to all the other hearts out there, to all of Mother Earth's creatures and plants, to the oceans, the mountains, the streams, and all of the biosphere. When your One heart breaks, all hearts feel it.

How can you become more emotionally resilient so you can navigate all this heartbreak and keep feeling the joy that emanates from me as I light up?

Practice surrender. When you resist life, you are vulnerable to the slings and arrows of what is happening outside yourself. When you trust life, it's easier to deal with whatever arises. Surrendering to life doesn't mean I won't tell you to pick up a protest sign! But if I do, it'll be with a calm, holy heart, guided by being a compassionate protector of the vulnerable.

Set and maintain healthy psychic boundaries. Get clear on what pain is yours and what is collective. Yes, we're all One, so you feel collective pain personally, but if you can't handle the amount of pain you're feeling right now, you can choose to boundary yourself against feeling all the collective pain. Make it clear with your intention that you need a break from the collective psychic pain. Allow yourself to keep feeling compassion for what hurts in others while also overdosing on joy, pleasure, and gratitude as an antidote to unbearable pain.

Surround yourself with people who uplift you and relax your nervous system.

Be aware of what you need in order to get by. If you're not sure what will help, ask me, "What do I need right now?" Then be brave enough to listen up and ask for what you need in a healthy, nondemanding way.

Come into right relationship with uncertainty. Meditation and contemplative prayer can help. If you lean into the pain that often accompanies uncertainty and the feelings of helplessness that may arise, the pain tends to ease off. When it flares up, soften into the pain. Let it move through you like a contraction. Ask someone to hold you if it helps.

Need someone always on call to hold you when it hurts?

My stat pager is turned on,

YOUR INNER PILOT LIGHT

348

Dear One,

When you can't decide, it's okay to wait.

Sometimes you get so worked up about the discomfort you feel when you're indecisive that you feel pressured to make a decision you're not yet ready to make.

Do you feel confused about a decision you're trying to make? If so, try tapping into me.

Maybe you've already made your decision, but you're in denial because your decision commands uncomfortable change and requires you to enter the land of uncertainty. If so, that's okay.

Maybe you're letting a fearful part keep you from acting upon your decision. That's okay too.

Maybe you're not in denial and you're not blending with a fearful part, but you still genuinely don't know what to do.

That's okay. *Wait.*

As singer-songwriter Karen Drucker sings in "Gentle with Myself," "I will only go as fast as the slowest part of me feels free to go."

Need help deciding? Need help loving the slowest part of you? Need help mustering up the moxie to take action when it's time?

I'm always here.

With faith that you'll be okay,
no matter what you decide,
YOUR INNER PILOT LIGHT

349

My Darling,

If ever you feel like you're the only person on this planet to ever face the struggle you're facing right now, take a step back.

Yeah, *way* back.

Keep backing up, darling, so far that you're way out in outer space, looking at the billions of bits of brilliance of all the other Inner Pilot Lights around you.

Notice how we all light up the planet in one interconnected web of woven stardust luminescence.

You are not alone.

Now come back. Closer.

Closer.

Look around.

What you feel, we all feel. Your loss, your grief, your anger, your feelings of betrayal, your disappointment, your fear . . . everyone else has felt *just like you*. Your joy, your ecstasy, your bliss, your excitement, your inner peace . . . all this is part of the human experience too. It's so easy to get lost in your own stories, to feel singled out and different, to feel isolated and disconnected, to take your stories so personally—because they *do* feel personal and through one lens they *are* personal—but they're also everyone's stories, binding you into an infinite web of transpersonal connectedness.

You are not alone. We are all in this together.

In wondrous awe,

YOUR INNER PILOT LIGHT

350

My Love,

I know it hurts to be around other people who aren't in touch with their Inner Pilot Lights. I know you feel sad, lonely, disappointed, and betrayed sometimes.

You know, my love, you can't change how everyone else behaves with you, because—*news flash—everyone is entitled to their own journey*.

But you *can* change how *you* respond. And you can choose who you let inside your inner circle.

> Ask what part you play in that difficult relationship dynamic you're struggling with.
>
> Ask how you might change not the other person but *yourself* and your response to the situation.
>
> Ask how you let yourself wind up vulnerable to something that doesn't feel right to you.
>
> Ask where you violated, betrayed, and disappointed yourself.

Then be extra kind to yourself, because beating yourself up is no more enlightened than beating up someone else.

> Ask me if you need to distance yourself from someone who isn't mature enough to treat you well.
>
> Ask me if you're being discerning enough about whom you choose to let close.
>
> Ask me if you have unmet needs you're not expressing, which are making you vulnerable to choosing relationships that don't uplift you.

If talking about this leaves you feeling tender, let me wrap my loving, nurturing arms around you, because I so love holding you close to my heart.

Free hugs,
YOUR INNER PILOT LIGHT

351

Sweetheart,

Next time you're at the grocery store or getting your driver's license or standing in the security line at the airport, look around you and marvel at the diversity.

Isn't it awesome that humans can look so different, sound so different, think so differently, pray so differently—and you can revel in the differences rather than be afraid of them, judge them, or need them to be more like you?

If you're having trouble appreciating the diversity, look into the eyes of those you might consider "others." You may just see the "other" person's Inner Pilot Light, and I will recognize that clear flame, and their Inner Pilot Light just might recognize me. Then . . . *voila!* Fireworks!

The great equalizer,
YOUR INNER PILOT LIGHT

352

Dear One,

Next time someone pisses you off, try this: Pay attention not to what that person is saying or doing but to the cry for help screaming underneath the surface. See if you can feel the wound, perhaps arising from the hurt inner child within that human.

> Is she lonely?
>
> Does he lack confidence?
>
> Is she jealous because she questions her own worth?
>
> Is he worried you'll withdraw your love?
>
> Is she threatened when you shine your sparkly, radiant light?
>
> Do you remind him of his mother, who always lashed out when he just wanted love?
>
> Does she feel insecure around you?
>
> Is he feeling uncomfortably vulnerable?
>
> Is he frightened by what he can't predict, control, or manipulate?

Take a deep breath, then pry underneath the surface, open your heart, and let yourself soften.

Instead of lashing out, how might you grant that person grace instead?

Don't trust yourself to behave this way?

Ask for my help.

I'm always infinitely compassionate, but I'll also protect you with my discernment and my clear boundaries.

Full of love,
YOUR INNER PILOT LIGHT

353

My Dear,

The world is full of people trying to change the things they can't, and not trying to change the things they can.

But you don't need to be one of them.

Give this a try, darling: Feel what you feel. Don't skip feeling frustrated or disappointed or scared or angry. But once you've let those emotions move, let me help you change the things you can. Let me help you let go of trying to change the things you can't.

If there's something you need to do, I'll guide you. If there's nothing to be done, I'll help you make peace with what is.

When you let me help you change the things you can and accept the things you can't, you create space in your life for more joy, more expansiveness, less stress, and less resentment.

Then . . . before you know it, miracles happen.

Here to help you change what you can,
YOUR INNER PILOT LIGHT

354

Dear One,

If you ever feel insufficiently loved, seek out not just those who will love you but also those you can love. The people hungry for your love are all around you. Go to the grocery store and see if anyone looks love deficient. Look around at the subway stop. Go to a church or temple or mosque and check out the back row. Volunteer at a hospital or orphanage or homeless shelter or animal shelter.

Find someone online who you sense might be in need of your love. Offer your attention and kindness as a gift, with no expectation of love in return. Be willing to let your love land flat if someone is unable to receive it, understanding that their lack of receptivity is most likely not a rejection of you but rather an inability to receive love, usually stemming from trauma and the resultant deep underlying sense of unworthiness.

Be willing to have your love embraced. Be willing to make someone's day. Be willing to hear laughter and see upturned smiles. Be willing to see tears and feel tears on your own face, because every single human craves love and belonging, and way too many are feeling love deficient.

When you seek to give love instead of complaining about how you're not getting loved up enough, a miracle happens. The energy of giving love is like a boomerang. Love rockets out of you, and then love comes bursting right back into your own heart. As the one opening your heart to give love, you are the lucky one.

If you long to feel loved, I dare you to try giving it. Then report back. What happened?

With eternal love,

YOUR INNER PILOT LIGHT

355

Beautiful Dear,

Do you realize how worthy you are of having needs and getting them met? Do you know how to cultivate awareness of your needs and get them met in a healthy way?

Let me give you some guidance, my love.

To express your needs feels vulnerable, so it's important to develop trust with those who will help you get your needs met. True intimacy requires both vulnerability and safety. Vulnerability without safety is a recipe for trauma. If you're opening yourself to someone who cannot hold your vulnerability with compassion, you have come face-to-face with a masochistic part in you. If you are repetitively refusing to meet the needs of someone you love when they are lying before you, naked and vulnerable, you are becoming intimate with a sadistic part.

Be gentle. Don't demonize these masochistic or sadistic parts. Just let me love them with you . . .

Be clear that if someone expresses a need to you, their need is not a criticism of you! It is simply an expression of need, desire, vulnerability, and the natural interdependency of human beings. It may sound like you're being blamed for their unmet need, but if you look beneath the charge you'll see what's really being expressed. Be aware of this tendency within yourself too. If your needs aren't being met and you wait too long to ask for what you need, you may lash out with the burden of resentment, anger, and frustration clouding your clear request.

I can help you make peace with human neediness. Realize that as long as you don't let yourself be needy, you cannot truly support someone else who is in need. (I know you might think you can but trust me . . . not *really*.) No matter how much you try to demonstrate loving behavior with others, if you are in denial of your own vulnerability and neediness, if you judge your needs as weaknesses and reject or exile those parts of yourself, then you will be unable to show up with true compassion for others when they need you. So if you're not motivated to get your needs met for self-loving reasons, do it for those you care about.

Sure, you can come to me first to help you get your needs met. But some needs require other humans. Let me help you find the humans who can help.

Always attuned to your beautiful, precious needs,
YOUR INNER PILOT LIGHT

356

Dearest Beloved,

Life is full of curveballs. So what can you do when one of them gets lobbed your way?

Don't be afraid to reschedule or cancel things. The culture teaches you to "force function," as if strong people power through such curveballs without missing a beat, as if it's a weakness to claim your right to make space for crises when they inevitably arise. You don't realize that people who have the mother lode of my strength behind them take the space they need to deal with what arises in a healthy way.

Get clear about what calms your nervous system and what doesn't. Be proactive about doing the things that calm you and, whenever possible, avoid the things that don't.

Take the time to digest and integrate the curveball. Meditation is important because we must take the time to digest, "Wow, that happened."

Instead of allowing the mind to go nuts as it tries to figure out how to control this curveball, trust that I've got you and I'll help you get through this. If there is something you need to do, I'll make it clear to you. So your mind can relax . . .

Feel what you feel. Move your body. Laugh your booty off. Sleep extra. Make love. Ask for lots of snuggles. Practice radical self-care—without apology. Create beauty. Find someone who knows how to hold space. Rest there.

And don't forget about me.

Always here with a catcher's mitt,
YOUR INNER PILOT LIGHT

357

Dear One,

I have good news and bad news.

However you're feeling right now, this too shall pass.

In fact, if you let yourself purely feel the emotion without complicating it with language, whatever you feel will most likely end in about ninety seconds.

> If you're sad, it's fleeting. (Phew!)
>
> If you're blissed out, it won't last either. (Bummer.)
>
> If you're enraged, it will move through you. (Grrrrr.)
>
> If you're bursting with obsessively romantic fervor, the crush will fade. (Sigh . . .)

Find comfort in this, darling. States are fleeting, but it's possible to have a deeper level of joy that is not dependent on transient states. When you're not grasping for feelings you like and resisting feelings you don't like, you're more likely to find gratitude in the moment for whatever experience of human emotion you're blessed to feel *right now*.

Don't like how you feel in this present moment?

Don't worry. I'm here with you every ninety seconds.

Nothing lasts but me,
YOUR INNER PILOT LIGHT

358

Great One,

Sometimes it can be hard to hold your ground when others are trying to sway you. But trust yourself. Don't let yourself get hooked or manipulated. Don't borrow anyone else's fearful parts. Trust me instead.

So many others are projecting their fears onto you. Their fears show up in the disguise of "advice" or "protection," but I know better. I can comfort your fearful parts, and you don't need to take responsibility for the fearful parts of others. As long as you let me take the lead, I'll help you swim deliciously in the love, peace, calmness, fulfillment, and faith that is your birthright. Even your fearful parts will want to come along for the joyride.

Sure, you can seek guidance from the select few you trust, the ones who have enough of a relationship with their Inner Pilot Light to offer you trustworthy feedback.

But in the end, let me filter everyone else's advice through the wisdom of my luminous truth meter.

Your best guidance,
YOUR INNER PILOT LIGHT

359

My Sweet,

Why do you judge yourself when you feel tired?

Why do you allow fatigue to turn into a story about how you're not enough?

Have you ever thought that perhaps I speak to you through feelings of exhaustion? Can you see that your fatigue might be a perfectly healthy rebellion against "business as usual," calling you to slow down, take stock, examine your priorities, and make changes that enliven you?

Perhaps you're not hearing my whispers, telling you to slow down. Perhaps fatigue is the spell I slap on you to help you listen to me.

If you're tired today, what do you think I might be telling you?

Listen up. I have a message for you . . .

Here while you nap,
YOUR INNER PILOT LIGHT

360

My Dear Mystic,

When was the last time you felt the wonder and awe of life? When did you last gasp at the beauty and mystery of it all? When was the last time you looked up at the stars and really took in their majestic vastness?

Have you marveled at the crazy magic of how a caterpillar dissolves into bug soup before emerging as a fully formed flight-worthy butterfly? Do you realize that these little creatures don't just sprout wings? They completely surrender to the full disintegration of all that they were in order to become all that they must.

Do you realize you are part of that same magical universe? Do you see that you are as much of a miracle as any marvelous creation on Earth? Do you realize that you have a choice: to see nothing as a miracle or everything as a miracle?

I'm here to help you remember that there is so much more than you can see and understand. There is a mystery to how your life unfolds, but the secrets of the mystery are part of the magic. You don't need to understand or be able to control the mystery in order to trust that the magic is real.

Don't give up five minutes before your miracle.

Abracadabra,

YOUR INNER PILOT LIGHT

361

My Dear Hero,

Brrrrringggg . . .

The phone is ringing, darling.

Pick up. Pick up! It's me, with a Divine Assignment just for you—a way you can be of service in a world that needs your love, a calling just for you that you can choose to accept or reject.

You may be tempted to reject the calling, because it's likely to feel scary and push you out of your comfort zone.

You have free will, so the choice is yours.

But I'm here to tell you that if you're brave enough to accept the call, not only will you be part of the healing of the world but you will also be blessed with a life of mission, service, abundance, love, connection, and an infinitely fulfilling sense of purpose.

You will become a blessing just by being *you*.

Will you muster up your courage, answer the call, and bring the full brilliance of my radiance into the world?

Holding the phone patiently,
YOUR INNER PILOT LIGHT

362

Dearest Lovebug,

I know you've tapped moments of bliss. You've felt the rush of true love or the perfect sunset. You've witnessed the face of a beloved child or tapped into a feeling of divine union. You've achieved a dream. You've listened in rapture to heart-opening music. You've touched the Divine through a piece of art or something you read or the rustle of leaves in a tree.

As French philosopher Pierre Teilhard de Chardin explained, "We are not human beings having a spiritual experience. We are spiritual beings having a human experience." Imagine what humans can experience that angels can't!

The Divine exists in our sensory experience of the world. It's surfing and skiing and hiking and touching your own skin and witnessing the Technicolor of spring.

Drink in these moments of ordinary bliss like precious nectar.

Enjoy heaven on Earth, darling. I will help you view it all with fresh eyes.

With rose-colored glasses,

YOUR INNER PILOT LIGHT

363

Dear One,

Just as the tree celebrates four seasons each year, life for humans goes through cycles too, so you must trust that nature will take its course.

Sometimes it's spring and everything is bursting into jubilant flower! Sometimes it's summer and the warmth of the sun is beating on your suntanned skin. Sometimes it's fall and things start to shed away, falling away like red autumn leaves. Then there are winter seasons, when it's time to rest, to hibernate, to turn inward on short days and long nights, when some things must die in order to make room for new birth the next time spring rolls around.

It's okay to have a preference about which season you like best, my love. You're allowed to like summer better than winter! But don't resist whatever season shows up. You can't fight winter any more than you can grasp hold of spring.

Regardless of the season, I shine all year round, through rain, wind, sleet, snow, sunshine, heat waves, tornados, and hurricanes.

My light might flicker. It might feel brighter some days than others. Like the moon, I may occasionally be eclipsed—but only to the outside eye, because inside of you I always burn brightly, always radiant, never extinguished, ever-present with the sparkle of hope, brilliance, and truth that represents the core of you and all you are becoming.

Seasonless,

YOUR INNER PILOT LIGHT

364

Dearest Starchild,

You may not see us or feel us, but I want you to know that, in this moment and always, you are completely supported, held in great arms of love by an army of Love Warriors. There are many other Inner Pilot Lights in the world, here on a mission to uplift and midwife planet Earth through this difficult birth transition that is underway.

We have come from far away, born of stardust from places of expanded consciousness, planted like star seeds on this beautiful planet to be beacons of light when Mother Gaia needs us most.

If you doubt me, feel into your own heart. Be curious. Wonder why you're here.

Have you always felt a bit different, as if you don't quite fit in with all the others who rape, plunder, and pillage beautiful Mother Earth? Have you always had a soft spot in your heart for the underdogs? Have you always felt the impulse to protect nature? Do you caretake children and elders? Do you yearn for a simpler life, one free from greed, narcissism, materialism, and the story of separation? Do you feel this great longing in your heart for something you can almost remember, this great Oneness where all beings live in harmony and reunion?

Yes, love. I know you feel it. That's because you're one of us. And we are all here to wake each other up, to remember who we are and why we're here. A great number of beings are all converging on this planet right now, on a Divine Assignment, as a mission of love.

You are not alone, my love.

Your star tribe is here, wrapping you in loving arms and lifting you up with moonbows.

The Universe is here, holding you, guiding you, sending you signs so you don't lose your way.

I am here, whispering the truth, reflecting back your beauty and brilliance, always aligned and never betraying you.

Sparkling with stardust,
YOUR INNER PILOT LIGHT

PS: Curious to learn more about your fellow star tribe? Listen to "A Gathering of the Tribe" at InnerPilotLight.com.

365

My Love,

Today is a new beginning, a fresh slate, a clean start, your chance to start anew.

So please, darling, take my hand. Come with me. Let me guide you, this day and always.

With me by your side, we will blaze new trails into unknown places of great delight. We will explore untapped desires and stray into uncertain territory. We will take risks. We will say yes often. We will say no when it's time. We will set boundaries we should have set years ago. We will open doors we're longing to swing free.

We will try new things. We will let go of old things that no longer serve us. We will free ourselves from society's expectations and give ourselves permission to be unapologetically who we really are.

We will be fearless. We will choose love. We will create miracles.

But only if you're ready.

Are you ready, darling?

Will you *be* me? Now is the time . . .

Holding out my hand and ready to merge,
YOUR INNER PILOT LIGHT

Taking Your Inner Pilot Light into the World

You did it! You devoted 365 days to communing with your Inner Pilot Light! So now what? Now, my darling, the journey is just beginning as you continue your relationship with your Inner Pilot Light on your own. If you haven't started doing so already, you are invited to wake up every morning and ask your Inner Pilot Light what it wants you to know. Simply ask, "Dear Inner Pilot Light, what do I need to know today?" Drop your consciousness into your heart and listen to what arises. You can do this as a meditation or as a journal practice. If you need love, comfort, awareness, or a cosmic kick in the patooty, let your Inner Pilot Light illuminate you. This great love affair is just beginning.

You might find that healing the illusion of separation between your Inner Pilot Light and what you consider to be "you" happens quite naturally. Especially if you engage in some sort of meditation practice, prayer, or quiet, reflective time in nature, your painful inner dialogues begin to quiet down. As your mind quiets, you hear much less from your fearful, critical, micromanaging, protective, intellectual, and wounded parts, which creates more space for your Inner Pilot Light to take the lead. You may not even have to do any sort of formal meditation after a while. Your life becomes a living meditation as you become aware that you're aware, with the consciousness of your Inner Pilot Light permeating all aspects of your life, whether you're cross-legged in a yoga class, doing the dishes, or dealing with conflict with a loved one.

As your noisy parts settle down and relax, your Inner Pilot Light becomes easier to hear. At this point, the messages that do come through are more likely to be arising directly from your Inner Pilot Light. This can feel quite mysterious. Sometimes the instructions that come from your inner wisdom may feel strange. You hear an instruction to phone a friend. You may not know why. Your nervous system is calm and relaxed, but because you trust this instruction and recognize it as a guiding force in your life, you pick up the phone, call your friend, and find out she needs you desperately right here, right now. Without any effort or self-sacrifice, you just became someone else's miracle.

As your Inner Pilot Light heals that which is in need of healing in you, the messages are likely to shift their focus. Instead of focusing so much on what *you* need, your Inner Pilot Light may start telling you what the collective "we" needs. You may get "downloads" that feel very specific and exciting, as your Inner Pilot Light guides you, one breadcrumb at a time, in the direction of your sacred purpose. You may begin to receive very clear signs that guide you toward that unique reason you were sent here to Earth School—so you can participate in the transformation of consciousness that is underway to restore balance on the planet.

You may wake up one morning and hear your Inner Pilot Light give you instructions for a nonprofit you're meant to spearhead. Or maybe your Inner Pilot Light will show you that you're meant to go read to the lonely elder down the street who needs love, attention, and a hot meal. Or maybe you'll be told to stop depleting yourself in the name of helping others so you can go soak your body in a lavender salt bath while you read a book, because your emotional, physical, and spiritual needs matter as much as everyone else's do. Over time, you may not even think of your Inner Pilot Light as some separate part of you. It may burn through you so fully that it simply lives inside your body and looks out of you as magical eyes, blessing everyone with the love that pours out of you.

Don't be surprised if things change and shift as your heart opens and your Inner Pilot Light takes over. This is nothing to fear, though it can feel disruptive to the adorably human parts of you. You won't lose those beloved parts. They are a precious contribution to your unique expression, and they will stay with you as valued consultants, even as your Inner Pilot Light takes more of a leadership role in the system of *you*.

As this transition happens, you'll be purified by the ignition of a flame so great it relaxes into the background everything that is not love, leaving a precious benevolent presence that blesses the world and experiences the deep joy, peace, and gratitude of someone who lives the human experience at full volume, with all its bliss and pain and vitality and glory. As Glennon Doyle Melton says, it's a brutal and beautiful process. Life becomes "brutiful" when you stop grasping for what you want and resisting what you don't want, just letting this eternal flame of love burn through you.

As your unique journey from the head to the heart ensues, you are likely to take three steps forward and one step back. You may experience a honeymoon period during which life feels full of magic, synchronicity, and miracles. After the seductive bliss of the honeymoon wears off, the journey deepens and may feel bewildering, disorienting, or even downright dark. Do not despair. No matter what obstacles you encounter on your journey, your Inner Pilot Light will shine the light so you can find your way back to your true home.

Welcome home, darling. As a homecoming gift, let me leave you with this prayer.

Inner Pilot Light Manifesto

- May I always know that wherever I am, I am home.

- Help me surrender to my Inner Pilot Light, so that my mind can relax and my heart can lead the way.

- Remind me to listen to the subtle whispers that guide my path.

- Strengthen me to muster up the courage to follow my guidance, even when it's scary.

- Fill me with the peace of knowing that I am the one I've been waiting for.

- May that which illuminates me heal and unblock all physical, emotional, mental, and spiritual illness.

- Help me choose love, especially when I am challenged to stay in love.

- Support my generosity with clear boundaries and healthy self-respect.

- Use me as a vessel of pure service, but don't let me give when I'm not resourced.

- May divine abundance shower upon me so I may fill myself and pour the overflow onto those in need.

- When the muse uses me, help me always remain humble and give credit where credit is due.

- Let my light attract the light within others so I may be blessed with a healthy soul tribe.
- Make me a blessing to those around me.
- Protect me from ever abusing the power of my Inner Pilot Light's luminescence.
- Allow the fire that burns through me to ignite and offer grace to a world in need of my love.
- When it is my time, let me leave this world with the song within me fully expressed.
- Let me bow in devotion to the eternal flame that flows through me.
- May I always remember that love is who I am.

Acknowledgments

Thank you first and foremost to my Inner Pilot Light, without which *The Daily Flame* would be nothing more than a twinkle in God/Goddess's eye. This whole creation belongs to the Divine Beloved who wrote it through me. I feel incredibly blessed to have been chosen to be the conduit for this book. I bow with all my love and devotion before this Force of Love that burns within us all.

To all the Daily Flame readers who have been reading "Love Letters from Your Inner Pilot Light" since 2009, you have my eternal gratitude. You inspire me daily and remind me to check in. Without you, this book wouldn't exist.

To Tami Simon, Jennifer Y. Brown, Gretel Hakanson, Jade Lascelles, Bridgette Boudreau, and everyone else at Sounds True, who took what was intended as a little pet project for my Daily Flame readers and had the vision to turn it into this beautiful book. To Jaidree Braddix, Celeste Fine, and Michele Martin, thank you for bearing with me as my little pet project became an unexpected book.

To my mother, Trish Rankin, to whom this book is dedicated and who transitioned out of her body as I wrote this beside her, I am forever grateful that you brought my Inner Pilot Light into this human world and that your faith taught me to trust an invisible Force of Love whose presence I came to know and trust. When people ask me where I got my faith, I think of you. Your steadfast, unwavering faith gave me the courage to make choices in my life I might never have been capable of making if I didn't believe in this Force of Love. Thank you for being such a blessing in my life.

I might never have come into close contact with my Inner Pilot Light were it not for the guidance, illumination, and love of my mentor Rachel Naomi Remen. When I first met Rachel, she told me that she recognized me but that the part of me she recognized only had about 28 percent stock in the company of Lissa. "Maybe if we hang out together," she told me, "the part of you I recognize can get 51 percent stock. All you need is 51 percent stock in a company to make all the decisions." I now understand that the part of me Rachel recognized was the part I later came to call my Inner Pilot Light. I still don't know whether that part has 51 percent stock in the company of Lissa, but at least I hear the voice of that wise, old part of me, and I am forever grateful to Rachel for recognizing something in me and fertilizing it until it started to blossom. I know you don't like it when I gush, Rachel, but I thank my lucky stars every day that you are in my life. I love you and am in awe of how blessed I have been by your presence, your wisdom, and your unconditional love.

To my daughter, Siena, thank you for showing me how brilliantly a child's Inner Pilot Light can sparkle when it is uncorrupted by the conditioning of dominant culture, fostered in the nest of a Waldorf-inspired school, and nurtured in the soul tribe that we live amongst. The purity of the divine love that shines through your cornflower blue eyes every time I look at you inspired me to write this book so that all beings everywhere might radiate love the way you do. Imagine a world where that is possible! Wow. Just wow. I love you, pumpkin.

To April, my home tree, house spouse, tribe glue, and roomie, I adore you. Thank you for being and doing all that you be and do so that I can tackle projects like writing a book. I love and appreciate everything about you and am so glad you once asked me if I would be your family. Yes. Yes. A hundred times still—yes.

To Pearl, the wind beneath my professional wings: Thank you for making this book possible, for keeping me grounded, for tending to the Daily Flame every day, for loving InfusionSoft and Excel spreadsheets way more than I do, for keeping the tribe sane, for having the courage to speak the truth, for sanding over many of my rough edges, and, most of all, for sticking with me through all that we've been through over the years. I appreciate you.

To Diane, my bestie and soul sister, thank you for traveling the spiritual path right alongside me, for listening to me ramble as I question everything, and for remembering my wholeness whenever I forget. I respect and admire the hell out of you, and I love you more than words can say.

To my beloved husband, Olivier, your presence in my life is a blessing that fills me with awe at how unbelievably generous the Universe can be. Thank you for showing up with your tender, wise heart wide open when my Inner Pilot Light sent out the cosmic call to yours. I did not know the kind of endless intimacy that was possible until you came into my life. I awaken in your arms each day, bowing in devotion and grateful thanks to the Force of Love that brought us so mysteriously together. I choose you today.

To Mary, thank you for reminding me that Anne Lamott once said, "One secret of life is that the reason life works at all is that not everyone in your tribe is nuts on the same day." What a relief! Mary, Mary, I love your Inner Pilot Light. I love that you want to take all the wild animals home to sleep with you in your bed. I love that my smile muscles always ache from overuse when you leave. I love reading the killer blog you write for only eight people. Thank you for not being nuts on the same days I'm nuts.

To Maja, thank you for being the goddess of stillness in my life and proving to me that longtime meditators can still (cue the dubstep) rap like nobody's business! I am so grateful for you and the delicate petals of your blossoming heart.

To Rachel, my twin from a different mother, bless you for showing how I could be if my Inner Pilot Light was lit up all the way! Thank Goddess someone at Esalen once told me we needed to meet. I'll never forget the day I met you on that Santa Cruz beach, looked deep into your forever eyes, and knew from the shocking heart-opening I had never experienced before in the presence of a "stranger" that I must have met you in some life I don't remember. I'm so grateful we are reunited in this life.

To Dennis, my sky love, twin flame, soul brother, whose journey through the depths of mysticism opened me to understandings I never would have been able to express in this book had I not experienced them through the eyes of the Beloved in a dear friend. I cherish our unusual friendship beyond words, so I won't even try to express how grateful I am to have you in my life and how dearly I love you.

To Charles, who rocked my world, opened my heart, shifted my worldview, and lit up the love revolutionary activist in me. Bless you for holding the peacemaking vibration of nonpolarizing universal love and showing us all how to love one another, even when we hold opposing points of view. Your influence is all over this book. My life has been so enriched by having you in it. I carry you in my heart.

To my spiritual counselor, Ted, many thanks for helping me navigate what is often a bewildering spiritual path. I am so grateful for your wisdom, your intuition, your knowledge, your expertise, and your friendship. So many Daily Flames have been inspired by your teachings. I am blessed by your presence in my life.

To Asha, bless you for helping me clear some of the intense trauma I've experienced in the past three years so my Inner Pilot Light can continue to sparkle, even in the presence of deep pain. What a blessing to have met you at just the right time, and thank Goddess my projective identifications didn't keep you away from me. (Phew.)

To Brandy, thank you for teaching me to expand all the ways I can hear my Inner Pilot Light communicate with me, for teaching me to reach deeper and inquire further, for connecting me with a mysterious invisible world of love, energy, and magic. I adore that we get to be in Hogwarts together.

To Emma, what a blessing to have Aphrodite Incarnate sparkling her Inner Pilot Light in my tribe, my home, and my heart. I feel this bursting in my heart just invoking your sweet presence in my consciousness. I love you and appreciate you.

To Katsy, who has known me forever and is one of the few who keeps coming back, no matter what happens in my life.

To Sweigh, what a gift it's been to have you join our soul tribe.

To my family—Matt, Chris, Keli, Malan, Nick, Zay, Becca, Trudy, Larry, Jana, Lin, Tina—thank you especially for navigating Mom's transition with me and for holding the space for love in the midst of intense loss as I wrote this book. I am grateful for the community of support that helped our beloved Trish's transition in the arms of those who adore her still.

To Tosha, Monique, Eivind, Del, Kristen, Shiloh, Jonathan, Dawson, Christine, Anne, Karen, Victoria, Kristine, Sera, and so many more I could thank. Infinite gratitude to everyone who helped make this book a reality, to every spiritual teacher who facilitated my journey, to everyone who dances with me at Open Floor in Sausalito, and to everyone who touches my heart with your Inner Pilot Light. I think everyone should make a practice of writing book acknowledgments at least once a year, even if you never write a book. If I didn't mention you, and you're precious in my life, please know I love you, I'm grateful for you, and I am keenly aware that I couldn't birth any of the creative projects I midwife into the world without the incredibly loving, talented, reliable, and committed beloveds who make up my tribe.

Resources

For more resources to help you connect with your Inner Pilot Light:

- Listen to Sounds True's audio program *Your Inner Pilot Light* with Lissa Rankin & Sounds True founder Tami Simon.
- Visit InnerPilotLight.com, where you can access free audio downloads and sign up for Daily Flame emails.
- Join Lissa Rankin's Healing Soul Tribe at LissaRankin.com/pages/soultribecommunity.
- Register for Lissa Rankin's blog and newsletter at LissaRankin.com.
- Listen to Lissa and Rachel Naomi Remen's free teleclass "10 Ways Your Soul Guides You in Daily Life" at MedicineForTheSoulRx.com/freecall.
- For a more personalized experience, bring your Inner Pilot Light to one of Lissa's live workshops. Find out where she's teaching next at LissaRankin.com/events.
- Follow Your Inner Pilot Light and Lissa Rankin on Facebook.

About the Author

Lissa Rankin, MD, trained as an OB/GYN physician and practiced conventional medicine for ten years before her Inner Pilot Light insisted that she leave the medical system to pursue a different kind of healing work. She has written six books, including *The Fear Cure*, *The Anatomy of a Calling*, *What's Up Down There?*, *Encaustic Art*, and the *New York Times* bestseller *Mind Over Medicine*. Her work inspired two National Public Television specials featuring her work: *Heal Yourself: Mind Over Medicine* and *The Fear Cure*. Lissa delivered four TEDx talks about health and spirituality, which have garnered over four million views.

In 2012, she founded the Whole Health Medicine Institute, a training program about consciousness and spirituality in medicine for physicians and other health-care providers. She has spent the last six years researching sacred medicine, traveling the world, learning from shamans in Peru and Colombia, Qigong masters from China, kahunas from Hawaii, Balinese healers, and energy healers and faith healers in the United States, as she inquires into the nature of what causes disease and what facilitates the healing process.

Lissa's prayer is that every person on Earth awakens to his or her Inner Pilot Light and dissolves the separation that causes us to divide and polarize rather than reunite, heal, awaken, and connect in love, service, and delight. Lissa is passionate about helping people view illness and other forms of adversity as an opportunity for awakening. She's a love revolutionary on a grassroots mission to put the "care" back in health care, to reunite healing and spirituality, and to inspire sacred activists to participate in the transformation of consciousness that is sweeping across our planet.

Lissa blogs regularly at LissaRankin.com and hosts the Healing Soul Tribe online community for those who are committing to letting their Inner Pilot Light take the lead. Each year she leads the Whole Health Medicine Institute, mentors a small circle of visionaries for a nine-month gestation, teaches live workshops at retreat centers such as Esalen, Kripalu, Omega, and 1440 Multiversity, and facilitates virtual workshops online. Her Inner Pilot Light lights up from hiking in redwood forests, soaking in natural hot springs, skiing in fresh powder, kayaking on rivers, listening to live music of all types, painting with beeswax, singing and snuggling with her soul tribe, engaging in full moon rituals with her priestess sisters, and dancing barefoot anywhere there's a beat. Lissa lives where the redwoods and mountains meet the ocean in Marin County, California, with her Waldorf-educated daughter, Siena, her husband, Olivier, her chosen family, April, and the rest of her soul tribe.

About Sounds True

Sounds True is a multimedia publisher whose mission is to inspire and support personal transformation and spiritual awakening. Founded in 1985 and located in Boulder, Colorado, we work with many of the leading spiritual teachers, thinkers, healers, and visionary artists of our time. We strive with every title to preserve the essential "living wisdom" of the author or artist. It is our goal to create products that not only provide information to a reader or listener, but that also embody the quality of a wisdom transmission.

For those seeking genuine transformation, Sounds True is your trusted partner. At SoundsTrue.com you will find a wealth of free resources to support your journey, including exclusive weekly audio interviews, free downloads, interactive learning tools, and other special savings on all our titles.

To learn more, please visit SoundsTrue.com/freegifts or call us toll-free at 800.333.9185.